# Secrets of the Tarot

# Numerology and the Deeper Meanings of the Major Arcana

Carey Croft

SECRETS OF THE TAROT

All rights reserved.
Copyright © 2017 by Carey Croft

ISBN 978-0-692-05108-5
Published in the United States.

## Dedication

This book is dedicated to:

Rachel Pollack, whose tarot knowledge and advice are invaluable.

Zoe Matoff, who helped me develop the structure of this book.

Paula Scardamalia, who with a few wise words helped me bring my dream into reality.

# Table of Contents

Foreword   xi
Introduction   xiii

## Chapters

| | | |
|---|---|---|
| One | Methodology | 1 |
| Two | Zero and the Fool – Something Unique | 15 |

**First Group of Nine – Magician through the Hermit   26**

| | | |
|---|---|---|
| Three | One and the Magician | 26 |
| Four | Two and the High Priestess | 38 |
| Five | Three and the Empress | 49 |
| Six | Four and the Emperor | 57 |
| Seven | Commentary: The Four Archetypes of Creation | 67 |
| Eight | Five and the Hierophant | 69 |
| Nine | Six and the Lovers | 78 |
| Ten | Seven and the Chariot | 87 |
| Eleven | Eight and Strength | 94 |
| Twelve | Nine and the Hermit | 101 |

**Second Group of Nine – Wheel of Fortune through the Moon   109**

| | | |
|---|---|---|
| Thirteen | Ten and the Wheel of Fortune | 109 |
| Fourteen | Eleven and Justice | 119 |
| Fifteen | Twelve and Hanged Man | 129 |
| Sixteen | Thirteen and the Death | 140 |
| Seventeen | Fourteen and Temperance | 148 |
| Eighteen | Fifteen and the Devil | 156 |
| Nineteen | Sixteen and the Tower | 165 |
| Twenty | Seventeen and the Star | 175 |
| Twenty-One | Eighteen and the Moon | 182 |

**Last Group of Three – Sun, Judgement, and the World   190**

| | | |
|---|---|---|
| Twenty-Two | Nineteen and the Sun | 190 |
| Twenty-Three | Commentary: The Number Triads and The first Triad of Progression | 199 |
| Twenty-Four | Twenty and Judgement | 202 |
| Twenty-Five | Commentary: The Second Triad of Progression | 210 |
| Twenty-Six | Twenty-One and the World | 212 |
| Twenty-Seven | Commentary: The Third Triad of Progression | 221 |
| Twenty-Eight | Commentary: The Three Archetypes of Paradox | 223 |

Twenty-Nine     Discoveries    229

Glossary    237
Foundation Principles    239
List of Key Words    241
List of Analyzed Words by Chapter    242
List of Analyzed Words Alphabetized    244
Bibliography    261
About the Author    262

## Acknowledgments

A special thank you to my husband, Doug, whose support and love inspire me.

Thank you to my brother, Jon, for his time, invaluable advice, and keeping me on track.

Thank you to my editor, Katie Mills of The Manuscript Maker, www.themanusciptmaker.com.

Thank you to my friends, who are always encouraging.

## Foreword: The Legitimate Use of the Occult

For the rational, Enlightenment-era mind, the use of the senses defined the limits of truth. It wasn't until Sigmund Freud, a Jewish physician studying the nervous system, that the power of other truths emerged from the shadows into the light of legitimacy. After Freud, the Age of Reason included the power of witchcraft and fortune telling.

Whether Freud studied the Kabbalah is unknown to me. As other European Jewish kids did in the religious curriculum on Shabbat, while learning about the philosophical debates surrounding the ancient texts, he may have heard of the medieval arts of deciphering numerical systems—systems dating back to Pythagoras and to the Egyptians before him. A generation after Freud, Elie Wiesel earnestly pursued this study while Europe descended into hell around him. But Freud's discovery that an unconscious mind can control human behavior opened a door to new claims of legitimacy for the superstitions of the famous elite like Napoleon's Josephine and Reagan's Nancy.

Freud's associate and disciple, Carl Jung, wrote of "synchronicity" in fortune telling with the pentagrams of the *I Ching*. He did so with the Enlightenment faithfully at his back. His point, consistent with the new "science" of psychoanalysis, lay in the search for the content of the unconscious mind. What Freud had discovered (and demonstrated) was that some diseased people could cure themselves by understanding the content of their unconscious minds. What Jung added, in his foreword to Richard Wilhelm's translation of the *I Ching,* was that how one reacts to the "fortune telling" reveals much.

Synchronicity—events coinciding in time—carries power. Two phenomena happening simultaneously may be related, Jung observed. Thoughts happening at the same time as observation of a card, discussion of concepts in a number, the swing of a pendulum, or the interpretation of a pentagram reveal content of the mind: of the conscious mind and of the unconscious mind. In modern argot, we say "feelings." The content may be observed in a dream or any evocation—in free association or in the interpretation of an inkblot. Jung's key point was to enable the observation of something that is otherwise invisible.

Any tool that allows us to see more has value. Any man, who is rational, will seek to observe the invisible that has power over him. He merely needs to acknowledge: the unconscious is hidden from us, but it exists.

Observing the unconscious takes place by indirection, like in a mirror. The light waves of our image from the mirror are not us, but they are uniquely from us. In the same way, indicators of our unconscious mind are not the thing itself, but they emerge uniquely from the source. And they reveal the nature of the source.

The readings of ancient systems evoke crucial ideas from within ourselves. They evoke content other than our logical thinking about the subject: they evoke our feelings in that relationship. And feelings have the power to shape our behavior. They are ignored at our peril.

*Jon Mills*
*June 2015*

## Introduction

In the late sixties, I was introduced to tarot by a good friend. Initially I was interested in it as a metaphysical subject. Metaphysics is defined by Wikipedia as "a traditional branch of philosophy concerned with explaining the fundamental nature of being and the world that encompasses it." I put tarot aside after learning the basics as other subjects captured my attention, most notably numerology. After becoming a professional numerologist in 1995, I began focusing on tarot again.

Rachel Pollack, tarot Grand Master and internationally known author, deepened my knowledge of tarot through her classes held near my home. As my knowledge of tarot grew, it became apparent to me that numerology and tarot aligned nicely with each other. I studied the role numbers played in the two metaphysical subjects, which revealed differences and similarities. The discovered kinship between numerology and tarot led to an exploration of what numerology could reveal about the names of the major arcana.[1]

My book views the major arcana as archetypes and is an exploration into the numerology of the names and card numbers. You will see every major arcana card paired with its order number. Also included are words associated with the numbers and cards, their meanings, the concepts the numbers and cards raise, and free associations from the author as querent.

I developed a way of interpreting the tarot's major arcana names, as shown in the following chapters by my research and my understanding of numerology. The numerology methods used are based on the work of Shirley Blackwell Lawrence, author of *Behind Numerology* (New Castle Publishing Co, Inc., 1989). This book has been reprinted under the title *The Secret Science of Numerology: The Hidden Meanings of Numbers and Letters*.

In my book, you can work through the numerology analyses with the samples provided. The chapters are constructed so that you may follow the numerology methods I use. You can read individual chapters of the cards that interest you, or you can read the book cover to cover. I recommend the latter, if only because what is revealed by continuity is understood more fully if read this way. Toward the end of each chapter, the new meanings revealed by the numerological process are listed. In every chapter, there is also a sample reading using the revealed meanings. Don't forget there are

---

[1] Arthur Edward Waite in his 1909/1910 deck *The Rider-Waite Tarot,* which he created with artist Pamela Coleman Smith, established the names and order of the major arcana used in this book.

an alphabetical list of analyzed words and a list of analyzed words by chapter at the end of the book.

I discovered a wealth of hidden knowledge by adding numerology to my understanding of the major arcana, which I pass on to my readers. Much of the knowledge can be applied to readings and esoteric study. At the very center of what is revealed is a spiritual understanding of our physical reality, which numerology frames in the progression of numbers one through nine. This one through nine progression can also be used to frame the order of the major arcana.

This book will:

> * Expand your definitions and understandings of the major arcana cards as archetypes.
>
> * Add to your knowledge of the relationships between the cards and how they interact.
>
> * Expand your ability to read the tarot with more depth.
>
> * Deepen your esoteric knowledge of the Rider-Waite major arcana.

The cards speak to us personally, in ways that are always suited to our understanding of our world. That is, in part, what makes tarot such a wonderful tool for personal growth. If you are already familiar with the deck, cards, and meanings of tarot, this book will add another level of interpretation and understanding.

The major arcana's archetypal meanings expand with the numerological analysis of their names and related words. The analysis reveals a cohesive relationship between the major arcana archetypes as a type of numerological progression. Approached as a metaphysical subject, it is not surprising that the numerological analysis of the major arcana also reveals esoteric teachings about spirituality. After all, the study of numbers has captivated human intelligence since the days of Pythagoras, 2500 years ago. Pythagoras believed numbers were the ultimate reality. The search for fundamental principles that underlie the physical world, like the generalizations of science, may have begun with Pythagoras' assertions about numbers.

The numbers one through nine describe a complete cycle in numerology, with one as the beginning and nine as the ending. The major arcana lend themselves to this numerological arrangement and are divided into two groups of nine. The experienced tarot reader will know that zero and the Fool are not within the numerology cycle of one through nine. Zero and the Fool stand alone because although they are a part of everything, they are also the origin—the potential from which all else comes. This gives zero and the Fool individually unique characteristics which no other numbers or archetypes possess.

Numerology applies cycles of one through nine to the major arcana in the following way. The first cycle of one through nine includes card one, the Magician, through nine, the Hermit. The second cycle of nine includes ten, the Wheel of Fortune, through eighteen, the Moon. The last three cards—nineteen, the Sun; twenty, Judgement; and twenty-one, the World—are the beginning of a third numerological cycle, which operates beyond the physical.

There are twenty-two major arcana in a standard tarot deck. In numerology, twenty-two is the number of the master builder or master architect. The tarot helps us be the architects of our reality. The archetypes of tarot represent twenty-two interactive fields of spiritual experience possible within physical reality and beyond. These interactive fields guide us by providing feedback in perspective, as well as suggesting productive actions.

# Chapter One

## Methodology

In chapter one, you will find the step-by-step process of working with a numerological system. Numerology uncovers the hidden meanings of any word. It translates letters into numbers, and numbers into words and concepts in keeping with the ancient traditions of numerology. According to Carl Jung, archetypes are ancient patterns and images that come from the collective unconscious. These patterns are connected to our psychic abilities and instincts. Although Waite did not create the major arcana as archetypes, I believe viewing them as such to be a natural progression in working with the tarot. The numerological process used in this book reveals new interpretations of the major arcana and provides different ways of understanding them as archetypes while expanding the reader's personal relationship to them. A deeper spiritual message is revealed as well. However, not every reading in which major arcana cards appear will call for interpretation at this level.

Numerology focuses on the vibrations of sound, which has number values. These number values can also be associated with letters. Because the English alphabet starts with "A," "A" is associated with the number one. Numerology organizes the English alphabet into repetitive cycles of one through nine. The numbers one through nine form a basic numerology cycle.

The numerology cycles of one through nine can be applied to the order of the major arcana. In the major arcana, because the Fool is numbered zero and stands alone as the primal source, the first cycle starts with one, the Magician. The first cycle ends with card nine, the Hermit. The second cycle begins with card ten, the Wheel of Fortune, and ends with card eighteen, the Moon. The Wheel of Fortune is the first card in the second cycle because nine is the end of the numerology cycle and because ten can be reduced by addition to a one: $1 + 0 = 1$. One is the number of beginning in numerology. The Moon card is the last card in the second cycle because it is card eighteen: $1 + 8 = 9$. Nine is the number of ending in numerology.

The third cycle is partial, beginning with card nineteen, the Sun, and ending with card twenty-one, the World. The third cycle begins with the Sun because $1 + 9 = 10$, which can be reduced through addition to one.

The following sections explain the basic processes that are used throughout the book.

## Numerology Cycles

The basic cycle of energy in numerology is described by the numbers one through nine. Methods of numerology establish numerical values for each letter based on a repeating sequence of one to nine, creating a fundamental number cycle. The cycle one through nine represents the stages of development described as one, a beginning, through nine, the ending. Chart One shows the letters of the English alphabet and their assigned numbers.

Chart One
Letters and Corresponding Root Numbers

|  | A | B | C | D | E | F | G | H | I |
|---|---|---|---|---|---|---|---|---|---|
| Root numbers | 1 | 2 | 3 | 4 | 5 | 6 | 7 | 8 | 9 |

| J | K | L | M | N | O | P | Q | R |
|---|---|---|---|---|---|---|---|---|
| 1 | 2 | 3 | 4 | 5 | 6 | 7 | 8 | 9 |

| S | T | U | V | W | X | Y | Z |
|---|---|---|---|---|---|---|---|
| 1 | 2 | 3 | 4 | 5 | 6 | 7 | 8 |

The reader should note the following points from Chart One:

* Each letter has a single digit known as a root number (A and 1, B and 2, C and 3, etc.).

* There are two complete one-through-nine cycles and a last partial cycle, one through eight, in the 26-letter English alphabet.

* Starting with "J", the root numbers are the added result of the individual digits of the full number. J = 10 (full number), 1 + 0 = 1 (root number).

* Full numbers for the English alphabet are 1 through 26.

* Root numbers are written below the letters in a chart, distinguishing them from the *full* number for that letter.

## Chart Two
### Letters and Corresponding Full Numbers

| Full numbers | 1 | 2 | 3 | 4 | 5 | 6 | 7 | 8 | 9 |
|---|---|---|---|---|---|---|---|---|---|
| | A | B | C | D | E | F | G | H | I |
| | 10 | 11 | 12 | 13 | 14 | 15 | 16 | 17 | 18 |
| | J | K | L | M | N | O | P | Q | R |
| | 19 | 20 | 21 | 22 | 23 | 24 | 25 | 26 | |
| | S | T | U | V | W | X | Y | Z | |

The reader should note the following points from Chart Two:

* Full numbers represent the full or entire vibration of a letter.

* Full numbers are 1 through 26 because there are twenty-six letters in the English alphabet.

* Full numbers are written above the letters.

* Full numbers and root numbers are the same for the letters "A" through "I".

* "J" through "Z" have full numbers and root numbers.

> Example: "P" has a full number of 16. 1 + 6 = 7.
> 7 is the root number of the letter "P".

### Master Numbers

The letters "K" and "V" are assigned the master numbers 11 and 22. Master numbers are two-digit numbers with consecutive repeating digits. (For example: 33, 44, 77, etc.) Master numbers vibrate at a higher level of potential. For our purpose, any number with two repeating consecutive digits is considered a master number.

### The Numerology of the Word "Tarot"

What follows illustrates how to build the numerology chart for the word "tarot" using the full and root number assignments for each letter. These steps follow the processes used in this type of numerological analysis. A numerology chart for any word can be constructed using this method.

* Step One: Assign the letters their full numbers from Chart Two.

    20  1  18  15  20
    T   A   R    O   T

* Step Two: Assign letters their root numbers from Chart One.

    T  A  R  O  T
    2  1  9  6  2

* Step Three: Illustrate step one and two combining full and root numbers.

    20  1  18  15  20
    T   A   R    O   T
    2   1   9    6   2

* Step Four: Add up the full numbers.

    20 + 1 + 18 + 15 + 20 = 74
    T   A   R    O   T

* Step Five: Add up the root numbers.

    T  A  R  O  T
    2 + 1 + 9 + 6 + 2 = 20

The resulting chart for "tarot" will now look like Chart Three.

### Chart Three
### Numerology Chart of the Word "Tarot"

    20  1  18  15  20 = 74 (addition of full numbers)
    T   A   R    O   T
    2   1   9    6   2 = 20 (addition of root numbers)

* Step Six: Reduce the top number on the right side of the equal sign by adding its individual digits.

    7 + 4 = 11

11 as a master number is not further reduced.

\* Step Seven: Reduce the bottom number on the right side of the equal sign to a single digit by adding the individual digits.

$$2 + 0 = 2$$

In numerology, when reducing a multiple-digit number, a forward slash is used, and the resulting number is placed to the right. The example is highlighted in bold.

\* Example of the graphic for reducing a multiple-digit number:

```
20   1   18   15   20 = 74/11
T    A   R    O    T
2    1   9    6    2 = 20/2
```

In numerology, the full and root numbers reduce to the same single digit, which is a proof for the addition. In the example, the full numbers reduce to eleven, which as a master number is not reduced any further. However, the individual digits of eleven add to confirm the proof: $1 + 1 = 2$.

To review, first translate a word into numbers by assigning numbers to the letters. Next, add the digits of any multiple-digit number until a single digit is the result. Chart Four illustrates the complete English alphabet and its associated full and root numbers.

Chart Four
Letter Full and Root Number Values

| 1 | 2 | 3 | 4 | 5 | 6 | 7 | 8 | 9 |
|---|---|---|---|---|---|---|---|---|
| A | B | C | D | E | F | G | H | I |
| 1 | 2 | 3 | 4 | 5 | 6 | 7 | 8 | 9 |
| 10 | 11 | 12 | 13 | 14 | 15 | 16 | 17 | 18 |
| J | K | L | M | N | O | P | Q | R |
| 1 | (2) | 3 | 4 | 5 | 6 | 7 | 8 | 9 |
| 19 | 20 | 21 | 22 | 23 | 24 | 25 | 26 | |
| S | T | U | V | W | X | Y | Z | |
| 1 | 2 | 3 | (4) | 5 | 6 | 7 | 8 | |

The reader should note the following points from Chart Four:

* I have combined Chart One and Chart Two for ease of reference. The chart shows both full and root numbers.

* When illustrating our alphabet chart with full and root numbers, the root numbers of "K" and "V" are put in parentheses.

* The root numbers for "K and "V" are in parentheses because 11 and 22, as master numbers, are usually not reduced.

Reducing the added result of root numbers or reducing the added result of full numbers to a single-digit or master number results in what is called the expression number. In the example "tarot", the expression number is indicated by underlining. Expression numbers are single-digit or master numbers representing the characteristics of the word in the tradition of numerology. The full numbers above the letters of a word result in the spiritual and esoteric expression numbers, i.e., what is beyond the physical. The root numbers below the letters of a word result in the mundane expression numbers, i.e., what is part of everyday life. The translation for the numbers of the word "tarot" is explained in Chart Five, page 8.

* Definition of Expression Number: A number that reflects the way a word expresses.

## Translation Techniques

In order to translate numbers, numerology lists key words, which express attributes and concepts of each of the numbers from one through nine, eleven, and twenty-two. For any arithmetic sum of the digits in a word, the numerology analyst translates all the numbers to the right of the equal sign (the number eleven for "tarot" on page 5, for example). For the purposes of translation, the analyst uses a list of attributes or key words associated with the number.

Translation Technique One:
Per the conventions of numerology, first decide which attributes or key words to use for the translation of the numbers into words. Take into consideration the overall subject matter. Form a sentence that includes the words chosen. See page 9, translation of "tarot" full numbers 7, 4, 11.

Translation Technique Two:
Use a concept assigned by numerology as a translation for a given

number. See page 16, translation of full numbers of "zero" 6, 4, 1.

Translation Technique Three:
Use the chart word in the resulting sentence, rather than a key word. See page 17, translation of root numbers of "potential" 4, 0, 4.

Translation Technique Four:
Use a different word that has the same root number as the subject word. See page 17, translation of root numbers of "potential" 4, 0, 4.

Translation Technique Five:
Converting numbers into letters. When converting numbers back into letters, you have multiple letters to choose from. For example, the number 1 can be converted into the letters A, J, or S. Start with the first letter assigned to the number to see if it works for the particular translation purpose. If not, move on to the next letter. In the example, I use the letters chosen to represent a concept or idea. See page 19, full number translation of "hold".

Translation Technique Six:
Using a number's assigned letter as the first letter of a word. Once you have chosen which letter to represent the number, then use a word starting with that letter which makes the most sense. See page 23, conversion of "Fool" root numbers 2, 1, 3 into the letters B, A, C. The letter "B" is used as the first letter of the word "Be." The letter "A" is used as the first letter in the word "Able."

Translation Technique Seven:
Converting a letter that sounds like a word into that word: "C" becomes "see." See page 23, conversion of the root numbers of "Fool" into letters. In this example, the number 3 was converted into the letter "C," then the sound of the letter "C" was used as the word "see" for the translation.

Translation Technique Eight:
Using the letters assigned to a series of numbers to form a word. See page 23, "Fool": root numbers are converted into letters, then the letters are used to form a word.

## Translating Multiple-Digit Numbers into Words

Within the convention of numerology, each of the numbers one through nine has a group of words as a possible translation. Multiple-digit numbers cannot be translated as a complete number because there are no attributes for double- or multiple-digit numbers. The exception is double-digit numbers made up of repeating digits, such as eleven and twenty-two. Eleven and twenty-two have attributes as master numbers. As a result, multiple-digit numbers (with the exception of 11 and 22, as per the conventions of numerology) are analyzed one digit at a time or as a sum of digits.

The following chart shows the construction of the numerology chart for the word "tarot". The numbers have been added with the results after the equal sign.

Chart Five
Tarot

20   1   18   15   20 = 74/11
T    A   R    O    T
2    1   9    6    2 = 20/2

Translating numbers into words:

* Multiple-digit numbers are separated into their single digits.

* Numbers to the right of the equal sign are translated.

* Master numbers (always double digits, as is eleven in this example) are not usually separated into their single digits.

* For purposes of translation, some master numbers are separated at one's discretion.

All single-digit numbers, as well as master numbers in numerology, have specific characteristics, key words, and concepts. Attributes for the purpose of translation can be expressed as characteristics, key words, and concepts.

Following is an example using the number six.

* Definition of Key Words: Words that describe the essence of a number in the tradition of numerology.

Example of key words for 6: Family, Caregiver.

* Definition of Concepts: Words that bring to mind abstract ideas.

Example of Concepts for 6: Harmony, Beauty, Idealism.

* Definition of Characteristics: Words that describe attributes of the number.

Example of Characteristics for 6: Loyal, Giving, Loving.

The reader forms sentences from the key words, concepts, and characteristics of the numbers based on traditions of numerology. It is important to translate the numbers in the original order resulting from addition when translating numbers into words and sentences. This maintains the integrity of the translation. For the word "tarot", the numbers translated are 7, 4, 11, and 2, 0, 2.

Chart Six
Single Word Translations for Full Numbers 7, 4, 11 of "Tarot"

| **Seven** | **Four** | **Eleven** |
|---|---|---|
| perfection | stable | dreamy |
| study | **foundation** | illuminate |
| unique/different | practical | **understanding** |
| **spiritual** | organized | psychic |

The words used in the translation are in bold print in Chart Six.

* Translation of "tarot" numbers 7, 4, 11:
The **Spiritual** (7) nature of tarot can be used as a **Foundation** (4) for **Understanding** (11) life.

The reader should notice the following points of the translation.

* The number being translated appears in parentheses in the sentence after the word used for translation.

Example: The word spiritual is used as translation for the number 7. The number 7 appears in parentheses after the word spiritual.

\* The word used as a translation is capitalized. The word Spiritual is capitalized as the translation of the number 7.

\* Remember that the full expression numbers (above the word) tell how a word is articulating spiritually.

Chart Seven
Single Word Translations for the Mundane Numbers 2, 0, 2 of "Tarot"

| **Two** | **Zero** | **Two** |
|---|---|---|
| **dual** | potential | opposite |
| result | boundary | **differing** |
| sensitive | **reflection** | empathetic |

\* Translation of 20/2:
The **Dual** (2) nature of tarot is **Reflected** (0) through **Differing** (2) points of view.

### The Hidden Meanings within Archetype

For the twenty-two cards of the major arcana, I use the term archetypes. They represent archetypal energy. Archetype is defined by The Free Dictionary as "an original model or type after which other similar things are patterned." Archetypes are the originating energy model for all other similar types of energy. Following is the numerology chart of "archetype".

Chart Eight
Full Numbers of Archetype

| 1 | 18 | 3 | 8 | 5 | 20 | 25 | 16 | 5 | = 101/2 |
|---|---|---|---|---|---|---|---|---|---|
| A | R | C | H | E | T | Y | P | E | |

In the numerology of "archetype" we see the number one comes first in the result of adding the individual letters' corresponding numbers. A key word for the number one is divine. The word archetype points us toward the divine.

The numbers of "archetype" (101) further illustrate an important numerological observation about the mirroring characteristic of zero. Translating the full numbers (the right side of the equal sign) of "archetype", we discovered the number one represents the Divine.

Furthermore, zero represents a mirror image, as in the reflection of whatever number comes before the zero. Using the idea of mirroring and reflection in the translation of 101 illustrates the premise that the divine constantly reproduces itself to create two: the divine and its mirror image.

Notice the two (101/2) is on the right side of the forward slash. The two is the result of divinity creating a mirror image of itself. The number zero, whose key words include "reflection," often functions as a mirror in numerology.

Two, in this case, is duality, or the Duality, as in our world. The full numbers 101/2 show how the energy of archetype expresses in the context of spirit.

> \* Translation of full numbers 1, 0, 1, 2:
> The Divine (1) archetype Reflected (0) Itself (1) to create the Duality (2).
>
> \* Meaning of Duality: When capitalized, Duality refers to our world.
>
> \* Meaning of duality: When not capitalized, duality refers to dual nature.

The translation implies that archetypes, as patterns reflected within the Duality, originate from divinity. The Duality, as a divine reflection, is a part of the divine but appears separate, which is symbolically alluded to by the "dividing" line (the forward slash) between the one and two. The numerology of "archetype" shows the Divine reflected itself and is manifested in and is a part of the world of form. One might say the divine is the cosmic archetype.

### Chart Nine
### Root Numbers of Archetype

| A | R | C | H | E | T | Y | P | E | |
|---|---|---|---|---|---|---|---|---|---|
| 1 | 9 | 3 | 8 | 5 | 2 | 7 | 7 | 5 | = 47/11 |

> \* Translation of root numbers 4, 7, 11:
> The Foundation (4) of the archetypes' Spiritual (7) Insights (11) brings us deeper understanding about the Duality.

The root numbers (4, 7, 11) show how the energy of archetype expresses in the mundane world, the world of form, also known as the

Duality.

## Definitions
The following words are defined specifically for this book.

Beauty:
The innate natural state of being of all that is.

Core Vibration:
The single-digit number that shows the basic characteristics of a word or phrase.

Consciousness:
The collective power of subconscious and conscious combined.

Divine or Divinity:
A higher power such as God, Goddess, All That Is.

Duality:
Capitalized, Duality refers to our world or us as a reflection of the divine. Not capitalized, duality refers to the dual nature of something.

Vision:
The conceiving of and/or discernment of spiritual awareness and insight.

Master Numbers:
The numbers eleven and twenty-two, or in some cases any repeating double digit numbers. For example: 33, 44, 55, etc.

## Phrase Analysis – Charts of Two Words at a Time

Analysis of phrases follows a methodology similar to the analysis of a single word, but with some slight variations. The conventions of numerology dictate the construction of charts. Per these conventions, we assign numbers to the individual letters. Next, we add the numbers within each *word* and place the results above the initial line of numbers for the esoteric, or below the initial line of numbers for the mundane. The last step is to add the resulting multiple-digit numbers of the words together. This number is placed to the right of the equal sign. This method allows for the examination of the numerology of the whole concept of a phrase.

Analyzing the phrase "free will" results in the following chart.

Chart Ten
Free Will

```
      34                        56
6   18   5   5        23   9   12   12 = 90/9
F    R   E   E         W   I    L    L
6    9   5   5         5   9    3    3 = 45/9
      25                        20
```

Numerology analyzes each word of the phrase. In the phrase "free will", the numbers 34 and 56 are the results of adding the numbers that are assigned to the letters. The sum of the numbers 34 and 56 is 90, which is placed to the right of the equal sign. Any multiple-digit number on the right side of the equal sign is reduced to a single digit. The last step is to translate the numbers on the right of the equal sign as you would with single word analysis.

## Chapter Organization

In the chapters you will find:

* The translations of the major arcana cards' number, the name's translations, and the translations of associated words.

* Translation methods will be noted in selected chapters to clarify what method has been used in each case.

* Translation Review:
The translations, grouped together, without the numbers.

* Applying the Revealed Information includes:

  Acquired Meanings:
  A list of meanings generated by the analysis of the major arcana names.

  Relevant Questions:
  Questions that can be used in a reading.

  Practical Application:
  The major arcana cards interpreted in a reading using the new meanings.

Just a Thought:
Any thoughts that occurred to me while working with numerological analysis.

The Archetype's Dynamics:
Single words that describe the essence of the card's energy.

## Division of Major Arcana Cards

The major arcana are divided into three groups in keeping with numerological cycles. The first group is the Magician through the Hermit, cards one through nine. The second group is the Wheel of Fortune through the Moon, cards ten through eighteen. The last group is the Sun, Judgement, and the World.

The order numbering of the major arcana cards lends itself to this arrangement. Cards one through nine make up the first group. Note that card number ten, the Wheel of Fortune, reduces to a one (10, 1 + 0 = 1) and starts the second group. Card eighteen, the Moon, reduces through addition to a nine (18, 1 + 8 = 9) and is the last card in the second group. The last three cards, the Sun, Judgement, and the World, fit into their own group. Note the Sun, card number nineteen, reduces to one
(19, 1 + 9 = 10, 1 + 0 = 1) and is the first card in the last group. These last three archetypes are the beginning of a third numerological cycle of the next higher vibration.

Zero and the Fool are not within the numerological cycle of one through nine. Zero and the Fool stand alone because they are the origin: the potential from which all else comes. This gives zero and the Fool individually unique characteristics that no other numbers or archetypes possess.

I examine the major arcana as archetypes to reveal the deeper esoteric and spiritual aspects of these cards.

# Chapter Two

Tarot's major arcana cards have themes which relate to the meanings and concepts of numerology. The specific order of the cards is intentional, and, not surprisingly, follows our number order. Because of the correlation between the card meanings and their numbers, it made sense to investigate the concept of the archetype with the concept of its associated number. By following this model, we discover interesting ideas revealing the depth of correlation between tarot and numerology.

## Zero and the Fool – Something Unique

*Zero, as a pause, holds the beauty of the Duality within its eternal circular pattern of energy.*

### Zero – The Potential of All That Is

Zero is the un-manifested which holds infinite potential. As the cosmic egg, zero holds the space from which divine potential and all else manifests. As such, it is all, everything. Yet zero is a glyph denoting nothing. Zero is both all and nothing. Zero is perfect and complete within itself. It is the source of all archetypal patterns.

Zero, the word and the glyph, includes the potential and perfection of the circular form and the concepts associated with a circle. Concepts of a circle include circular motion, cycles, a closed system of energy, etc. Both the word and the glyph for zero contain meaning.

The divine came out of zero. The One, as in the divine, arose from zero as shown by the numerology of the word "zero", which has a root number of one (1). The numbers of Chart Ten show a direct relationship between zero and one. The infinite potential within zero is expressed by the one, the divine.

Chart Ten
Zero

| 26 | 5 | 18 | 15 | $26 + 5 + 18 + 15 = 64\ (6 + 4 = 10)\ 64/\mathbf{10}$ |
|----|---|----|----|---|
| Z  | E | R  | O  | |
| 8  | 5 | 9  | 6  | $8 + 5 + 9 + 6 = 28\ (2 + 8 = 10)\ 28/10/1$ |

\* Zero key words: *divine template, perfection, seed, infinite potential.*

\* Zero, as a circle, contains the Divine Template (10).

* Sixty-four is the full number of the word "zero".

* Ten, the reduction of sixty-four, is shown in bold type.

Ten, on the esoteric level, is the Divine (1) and all its potential (0). Ten is the number of divine perfection and existence because the initial steps of creation, represented by the numbers one through four, add up to ten (1 + 2 + 3 + 4 = 10). The root number of "zero", one, is zero's expression on the mundane level or our reality. On the mundane level, the number one denotes individualism, uniqueness, originality. The root number one of "zero" shows that zero expresses as unique and original.

Zero has various meanings and ideas associated with it. Arithmetically, zero added to any number results in that number, as if the number were reflected in a mirror. The numerology notation, 10/1, suggests a similar idea of mirroring.

The numerology reduction of ten, shown as 10/1, also illustrates the reflection principle: as above, so below. This reflection principle did not originate with numerology, but can be used to illustrate the idea that what is divine (above) is also mundane (below). The divine is reflected in the mundane as the Duality, or our world. The mundane is called the Duality because it is a mirror of the divine.

Eight is a particularly interesting number contained in the numerology of zero. Our glyph for the number eight—one of the root numbers for "zero"—contains meaning as a graphic symbol. The glyph represents a circular reflecting pattern of energy. The Duality is the reflected part of this pattern. The Duality has the ability to reflect and manifest divine potential.

The translation of zero's numbers illustrates that numbers can represent a concept or idea as well as characteristics and attributes.

* Reminder: The numbers above the letters express in a spiritual, esoteric level; the numbers below the letters express in the mundane, physical level.

* Translation of full esoteric numbers, Chart Ten "zero" 6, 4, 1, 0:
The Beautiful (6) Foundation (4) of Divine (1) Potential (0) is the first and original.

* Translation of mundane root numbers of "zero" 2, 8, 1, 0, 1:
The Duality's (2) Power (8) is derived from Divine (1) Potential (0) within the One (1) (as in the divine).

\* New Translation Method Used:
Using concepts or an idea as a translation for a number. In this case, the concept of beauty is used to translate the number 6 of the full numbers.

\* New Translation Method Used:
For the translation of the root numbers 2, 8, 1, 0, 1 into words, I have used key words to form sentences.

Let's look at the numerology of "potential" next.

Chart Eleven<br>Potential

| 16 | 15 | 20 | 5 | 14 | 20 | 9 | 1 | 12 = 112/4 |
|---|---|---|---|---|---|---|---|---|
| P | O | T | E | N | T | I | A | L |
| 7 | 6 | 2 | 5 | 5 | 2 | 9 | 1 | 3 = 40/4 |

\* Translation of esoteric full numbers 11, 2, 4:
The cosmic egg gave birth to Divine Light (11), the Duality (2), and all Manifestation (4). (A key word of 4 is manifestation.)

\* Translation of mundane root numbers 4, 0, 4:
Potential (4) is Reflected (0) as possibility within Divinity (4) and the Duality.

\* New Translation Method Used:
In translating the root numbers of the word "potential", potential is used as translation for the number four because "potential" has a root number of four.

\* New Translation Method Used:
In translating the root numbers of the word "potential", a different word, "divinity," with the same root number is used as translation of the number 4.

A circle is the glyph for zero. The word circle has interesting numerological implications. Here is the numerology of "circle".

## Chart Twelve
## Circle

| 3 | 9 | 18 | 3 | 12 | 5 = 50/5 |
|---|---|----|---|----|----------|
| C | I | R  | C | L  | E        |
| 3 | 9 | 9  | 3 | 3  | 5 = 32/5 |

    The number five represents a circle because "circle" has a five root number. Five, as half of ten, is the number of the center of all that exists because five is the center between one and ten. Also ten is the number of all that exists (divine and its potential) because it contains the four initial steps of creation: one, two, three, four, which add up to ten. Therefore, a circle represents the center of all that exists as well.

    The full numbers 5, 0, 5 of circle illustrate the concept that all things come from and go back to zero, "0", the cosmic egg. A key word of the number five is change. Starting with the circle, as the beginning, a change occurs (5) expressed as outgoing expanding energy. The expanding energy eventually contracts, returning to the circle or the center (0). Another change (5) takes place, resulting again in expanding energy. This dynamic, which can also be represented by our glyph for the number eight, is the constant circular pattern of expanding and contracting, outgoing and returning energy.

    Zero is the number of unlimited potential. The numbers one through nine express at their next higher potential when zero comes after them. Take for example the number five in this case. Five is the number of change. The full number count of the word "circle" is fifty. Fifty shows the meaning of the number five taken to a higher potential. The zero in fifty reveals the perfection of the universal principle of change. The universal principle of change states that everything changes except the origin or cosmic egg.

> \* Translation of the full numbers of "circle" 5, 0, 5:
> The principle of Change (5) has Unlimited Potential (0) within the dynamics of the Circle (5) and its motion of energy.

> \* Translation of the root numbers of "circle" 3, 2, 5:
> The Creative (3) template of the Duality (2) is activated by the principle of Change (5).

    The principle of change states that within the Duality everything changes.

    The word "hold" is analyzed because in math, zero holds a space.

## Chart Thirteen
## Hold

|   |   |   |   |
|---|---|---|---|
| 8 | 15 | 12 | 4 = 39/12/3 |
| H | O | L | D |
| 8 | 6 | 3 | 4 = 21/3 |

The full number 39 reduces to 12/3 or 1, 2, 3. The numbers 1, 2, 3 convert into the letters 1 = A, 2 = B, C = 3 or A, B, C. The ABC's of something represent the basics. The root number of "hold" is three (3), the number of creativity and expression. Hold contains a basic component of creativity.

> \* Translation of esoteric full numbers 3, 9, 1, 2, 3:
> Esoterically, hold, as a pause, allows Creativity (3) to come to its ultimate Fulfillment (9) using Basic Components (1 = A, 2 = B, 3 = C) to create. (The ABC's of something are the basics.)
>
> \* Translation of mundane root numbers 2, 1, 3:
> In the Duality (2), hold creates a pause, which facilitates an Individual (1) person's ability to Create (3).
>
> \* New Translation Method Used:
> Converting numbers into letters which represent a concept or idea. Using the concept or idea as the translation.

Zero, associated in mathematics with holding a space, can also represent a pause. The Duality's laws of physics affect divine energy when that energy crosses into the Duality, creating the illusion of time. The words "hold" and "pause" represent the idea of time passing. Creating something out of potentiality takes time from our perspective.

## Chart Fourteen
## Pause

|   |   |   |   |   |
|---|---|---|---|---|
| 16 | 1 | 21 | 19 | 5 = 62/8 |
| P | A | U | S | E |
| 7 | 1 | 3 | 1 | 5 = 17/8 |

The root number of "pause" is eight. The number eight illustrates a basic energy dynamic. Our glyph for eight is a symbol for the eternal outgoing and returning motion of energy. The motion of energy expressed by the root number eight of "pause" may also include the concept of time passing within the Duality.

> * Translation of full numbers 6, 2, 8:
> Zero holds the Beauty (6) of the Duality (2) within its Eternal (8) circular pattern of energy.

> * Translation of root numbers 1, 7, 8:
> Zero, as a pause before the One (1), is unknowable, Spiritual (7), and Powerful (8).

Zero, as a pause before the divine is created, is unknowable, spiritual, and powerful. Hold is an important component of creativity. Hold implies that there is a waiting period when something is created (root number three) in the Duality. Pause is powerful, as shown by its root number eight. It is powerful within the concept of creation as well as what came before the divine.

### The Fool – Unlimited Potential; The First Archetype of Paradox

In numerology, the article "the" is omitted in the development of a chart. The word "Fool" becomes the numerology subject without the word "the." All major arcana names eliminate the article for analysis.

The Fool, the empty innocent, embodies the unlimited potential of the divine, the unlimited potential within creativity. The archetype of the Fool is both empty and full. He is empty because he has no content; his content is not yet manifested. He is full because his content can be anything when it is manifested. His potential is without limits. No other major arcana is vacuous. The Fool is unique.

As both empty and full, the Fool is a paradox—the first paradox within the major arcana. A paradox is like a hall of mirrors. The more you look, the more confusing your point of view until you understand the originating principle that is being reflected. The Duality, our world, contains the potential of paradox as a reflection of the divine. The Fool is a part of us, therefore we contain paradox as well.

The root numbers of the first three letters of "Fool" (F, O, O) are 6, 6, 6. The mark of the beast in Revelations is 666. Beast can refer to the basic primal nature of something, as postulated by Shirley Blackwell Lawrence in her book, *The Secret Science of Numerology.* The sixes show there is primal energy within the Fool. Six is the number of beauty and harmony, so there is the potential of beauty and harmony within this primal energy. According to Ms. Lawrence, the number six also represents the knowledge of good and evil. This is because six has the creative impulse within it as

3 + 3, which can be used for good or evil. The word "primal" has a root number of six. Primal and Fool are numerologically related because three, the root number of "Fool", is half of six, the root number of "primal". To create (3) is primal (6). Let's look at the numbers of "Fool".

Chart Fifteen
Fool

|   |   |   |   |
|---|---|---|---|
| 6 | 15 | 15 | 12 = 48/12/3 |
| F | O | O | L |
| 6 | 6 | 6 | 3 = 21/3 |

* Translation of full numbers 4, 8, 1, 2, 3:
The Foundation (4) of Power (8) within the Fool is manifested infinitely within the Divine (1) and the Duality (2) as Creative (3) potential.

* Translation of root numbers 2, 1, 3:
The Fool holds within it the potentiality of the Dual (2) nature of the One (1) divinely Expressed (3).

* A key word of the number three is *expression*.

"Fool" and "evil" have a root number of three. The Fool archetype contains the potential of good and evil, two basic archetypal patterns. These basic patterns are the higher and lower potential of primal energy. The Fool contains the potential for the expression of primal energy, beauty, harmony, good, and evil as well as the potential to express all else.

Chart Sixteen
Good

|   |   |   |   |
|---|---|---|---|
| 7 | 15 | 15 | 4 = 41/5 |
| G | O | O | D |
| 7 | 6 | 6 | 4 = 23/5 |

* Translation of full numbers 4, 1, 5:
Potential (4) within the Divine (1) creates Change (5).

* Translation of root numbers 2, 3, 5:
Choice (2) in creative Expression (3) leads to Change (5).

## Chart Seventeen
## Choice

| C | H | O | I | C | E |
|---|---|---|---|---|---|
| 3 | 8 | 6 | 9 | 3 | 5 = 34/7 |

* Translation of root numbers 3, 4, 7:
Expression (3) within the Foundation (4) of Choice (7) is an innate part of divine potential.

Forty-eight (48), the full number of "Fool", reduces to 12/3 or 1, 2, 3. This series of numbers is called the Creative Trinity. The root number three shows the Fool is an archetype that holds the Creative Trinity as unlimited potential. The Creative Trinity is expressed as the equation $1 + 2 = 3$. The potential of all creativity is within the Fool, as shown by the Creative Trinity. The divine (1) and its reflection (2) are combined $(1 + 2 = 3)$ to create something new.

The root number three in "Fool" shows this archetype is specifically related to the Empress, card number three. The Fool and the number three relate to the Empress as the potential expression of divine creativity. This relationship will be explained further in Chapter Five: Three and the Empress.

Twenty-one on the mundane level of "Fool" (Chart Fifteen, page 21) is the reflection of twelve on the esoteric level of that chart. What is above is reflected below. This mirroring adds importance to the numbers reflected. The number reflected is 12 as 21. When translating the 2 in 21, the 2 comes first on the mundane level, and therefore it is emphasized. On the esoteric level, the 1 comes first in 12, therefore the 1 is emphasized.

Six plus six plus six (666) from the first three letters of "Fool" equals eighteen (18), and $1 + 8 = 9$. These numbers show the Fool is the Beginning (1), Power (8), and the potential End (9). The Fool as the beginning and the end is illustrated within tarot literally, as the Fool is sometimes the first card, zero, or the last card, twenty-two. The Fool as the last card and master number twenty-two would be the Master Architect (22) (Matthew Oliver Goodwin, *Numerology the Complete Guide, Volume One*). As a Master Architect, the Fool has all the potential master plans. Using additional translation techniques, further meanings emerge.

* Conversion of "Fool" root numbers 2, 1, 3 into letters:
$2 = B, 1 = A, 3 = C$.

\* Translation of letters B, A, C:
To understand this archetype, it helps to Be (B) Able (A) to See (C) the unlimited potential and creativity of the Fool as a part of the Duality.

Here I mixed two different translation methods to form the sequence of words, "be able to see."

\* New Translation Method Used:
Using a number's assigned letter as the first letter of a word. "B" used in the word Be, and "A" in Able.

\* New Translation Method Used:
Using the sound of a letter as a word. "C" is translated as the word "see."

\* Conversion of "Fool" root numbers into letters and using the letters as a word: the letters "B", "A", "C" used as the word "back."

\* The Fool takes us <u>B</u> (2) <u>A</u> (1) <u>C</u> (3) or bac(k) to the primal state.

\* New Translation Method Used:
Using the letters assigned to a series of numbers to form a word.

## Translation Review

The Beautiful Foundation of Divine Potential is the first and original. The Duality's Power is derived from Divine Potential within the One. The cosmic egg gave birth to Divine Light, the Duality, and all Manifestation. Potential is Reflected as possibility within Divinity and the Duality. The principle of Change has Unlimited Potential within the dynamics of the Circle and its motion of energy. The Creative template of the Duality is activated by the principle of Change.

Esoterically, hold, as a pause, allows Creativity to come to its ultimate Fulfillment using Basic Components to create. In the Duality, hold creates a pause, which facilitates an Individual person's ability to Create. Zero holds the Beauty of the Duality within its Eternal circular pattern of energy. Zero, as a pause before the One, is unknowable, Spiritual, and Powerful.

The Foundation of Power within the Fool is manifested infinitely within the Divine and the Duality as Creative potential. The Fool holds within it the potentiality of the Dual nature of the One divinely Expressed. Potential within the Divine creates Change. Choice in creative Expression leads to Change. Expression within the Foundation of Choice is an innate part of divine potential. To understand this archetype, it helps to Be Able to See the unlimited potential and creativity of the Fool as a part of the Duality. The Fool takes us BAC(k) to the primal state.

**Applying the Revealed Information**

As a result of translating the numbers for the words associated with zero and Fool, new meanings have emerged.

**Acquired Meanings – New Meanings Revealed by Numerology**

Unlimited potential, a pause, origins, reflection, raise to the next level, circular motion, cycles, possibility, creative potential, primal energy.

**Relevant Questions**

The following questions might be asked in a reading related to the archetype of the Fool. What potential should I bring forth at this time? What is being amplified? What needs to be or can be taken to the next level? What has come full circle? Where am I within a cycle? What primal energy is active at this time? Within what area is change possible for me? What is the best way for me to use my creative potential?

**Practical Application**

In the practical application section of each chapter, I use the new meanings of the major arcana cards as revealed by numerology in a reading. Using this numerological analysis for the names of the minor arcana, however, would be too repetitive because of the suit names.

Reading: the Nine of Wands, the Hierophant, the Fool.

Sometimes standing our ground can be difficult, especially when we are being personally challenged. If the querent has faith in the guidance of spirit, it can give him or her strength when it is needed. The Hierophant represents that kind of support. The Fool brings added power and potential to the idea of belief in something greater than ourselves that supports us in our time of need. The Fool also indicates there is the potential to deepen the querent's faith and spiritual understanding.

**Just a Thought**

The sun on the Fool card is the only sun in this deck that is white. All the other suns are yellow. The white sun represents the light of purity. It also represents the purity and potential (0) within us. White symbolizes the undefined purity of divine consciousness. The white dog is a symbol of the Fool's pure, subconscious, primal energy. The white shirt under the Fool's tunic is a symbol of Fool's primal energy that is pure in form. The white rose symbolizes the heavenly perfection (white), passion (rose), and purity of the primal energy. Yellow, the predominant background color, is the color of enlightenment. The Fool's boots are yellow, indicating he is grounded in an enlightened state.

**Fool Dynamics:**
Reflecting
Activating
Pausing
Emphasize

# First Group of Nine – Magician through the Hermit

## Chapter Three

### One and the Magician

*One is the seed originating from the cosmic egg,
germinating as divine energy.*

#### One – All That Is, the Divine

In the tarot archetypes, the number one refers to the Magician and also the divine. In numerology, one is the number of individuality. The characteristics of one imply a connection between the divine and the individual. This concept is reflected in the graphic representation of the glyph. The glyph for one is the symbol of the singular pronoun "I." The Roman numeral for one and our capital "I" are both symbols for one. The likeness of the two symbols demonstrates that the same symbol denotes both the divine and the individual.

One is singularity, generator, and the divine. The singleness and yet generating nature of the number one is an attribute unique to this number. The generating ability of one is shown by the fact that one, as a single entity, added to itself creates all other whole numbers. An illustration of this idea is the equations $1 + 1 = 2$, $1 + 1 + 1 = 3$, etc. One represents the macrocosm as divinity, and one as the individual represents the microcosm. The expression of one as divinity is the first change from unlimited potential. The number one is a beginning, originality, and origin.

The word "one" and the word "all" both have a root number of seven. There is a relationship between one and all. Seven's key words "spirit," "spiritual," and "spirituality" show that one and all are related spiritually. One as the divine, and all as spirit expressing as individuals, are the same in the eyes of spirit because "all" and "one" have the same root number. There is no distinction. The tarot is full of these types of paradoxical ideas. All is one and one is all. If all and one are indistinguishable, then the divine is in the individual, as the individual is in the divine.

The microcosm reflects the idea of the sameness of divine and the individual within the similarity of the Roman numeral for one "I" and the personal pronoun "I."

## Chart Eighteen
## One

| 15 | 14 | 5 = 34/7 |
|----|----|----------|
| O  | N  | E        |
| 6  | 5  | 5 = 16/7 |

\* One key words: *active, unity, initiating, original.*

\* Translation of full numbers 3, 4, 7:
Creativity (3) is a Foundation (4) of the Duality infused with Spirit (7).

\* Conversion of full numbers 3, 4, 7 to letters:
3 = C, 4 = D, 7 = G.

\* Translation of C, D, G as letters:
One is a Seed (C, D; phonetically sounding C and D together) originating from the cosmic egg Germinating (G) as divine creation.

\* Translation of root numbers 1, 6, 7:
One (1), as in the divine, is also the Beauty (6) within Spirit (7).

Man as a part of the Duality contains will: the will to create and ability to decide on a course of action. All of the Duality, as a reflection of the divine, interacts with the power of will.

## Chart Nineteen
## Will

| 23 | 9 | 12 | 12 = 56/11 |
|----|---|----|------------|
| W  | I | L  | L          |
| 5  | 9 | 3  | 3 = 20/2   |

\* Translation of full numbers 5, 6, 11:
It is divine will that Man (5), by Vision (6), is brought into the Light (11). ("Light" has a root number of eleven.)

\* Six key word: *vision.*

\* Definition of Vision: The conceiving of and/or discernment of spiritual awareness and insight.

\* Translation of 2, 0, 2:
Divine Will (2) is Reflected (0) within the Duality (2).

## The Magician – Archetype of the Divine

The Magician is the first of four powerful interacting archetypes (Magician, High Priestess, Empress, and Emperor). These archetypes describe a progression from creation to physical manifestation. The Magician is the archetype of the divine, our creator. The creator is the generator of our reality.

Of particular interest are the symbols on the Rider-Waite major arcana cards. Some of these symbols are repeated on multiple cards. The Magician card has the most important symbol: the lemniscate.

We know the lemniscate as the symbol of infinity, but it is much more than that. The lines of the lemniscate illustrate the reflection dynamic. The left side of the lemniscate is the divine. The right side is the reflection of the divine. The reflection allows the creator to know itself and at the same time create our reality. Reflection implies that certain dynamics are active.

The lemniscate—the sideways figure 8—symbolizes this "reflection dynamic" and the motion of divine energy. The reflection dynamic describes how reflection influences energy. In the act of creation, the divine makes a reflection of itself by sending energy outward.

Close examination of the lemniscate reveals hidden secrets about the creation of divine reflection. By envisioning the line as the movement of energy, we can trace the flow as it moves away and returns to its source. Starting on the left side of the lemniscate, the energy of creation proceeds upward. Following the ellipse of the left side of the lemniscate, forming the top half as one continuous clockwise arc, the original outgoing energy then changes to move into a counterclockwise ellipse, forming the bottom half of the right side of the lemniscate. The energy now flows in a counterclockwise direction, crossing over itself on its return to the source.

The lemniscate is a paradigm that also applies to human creativity, as it does to the Magician or divine creativity. We experience this paradigm most directly as our outgoing energy reflected back to us. The reflection dynamic allows us to see what we create: a work of art, our homes, our family, and our personal reality.

The right side of the lemniscate is the divine's reflection, a kind of duplicate, which I refer to as the Duality. The process of creating the reflection dynamic gives rise to the Duality. The reflection dynamic causes things to be, or appear to be, reversed in the Duality as in a mirror. The reflection dynamic also produces unending creativity within the Duality.

Within the image of the lemniscate, the point where the reflected energy crosses over the original outgoing energy forms an "X." The "X" is the origin point of the reflection. All the elements of the original outgoing energy are included in the reflection. The origin of reflection represents a primal connection to the divine. We say "X marks the spot" perhaps because it is a part of our unconscious knowledge of the point of origin.

The archetype of the divine has the potential of self-procreation. This self-procreation is demonstrated by the Magician's ability to multiply itself by the attributes of the number one. This idea is represented by the equation, $1 + 1 + 1...$, infinitely. The Magician as one imbues all other archetypes, whose numbers are made up of sequential ones. One also adds to the development of their potential expression. As $1 + 1 = 2$ shows, the whole is greater than the sum of its parts. Two conceptually has greater implications than the mathematical definition of $1 + 1$.

The Magician uses primal energy to create the four elements: Earth, Air, Fire, and Water, represented by the symbols Pentacles, Swords, Wands, and Cups. The card shows these symbols on the Magician's table as a reminder that he is the divine origin of the four elements. The four elements are used alone and in combination to create.

As a part of my personal investigation into the role of the four elements, I assigned numbers to their first letters: "E", "A", "F", "W". It may occur to the reader to investigate his or her own personal associations for analysis in a similar vein.

## Chart Twenty
### E, A, F, W

| E | A | F | W |
|---|---|---|---|
| 5 | 1 | 6 | 5 = 17/8 |

\* Conversion of root numbers 1, 7, 8:
1 = A, 7 = G, 8 = H.

\* Translation of A, G, H:
The Magician's four elements Abundantly (A) Give (G) us the Highest (H) energy to work with.

\* Translation of root numbers 1, 7, 8:
The four elements are the Divine's (1) basic building components which enable Spirit (7) to use and express its own Power (8) in the Duality.

The Magician holds a white wand. "Wand" has a root number of 6, the same as magic. A wand is an aid for magic and is a symbol of focused energy. Following is the numerology of "wand".

Chart Twenty-one
Wand

| 23 | 1 | 14 | 4 = 42/6 |
|----|---|----|----------|
| W  | A | N  | D        |
| 5  | 1 | 5  | 4 = 15/6 |

\* Translation of full numbers 4, 2, 6:
A wand channels a Foundation (4) of energy directed by Choice (2) guided by a Vision (6) (as in an imagined image).

\* Translation of root numbers 1, 5, 6:
The Divine (1) Manipulates (5) and focuses energy to manifest his Vision (6) in the Duality. ("Manipulates" has a root number of five.)

Creation can seem like magic. Next is the numerology of "magic".

Chart Twenty-two
Magic

| 13 | 1 | 7 | 9 | 3 = 33/6 |
|----|---|---|---|----------|
| M  | A | G | I | C        |
| 4  | 1 | 7 | 9 | 3 = 24/6 |

\* Translation of full numbers 3, 3, 6:
Divine energy is Creative (3) potential Expressed (3) as beauty and Vision (6).

\* Translation of root numbers of Magic 2, 4, 6:
The Duality (2) is given the magic of co-creation as a Foundation (4) stabilized by Vision (6).

The number thirty-three is sometimes called the number of selfless giving. Some of three's attributes are empathy and compassion. "Magic" has an expression of thirty-three, made up of two 3's, as shown in Chart Twenty-two. The presence of three links magic with the Magician archetype. The Magician, with a root number of three, has empathy and compassion, which are divine attributes.

The word "magic" has an expression of six, which is three doubled. When the Magician, as the archetype of the divine, doubles his creativity, he produces magical results. Pure potential, as a form of energy, has the possibility of being transformed by the divine into everything that exists.

The word "will" is associated closely with other words, perhaps most notably with "free." Next is the analysis of "free will". On the mundane level, twenty is the sum of the individual letters in "will", and two is the root number of "will". The zero after the two elevates the expression of the number two from the mundane to the esoteric and signifies the divine aspect of will. The Magician's divine will can be reflected as personal will (free will) within the individual.

Chart Twenty-three<br>Free Will

|   | 34 |   |   |   | 56 |   |   |          |
|---|----|---|---|---|----|---|---|----------|
| 6 | 18 | 5 | 5 | 23| 9  | 12| 12| 12 = 90/9|
| F | R  | E | E | W | I  | L | L |          |
| 6 | 9  | 5 | 5 | 5 | 9  | 3 | 3 | 3 = 45/9 |
|   | 25 |   |   |   | 20 |   |   |          |

* Translation of full numbers 9, 0, 9:
Divine energy Initiates (9) the creation of its Reflection (0) with the emanation of Unconditional Love (9). ("Love" has a root number of 9.)

* Translation of root numbers 4, 5, 9:
Free will is a Foundational (4) element of Change (5) enabling us to bring about a desired End (9).

The translation of numbers 9, 0, 9 show that the Duality, as the reflection, is imbued with the essence of divine unconditional love. On the mundane level, the root of 25 and 20 reduce to 7 and 2, and their total is 9. The numbers 7, 2, 9 are translated for further information.

* Translation of 7, 2, 9:
Free Will is also a Spiritual (7) component of the Duality (2). To have free will is part of spirit's Initiation (9) into the Duality.

Spirit's entry into the Duality is a first step, a seminal initiation. The divine gives spirit the free will to express itself within the Duality as part of spirit's growth. The nature of the Duality allows for the beginning of individual self-expression. A question evoked by the translation of 7, 2, 9 is: if free will is *part* of spirit's initiation, what is the other part? The answer is creative consciousness, which is discussed in Chapter Four: Two and the High Priestess. The numbers 7, 2, 9 also show that the divine, as part of unconditional love, gives us free will. Free will and divine love unlock spirit's potential. Love is the master key that unlocks all potential.

The Magician unlocks our personal potential as we spiritually mature. Here is the numerology of "Magician".

Chart Twenty-four
Magician

| 13 | 1 | 7 | 9 | 3 | 9 | 1 | 14 | = 57/12/3 |
|----|---|---|---|---|---|---|----|-----------|
| M  | A | G | I | C | I | A | N  |           |
| 4  | 1 | 7 | 9 | 3 | 9 | 1 | 5  | = 39/12/3 |

The numbers 1, 2, 3 show the formula of creation is part of the Magician. The creative dynamic of 1, 2, 3 is part of the Magician's expression on both the esoteric and the mundane levels.

* Conversion of 1, 2, 3 into letters:
1 = A, 2 = B, 3 = C.

The ABC's of something are the basics or building blocks.

* Translation of letters A, B, C:
The Magician archetype contains the basic building blocks (A, B, C).

The identity of the building blocks will be revealed shortly. Another word whose expression number is three is "intention".

Chart Twenty-five
Intention

| 9 | 14 | 20 | 5 | 14 | 20 | 9 | 15 | 14 | = 120/3 |
|---|----|----|---|----|----|---|----|----|---------|
| I | N  | T  | E | N  | T  | I | O  | N  |         |
| 9 | 5  | 2  | 5 | 5  | 2  | 9 | 6  | 5  | = 48/12/3 |

* Translation of full numbers 1, 2, 0, 3:
Divine (1) intention as Will (2) is Reflected (0) throughout

Creation (3).

\* Translation of root numbers 4, 8:
Intention is a Foundational (4) Power (8) of magic (as in creation).

Three is the connection between "magic" (6), "Magician" (3), and "intention" (3). Three, as the root number of "intention" and "Magician", is half of six, the root number of "magic". Intention and the Magician facilitate creation. As metaphorical magicians, we use intention to express ourselves when creating something. We see that Magician (3) is a part of magic (6) because three plus three equals six. It is important to focus one's intention when doing magic, which makes magic a part of the Magician.

Let's go back to the identity of the Magician's building blocks of A, B, C. The building blocks, represented by A, B, C (Chart Twenty-four) are letters that in this case represent the building blocks of life on Earth.

A = Air – Air contains Oxygen, which we need to survive.

B = Biopolymers – One of which is DNA. Biopolymers are the nucleic acids which are in all living things.

C = Carbon – Necessary for life on earth.

Taking the last letter first, "C" is for carbon. All life on Earth is carbon-based. We are carbon-based life forms. Carbon is the chemical equivalent of the number one, whose unique characteristic is to add itself to itself, or to other things, to make everything else.

The characteristics of the number one may be summarized as the One Principle: two of the same thing added together creates something which includes the original but is qualitatively different from it. One plus one creates two. Carbon is the physical manifestation of the One Principle because when it bonds, or adds itself to something else, it includes the original while also making the original more than it was. The number one can add to itself infinitely to create. Carbon can bond with itself and almost all other non-metallic elements to create an unending string and variety of complex molecules.

Wikipedia explains the Carbon-Carbon Bond: "Carbon is one of the few elements that can form long chains of its own atoms, a property called catenation. This coupled with the strength of the carbon-carbon bond gives rise to an enormous number of molecular forms, many of which are important structural elements of life."

Carbon can also bond with the three other basic building blocks because it has four electrons available to form chemical bonds. It seeks four other electrons to stabilize the bond for a total of eight electrons (4, foundation, plus 4, stability). The word "carbon" has a root number of 8; the same number of electrons it wants. Eight, the number of power, reflects the power of carbon when it has eight electrons. Carbon's power comes from its ability to bond in infinite combinations. Carbon gets the additional electrons from the three other building blocks. The three other most common building blocks are Oxygen, Hydrogen, and Nitrogen.

Because four in numerology is the number of foundation, stability, and physical manifestation, it makes sense to have four components of life on earth. The four basic components for life on earth are: Carbon, Oxygen, Nitrogen, and Hydrogen.

Chart Twenty-six
Carbon

| 3 | 1 | 18 | 2 | 15 | 14 = 53/8 |
|---|---|----|---|----|-----------|
| C | A | R  | B | O  | N         |
| 3 | 1 | 9  | 2 | 6  | 5 = 26/8  |

\* Translation of full numbers 5, 3, 8:
The Universe (5) is Created (3) by the Power (8) of the divine and carbon.

\* Translation of root numbers 2, 6, 8:
The Duality's (2) creative Magic (6) is based in the power of Carbon (8).

The numerology of "carbon" joins the concepts of the divine, power, and carbon. By the divine, carbon is given the power (8) to create.

**Translation Review**
Creativity is a Foundation of the Duality infused with Spirit. One is a Seed originating from the cosmic egg Germinating as divine creation. One, as in the divine, is also the Beauty within Spirit. It is divine will that Man, by Vision, is brought into the Light. Divine Will is Reflected within the Duality. The Magician's four elements Abundantly Give us the Highest energy to work with. The four elements are the Divine's basic building components which enable Spirit to use and express its own Power in the Duality. A wand channels a Foundation of energy directed by Choice guided by a Vision. The Divine Manipulates and focuses energy to manifest his Vision in the Duality. Divine energy is Creative potential

Expressed as beauty and Vision. The Duality is given the magic of co-creation as a Foundation stabilized by Vision.

Divine energy Initiates the creation of its Reflection with the emanation of Unconditional Love. Free will is a Foundational element of Change enabling us to bring about a desired End. Free Will is also a Spiritual component of the Duality. To have free will is part of spirit's Initiation into the Duality.

The Magician archetype contains the basic building blocks. Divine intention as Will is Reflected throughout Creation. Intention is a Foundational Power of Magic. The Universe is Created by the Power of the divine and Carbon. The Duality's creative Magic is based in the power of Carbon.

## Applying the Revealed Information

### Acquired Meanings – New Meanings Revealed by Numerology

Inclusive, divinity, connection, unity, opposites/polarities, unlimited, power, active and passive energy, creative consciousness, unconditional love, Divine Will, free will, initiating principle, basics, building blocks, seed.

### Relevant Questions

How can I best align myself with Divine intention? How can I claim my power? What is the best way to express my higher sense of who I am at this time? What building blocks do I need to work with in order to reach my goal? What seed has been planted? How can I best use my creative abilities? What part does free will play in the present situation? What is the connecting element between things, people, or situations? In what way am I limited and unlimited?

## Practical Application

Reading: the Queen of Swords, the Magician, the Page of Cups.

The Queen of Swords, as the querent, indicates that the querent's powers of study and analysis are prominent. It may be that the querent should focus his or her powers of analysis and creative thinking. The querent may also need to embrace his or her abilities through the appropriate expression of the element of Swords.

The Queen of Swords and her throne are facing the Magician, indicating the querent is seeking the higher mind and divine guidance. The Page of Cups indicates the Queen has an innate curiosity about life. Following one's curiosity can bring new understanding. The cards also show this is a good time to connect the higher mind to the emotional experience of the inner child (Page of Cups) for greater personal insight.

## Just a Thought

The Magician brings to mind the question: what is the connection between the Queen of Swords and the Page of Cups? The answer depends on a person's perspective. The lemniscate over the Magician's head represents infinity, eternity, power, or cycles. The lemniscate can indicate there are cycles or repeated interactions between two people, things, etc., that keep them connected. In this case, the lemniscate indicates a possible connection between two people because there are court cards on either side of the Magician.

The background behind the Magician is yellow. The idea of enlightenment or higher understanding is symbolized by the color yellow. The color white on the wand and the Magician's tunic is the color of purity. Whenever the Magician card is present, it may indicate the possibility of an "ah ha" moment, that sudden flash of deeper understanding.

**Magician Dynamics:**
Magnifying
Connecting
Unifying
Initiating

# Chapter Four

## Two and the High Priestess

*The Duality holds within it the divine creative spark which contains the foundational principle of creation and change.*

### Two – The Duality, Reflection of the Divine

One plus one equals two. The divine (1) recreated itself (1) by projecting its energy outward to become two, a duality (2). The resulting image, the outward re-creation of the divine, is therefore mirrored. Mirroring produces reversals. This same mirroring happens when we see our image projected outward and reflected back to us using a glass mirror. Two is the first energy that is differentiated from one. Two is the reflection of the divine. Two, and the dual nature of all things reflected, represent our reality. Our reality is the reflection of the divine, and so it is reversed as in a mirror. The Duality, because it is the reflection, operates within the reflection dynamic (The Magician, page 32). The Duality's fabric is a matrix that is both interactive and reflective in nature.

In numerology, two is receptive and passive, compared to one as a generator, the source of outgoing energy. The idea of a dual nature, embodied in two as a fundamental principle, includes both polarity and paradox. As to polarity, two implies the opposite nature of things. The idea that two includes polarity implies that two is both male and female, positive and negative, good and evil, etc. But how is it possible for opposites to exist within the nature of two?

The dynamic of reflection is the answer. The reflection dynamic creates polarity within the one. Two generates paradox in part because the origin of two is only possible with the existence of one. Therefore, stated as a paradox, two is two of the one. As a paradox, two is included in the one, but contains attributes that are only possible as a reflection of one, which makes it different because of the dynamics of reflection, but makes it the same because it contains all the attributes of the one.

Another way of understanding the paradox of two is to contemplate a classic assertion of philosophers. They will say, "If you have a 'yes,' it implies that there is a 'no.'" Similarly, if you have a one, it implies that there is a two. The paradox is that if there is one, then there must be two, and therefore one does not stand alone. There is not one. The paradox exists: there is one and there is not one at the same time.

The uniqueness of the one is contained within two. Two is the first prime number, divisible only by itself and one. Two is the only even prime number. As one added to itself creates other numbers, all that is within one is included in the other numbers. But at the same time these new numbers made up of ones, having the attributes of one, also have their own unique qualities.

Chart Twenty-seven
Two

| 20 | 23 | 15 = 58/13/4 |
|----|----|--------------|
| T  | W  | O            |
| 2  | 5  | 6 = 13/4     |

* Two Key Words: *duality, choice, reflection, differentiation.*

* Conversion of root numbers 13, 4 to letters:
13 = M, 4 = D.

* Translation of M, D:
The Duality is Multi-Dimensional (M, D).

* Translations of full numbers 5, 8, 1, 3, 4:
Changes (5) inherent within the Reflection (8) principle allow the Divine (1) to Create (3) multi-dimensional Foundations (4).

* Translation of root numbers 1, 3, 4:
Man as an Individual (1) Creates (3) and Constructs (4) foundations through the choices he makes.

* Alternate translation of 1, 3, 4:
The Duality holds within the Divine (1) Creative (3) spark that which contains the Foundational (4) principle of creation and change.

The numbers of the word "two" add up to what is called in numerology a karmic number. The karmic number in this case is thirteen. Numerology's focus is on the negative attributes of the number four. The thirteen warns: The One (1) who puts selfish needs first, wasting time in Frivolous (3) superficial activities to avoid Work (4), will incur more work for themselves. The root number of the word "two" is four. A key word for the number four is work. Two represents the Duality, therefore the Duality is a place for spirit to work. We do not only do literal work here, but spiritual work as well.

The reflection dynamic is an important component of the Duality. Following is the numerology of "reflection".

## Chart Twenty-eight
## Reflection

| 18 | 5 | 6 | 12 | 5 | 3 | 20 | 9 | 15 | 14 = 107/8 |
|---|---|---|---|---|---|---|---|---|---|
| R | E | F | L | E | C | T | I | O | N |
| 9 | 5 | 6 | 3 | 5 | 3 | 2 | 9 | 6 | 5 = 53/8 |

* Translation of full numbers 1, 0, 7, 8:
Divine (1) energy Mirrored (0) in Spirit (7) is Powerful (8) and eternal.

* Translation of root numbers 5, 3, 8:
Man's (5) Creations (3) are Reflected (8) within the Duality.

Let's go back to the numbers of the word "two" for a moment. (See Chart Twenty-seven.)

* Conversion of full numbers of "two" 5, 8, 1, 3, 4 into letters:
5 = E, 8 = H, 1 = A, 3 = C, 4 = D.

* Translation of E, H, A, C, D:
Ego (E) Has (H) almost Always (A) Chosen (C) to focus on the Duality (D), or some aspect of it, instead of the divine.

When ego focuses on the Duality instead of the divine, the person may become involved in a cycle of reincarnation.

* Conversion of root numbers 1, 3, 4 into letters:
1 = A, 3 = C, 4 = D.

* Translation of A, C, D:
The Duality is A (A) Creatively (C) multi-Dimensional (D) interactive matrix for self-expression.

Exploring the numerology of "duality" leads us to further ideas about the relationship between spirit, duality (as in dual nature), and the Duality matrix.

## Chart Twenty-nine
## Duality

| D | U | A | L | I | T | Y |
|---|---|---|---|---|---|---|
| 4 | 3 | 1 | 3 | 9 | 2 | 7 = 29/11 |

\* Translation of root numbers 2, 9, 11:
By the nature of the Duality (2) we gain Wisdom (9) and spiritual Understanding (11).

The reflective nature of the Duality teaches us about ourselves and divinity through mirroring.

## Chart Thirty
## Mirror Image

| M | I | R | R | O | R | I | M | A | G | E |
|---|---|---|---|---|---|---|---|---|---|---|
| 4 | 9 | 9 | 9 | 6 | 9 | 9 | 4 | 1 | 7 | 5 = 72/9 |
|   |   | 46 |   |   |   |   | 26 |   |   |   |

\* Translation of root numbers 7, 2, 9:
Spiritual (7) aspects of the divine are passed on to the Duality (2) by the reflective nature of the divine's Mirror Image (9).

All the things we see are many forms of the One. Many spiritual philosophies teach that the great diversity and variety of form within the Duality is an illusion.

"Mirror image" has a root number of nine. In numerology, nine is the last number at the end of an evolving cycle. It is the number that denotes the end of something. As a mirror image, the Duality can be seen as a closed system. Everything has a limited existence in the Duality. The root number nine of "mirror image", using free association, led me to the phrase "dead end."

## Chart Thirty-one
## Dead End

| D | E | A | D | E | N | D |
|---|---|---|---|---|---|---|
| 4 | 5 | 1 | 4 | 5 | 5 | 4 = 10/1 |
|   | 5 (14) |   |   |   | 5 (14) |   |

\* Translation of mundane numbers of "dead" and "end" 14, 5:
Dead end leads back to the divine through Death (14) and End (5).

Note that both "dead" and "end" have the same full number, 14. Because the words have the same full number, they also have the same root number 5 (1 + 4 = 5). Coincidence inspires further investigation.

In single word analysis, numbers to the left of the equal sign are not often used for translation. In this case, the numbers to the left are translated to reveal further information because the numbers are the same and because the analysis is of a phrase.

The reduction of 14 into 5 reveals that "dead" and "end" represent change because five is the number of change. In this case, change occurs by death. 10/1, the root number of "dead end", shows that this kind of change ultimately leads back to the divine.

## High Priestess – The Continuum; The Second Archetype of Paradox

The High Priestess is the second archetype of creation and paradox. As a paradox, she is the two of the one. She is also the continuum, and as such represents the connection between all things within the Duality. In the illustration by Pamela Coleman Smith, the flowing water behind the two pillars symbolizes the continuum.

The Google web dictionary defines continuum as "a continuous sequence in which adjacent elements are not perceptibly different from each other, although the extremes are quite distinct."

The black and white of the illustrated pillars represent the distinctness of extremes or opposites contained within the continuum. Energy that crosses into the Duality can appear to have opposites, and also polarity. What appears as opposite, or polar, is in fact a sequence of minute changes within one thing.

A horizontal line can represent opposites of light and polarity, each end being the extreme expression of the other. In the case of light, that would mean one end is white, and the other end is black. Starting at the white end, a continuum moves toward the other end, which is black. White changes, becoming less white by minute increments, moving through gray, slowly becoming black.

In the Duality, opposites attract each other, drawing the two ends together to make the line into a circle or a lemniscate. The lemniscate, or twisted circle, as a metaphor represents divine energy and its reflection, the Duality. Energy seeks completeness and stability. A circle, or a lemniscate, is an unending movement of energy that is complete within itself. The joining together of the ends, stabilizing the energy, completes the circular movement of energy. The formation of the energy pattern from the joining of opposites and polarities suggests that the existence of polarity and opposites are a fabrication of duality and consciousness.

From our limited point of view, we see a very small part of our universe and reality, making what is connected appear linear or disconnected. A lemniscate is made of energy that is innately and infinitely changing, but ultimately compelled to return to its original stable state. The reinstatement of stability results in the formation of a closed system of energy. This closed energy system can be seen as the end result, but, in a cosmic sense, it is also the beginning.

What we previously thought of as unconnected is a small section of a much larger whole, one of many mystery teachings of the High Priestess. If we could see in totality the progression of minute changes, we would see the two as one. The High Priestess contains the dynamic of polarity: positive, negative, and the dynamic of opposites: active, passive; light becoming black.

Let's look at the chart of the phrase "High Priestess".

### Chart Thirty-two
### High Priestess

```
        32                              130
  8  9  7  8    16  18  9  5  19  20  5  19   19 = 162/9
  H  I  G  H     P   R  I  E   S   T  E   S    S
  8  9  7  8     7   9  9  5   1   2  5   1    1 = 72/9
        32                               40
```

* Translation of full numbers 1, 6, 2, 9:
High Priestess is the One (1) that contains the Vision (6), which is passed on through the mysteries to Us (2) to aid Humanity (9).

* Definition of Vision: The conceiving of and/or discernment of spiritual awareness and insight.

* Translation of the root numbers of the entire phrase 7, 2, 9:
The Paradox (7) of the Duality (2) contains hidden Wisdom (9).

* Translation of the mundane root numbers of the individual words 5, 4:
Changes (5) and paradoxes that occur within this archetype Serve (4) a higher purpose.

For the purpose of translation, I added the mundane numbers 32 and 40 of High Priestess to get 72. After translating 72/9, I translated 5 (3 + 2), and 4 (4 + 0), which are the root numbers of "High" and "Priestess" on the mundane level. The last step is to translate 5, 4, and 9.

> \* Translation of numbers (5), (4), 9:
> She passes on to Man (5) elemental mysteries as a Foundation (4) of an initiate's Wisdom (9).

The High Priestess passes on wisdom by the mystery teachings of duality and paradox. We gain more insight into the mystery teachings as we learn more about our spiritual nature and the nature of the duality matrix.

Let's look at free will again using different key words in the translation for additional information. I have repeated the chart of "free will" for ease of reference.

Chart Thirty-three
Free Will

|   | 34 |   |   |   | 56 |   |   |          |
|---|----|---|---|---|----|---|---|----------|
| 6 | 18 | 5 | 5 |   | 23 | 9 | 12 | 12 = 90/9 |
| F | R  | E | E |   | W  | I | L | L         |
| 6 | 9  | 5 | 5 |   | 5  | 9 | 3 | 3 = 9     |
|   | 7  |   |   |   | 2  |   |   |           |

> \* Alternate Translation of esoteric numbers 9, 0, 9:
> Free will contains the Wisdom (9) of Divine Potential (0), which is a part of Unconditional Love (9).

The numbers 7, 2, 9 answer free will's question: if free will is a *part* of spirit's initiation into the Duality, what is the other part of the initiation? (Chapter Three, page 32.)

> \* Alternate Translation of root numbers 7, 2, 9:
> Spiritual Intelligence (7) is given to Us (2) for Initiation (9) into creative consciousness.

The first part of spirit's initiation into the Duality is free will. The second part of spirit's initiation into the Duality is the expression of creative consciousness.

The archetypal expression and principles of the Fool, Magician, and High Priestess give us the first three building blocks or steps toward creation and the Duality. They represent pure potential (the Fool), divine energy (the Magician), and the continuum (the High Priestess). The High Priestess, representing the reflected energy bringing paradox into the Duality, is placed between the Magician, representing the creation, power, and potential of Divine energy, and the Empress, representing the foundational creative support matrix, also known as the duality matrix.

By combining the full numbers of chosen words, we can gain more information. As an example, I have combined the full numbers of "Magician", 57, and "High Priestess", 162, to learn more about these two archetypes. The numerology chart of "Magician" is repeated for ease of reference.

### Chart Thirty-four
### Magician

| 13 | 1 | 7 | 9 | 3 | 9 | 1 | 14 | = 57/12/3 |
|----|---|---|---|---|---|---|----|-----------|
| M  | A | G | I | C | I | A | N  |           |

* The full number of "Magician" is 57.

* The full number of "High Priestess" is 162 (Chart Thirty-two, page 43).

* The sum of 57 and 162 is 219.

* Conversion of 2, 1, 9 into letters:
2 = B, 1 = A, 9 = I.

* Translation of letters B, A, I:
The combined energies of the Magician and the High Priestess are Beyond (B) Any (A) Intelligence (I).

What these two archetypes represent is beyond our minds' intelligence. We can use our intellect to try to understand them, but the totality of them is beyond our mental capacity. There are aspects of these two archetypes that cannot be fully understood, explained, or expressed in words.

By adding the root numbers, 3 and 9, of "Magician" and "High Priestess", the equation is $3 + 9 = 12/3$.

* 1, 2, 3 or the A, B, C's as the basics or the building blocks.

What are these building blocks for? Together these energies, represented as archetypes, are building blocks for creation on different planes; in this particular case, the spiritual and the physical planes. In the equation $1 + 2 = 3$, three represents a plane. Three represents a plane because one represents point. Two represents a line when two points are joined together. Three, a third point connected to the first two points by a second line, forms a plane. One is a point, two is a line, three is a plane.

By combining the archetypes of the Magician (the divine) and the High Priestess (the reflection dynamic and continuum), you get the basic founding principles that actively create another plane of existence. The combination of these archetypal energies $(1 + 2)$ gives birth to the creative matrix, three $(1 + 2 = 3)$. The number three represents the creative matrix, which is the invisible supporting latticework for all energy within the reflection. This supporting latticework is the interactive reflective duality matrix.

**Translation Review**

The Duality is Multi-Dimensional. Changes inherent in the Reflection principle allow the Divine to Create multi-dimensional Foundations. Man as an Individual Creates and Constructs foundations through the choices he makes. The Duality holds within the Divine Creative spark that which contains the Foundational principle of creation and change. Divine energy Mirrored in Spirit is Powerful and eternal. Man's Creations are Reflected within the Duality.

Ego Has almost Always Chosen to focus on the Duality, or some aspect of it, instead of the divine. The Duality is A Creatively multi-Dimensional interactive matrix for self-expression. By the nature of the Duality we gain Wisdom and spiritual Understanding. Spiritual aspects of the divine are passed on to the Duality by the reflective nature of the divine's Mirror Image. Dead end leads back to the divine through Death and End.

High Priestess is the One that contains the Vision, which is passed on through the mysteries to Us to aid Humanity. The Paradox of the Duality contains hidden Wisdom. Changes and paradoxes that occur within this archetype Serve a higher purpose. She passes on to Man elemental mysteries as a Foundation of an initiate's Wisdom. Free will contains the Wisdom of Divine Potential, which is a part of Unconditional Love. Spiritual Intelligence is given to Us for Initiation into creative consciousness. The combined energies of the Magician and the High Priestess are Beyond Any Intelligence.

## Applying the Revealed Information

### Acquired Meanings – New Meanings Revealed by Numerology
Division, duality, differentiation, choice, conflict, dual nature, paradox, intuition, continuum, two that is one, serve a higher purpose.

### Relevant Questions
What are my choices? What is the dual nature of this situation? What is the teaching within a particular paradox about? When two things seem unrelated, what is their unifying element? What higher purpose is there being served in this situation?

### Practical Application
Reading: The Wheel of Fortune, the Four of Wands, the High Priestess, the Three of Wands.

The Wheel of Fortune brings a change of circumstance for the querent. The Four of Wands indicates that the change of circumstances can serve as a new foundation. The High Priestess shows that there are connections which are not obvious and that there is something yet to be resolved. A way to resolution may be revealed when connections are made between the Four of Wands and the Three of Wands. A choice is made and the course set in the Three of Wands, but there are aspects over which the querent has no control. The querent will have to wait to see the result.

### Just a Thought
The High Priestess represents a process of minute changes. As the archetype that embodies the continuum, the High Priestess hints there are connections, whether we are aware of them or not. The High Priestess points to a connection possibly obscured by our focus on one element or aspect, a small portion of the larger picture.

Rachel Pollack calls a reading that is not in response to a personal question, a wisdom reading. Consider this spread within that context. Change (the Wheel of Fortune) creates new foundations (Four of Wands) on many levels. Every action we take creates change and is therefore part of a continuum (High Priestess). Some actions we take (Three of Wands) lead to obvious results, while other results are more subtle.

The pomegranates on the curtain behind the High Priestess, which we also see on the Empress card, are a symbol of promoting abundance and fertility, in this case by the dynamics of change. Fertility within the human body implies cell division, which we all experience on a very basic level.

**High Priestess Dynamics:**
Connecting
Reflecting
Changing
Polarizing

## Chapter Five

### Three and the Empress

*The creative matrix altered within dimensional space to take form within Duality.*

**Three – The Creative Principle and Diversity**

Three represents the foundation principle of creation as the dynamic interaction between one and two. Three is the first result of an interacting pair and is the last number in what is called the Creative Trinity in numerology. The Creative Trinity is the numbers 1, 2, 3. As the result of one plus two, three is the number of creativity, diversity, and expression. Three also represents the triangle—the first geometric figure. To review: one gives you a point, which has no spatial dimensions. Two points give you a line, which has one spatial dimension of length. Three gives you a plane, which has two spatial dimensions of infinite length and infinite width. All geometric figures start with point, line, plane.

Three non-linear points connected by three lines gives us the first basic geometric form: the two-dimensional triangle. The triangle is a geometric result of the interaction of one plus two. The three connected points of the triangle form the basic skeletal foundation that supports physical manifestation within the Duality. The third line connecting the third point to the first point gives the other two lines support. Three supports creation by providing a skeletal structure. Three represents the support matrix within three-dimensional space. The number three, in three dimensions, has a fourth point in space and is represented by the triangular pyramid.

Three also represents time as past, present, future. Everything that manifests physically goes through three basic stages of creation, formation, destruction. Let's take a look at the numerology of the word "three".

Chart Thirty-five
Three

| 20 | 8 | 18 | 5 | 5 | = 56/11 |
|---|---|---|---|---|---|
| T | H | R | E | E | |
| 2 | 8 | 9 | 5 | 5 | = 29/11 |

\* Three key words: *creative trinity, expression, support matrix.*

\* Translation of full numbers 5, 6, 11:
Man (5) is Responsible (6) on a Spiritual (11) and physical level

for what he creates.

\* Translation of root numbers 2, 9, 11:
It is important We (2) use Integrity (9) when creating and gain Understanding (11) and insight from what is created.

Notice in the numerology of "create", the full number is reversed in the root number. The full number is 52. On the mundane level, the digits of 52 are reversed. This is called mirroring. If the number order is reversed, it calls attention to which digits are being emphasized. The digit that comes first is the one emphasized in the translation. In this example, the digit 5 of 52 and the digit 2 of 25 would be emphasized.

### Chart Thirty-six
### Create

| 3 | 18 | 5 | 1 | 20 | 5 = 52/7 |
|---|----|---|---|----|----------|
| C | R  | E | A | T  | E        |
| 3 | 9  | 5 | 1 | 2  | 5 = 25/7 |

\* Note that the esoteric number 52 is mirrored on the mundane level as 25.

\* Translation of full numbers 5, 2, 7:
Changes (5) within the Duality (2) are a part of the divine's and our Spiritual (7) expression.

\* Translation of root numbers 2, 5, 7:
The Duality (2) brings about Change (5) by the act of creating as a process of Spiritual Intelligence (7) and therefore an extension of spirit.

The seven root number of "create" indicates that to create is an action based in the spiritual. To create in the Duality takes time. Here is the numerology of "time".

### Chart Thirty-seven
### Time

| 20 | 9 | 13 | 5 = 47/11 |
|----|---|----|-----------|
| T  | I | M  | E         |
| 2  | 9 | 4  | 5 = 20/2  |

\* Translation of full numbers 4, 7, 11:
Time is a Foundational (4) aspect of Intellect (7) and Spiritual Understanding (11) within the Duality.

\* Translation of root numbers 2, 0, 2:
Time gives Us (2) space to reflect (0) on the nature of the Duality (2).

Time also creates the illusion of progression, as in an ongoing process of development. Time creates space for us to consider our creations.

### The Empress – Multi-Dimensional Creative Matrix

The Empress is the third archetype of creation. As a conduit, the Empress receives information from the divine and the continuum to form an energy matrix. The archetype of the Empress creates the patterns as part of the matrix for everything that enters three-dimensional space. The Empress expresses these patterns and the energy matrix, which facilitate creation within the Duality. The Duality uses the energy matrix and patterns as a medium for expression.

Chart Thirty-eight
Empress

| 5 | 13 | 16 | 18 | 5 | 19 | 19 = 95/14/5 |
|---|----|----|----|---|----|--------------|
| E | M  | P  | R  | E | S  | S            |
| 5 | 4  | 7  | 9  | 5 | 1  | 1 – 32/5     |

\* Translation of full esoteric numbers 9, 5, 1, 4, 5:
The Empress aids the Initiation (9) of Change (5) in the Duality while also facilitating the Divine (1) plan by providing the support Matrix (4) needed for Change (5) and variety.

Nine is the number of initiation, as explained by Shirley Blackwell Lawrence in her book *The Secret Science of Numerology*. The word "matrix", with a root number of 4, is used as a translation for the number four.

\* Conversion of full numbers 1, 4, 5, into letters:
1 = A, 4 = D, 5 = E.

\* Translation of letters A, D, E:
The Empress is an ADE (aid) to creativity.

\* Conversion of root numbers 3, 2, 5 to letters:
3 = C, 2 = B, 5 = E.

\* Translation of C, B, E:
She Transmits (CB, as in CB radio) her Energy (E) as the duality matrix.

\* Translation method used for C, B; A, D, E:
Taking letters whose sound represents a word; CB, as in citizens band radio, and the homonyms ADE and aid.

Five, the root number of "Empress", shows this archetype promotes variety and abundance by change. Every matrix pattern has infinite variations. The matrix patterns of the Empress permeate the Duality. The Duality as we know it would not exist without these patterns. As an archetype, the Empress is reproductive.

On the esoteric level, notice the 14/5 karmic number of "Empress" (Chart Thirty-eight, page 51). The 14/5 karmic number warns that why we create and what we create need careful consideration, because what we create is an extension of our spiritual persona. On the level of spirit, what we create is a reflection of ourselves. A self-centered focus (the negatively expressed attribute of the number one) paired with a lack of accountability (the negatively expressed attribute of the number four) is an abuse of personal freedom. Personal freedom is abused when we create with negative intent or lack of responsibility.

Because of the Empress, all physical manifestations can exist in the Duality. Let's look at the numbers of "exist".

Chart Thirty-nine
Exist

| 5 | 24 | 9 | 19 | 20 = 77 |
|---|----|---|----|---------|
| E | X  | I | S  | T       |
| 5 | 6  | 9 | 1  | 2 = 23/5 |

Seventy-seven is considered the number of Christ consciousness because the word "Christ" has a full number of seventy-seven. Christ consciousness is an innate part of our divine spiritual essence. It is a pattern of pure divine energy. "Exist" has the same full number. To exist is to have the pattern of Christ consciousness and the potential to express it.

The interactive component of the support matrix is an integral part of existence within the Duality. Nothing could exist, energetically or physically in the Duality, without the interactive nature of the support matrix. Following are the numbers of "support matrix".

Chart Forty
Support Matrix

```
           125                              85
19  21  16  16  15  18  20   13   1  20  18  9  24 = 210/3
 S   U   P   P   O   R   T    M   A   T   R  I   X
 1   3   7   7   6   9   2    4   1   2   9  9   6  = 12/3
            8 (35)                     4 (31)
```

* Translation of esoteric full numbers 2, 1, 0, 3:
The Duality's (2) Divine (1) foundations are Reflected (0) from the Expression (3) of the Magician, High Priestess, and Empress.

* Conversion of full numbers of "matrix" 3, 1, 4 into letters:
3 = C, 1 = A, 4 = D.

* Translation of 3, 1, 4 as letters:
The Creative (C) matrix is Altered (A) within Dimensional (D) space and in the Duality so the energy of the creative matrix can take form.

* Translation of root numbers of "support" and "matrix" 8, 4, 3:
The Empress is an eternally Powerful (8) creative Foundation (4) for this type of dimensional Expression (3).

Let's go back to the numbers of "Empress" for a moment. (Chart Thirty-eight, page 51.)

* Conversion of full numbers 9, 5 to letters:
9 = I, 5 = E.

* Translation of letters I, E:
She is the Integrated (I) energy matrix within Everything (E).

**Translation Review**
Man is Responsible on a Spiritual and physical level for what he creates. It is important We use Integrity when creating and gain Understanding and insight from what is created. Changes within the Duality are a part of the divine's and our Spiritual expression.

The Duality brings about Change by the act of creating as a process of Spiritual Intelligence and therefore an extension of spirit. Time is a Foundational aspect of Intellect and Spiritual Understanding within the Duality. Time gives Us space to reflect on the nature of the Duality. The Empress aids the Initiation of Change in the Duality while also facilitating the Divine plan by providing the support Matrix needed for Change and variety. The Empress is an ADE (aid) to creativity. She Transmits her Energy as the duality matrix.

The Duality's Divine foundations are Reflected from the Expression of the Magician, High Priestess, and Empress. The Creative matrix is Altered within Dimensional space and in the Duality so the energy of the creative matrix can take form. The Empress is an eternally Powerful creative Foundation for this type of dimensional Expression. She is the Integrated energy matrix within Everything.

**Applying the Revealed Information**

**Acquired Meanings – New Meanings Revealed by Numerology**
The dynamic interaction, support matrix, divine expression, creativity, time, infinite variety, abundance, cooperation, cohesion, basic stages, result.

**Relevant Questions**
What components are needed to manifest my ideas? What three things support me at this time? What is the best way to express my creative energy? What matrix can I create to promote success? What do I need to promote growth and expansion at this time?

**Practical Application**
Reading: the King of Wands, the Empress, the Sun.

These three cards represent fire energy: Wands, the element of fire; Empress, the fire of creation; Sun, the light and heat of elemental fire. There is a dynamic interaction between the querent's mastery of decisive action and creative energy at this time. In general, the querent is likely to be experiencing a time of abundance, variety, and expansion. Plans that the querent puts into action are likely to bring about desired results. Creativity and self-expression are at a higher level.

The mastery of spirit expressing itself creatively within the Duality will lift spirit to the next level of creation. In these three cards, we see all four elements: fire and spiritual energy, King of Wands; water and emotion, the stream in the Empress card; air and mental energy, the sky in the Sun card; earth and creative abundance, Empress.

There is a strong relation between action (Wands), creation (Empress), and possible result (Sun, bringing something into the light of day). These cards indicate a deeper understanding of what is needed to bring about a desired result. Take the right action to create the environment for a desired result.

**Just a Thought**
The Empress card has a stream in the background on the right side. Water can have many meanings, but continuing the idea of water representing a continuum, as was discussed under the High Priestess (Chapter Four, page 42), drew my thinking to what is common to the cards of this reading. The element of fire was immediately apparent. The fire

element is represented by the suit of Wands and the red material the Empress sits on. The large red banner the child holds in the Sun card represents fire energy and its dynamics, as well as the fiery energy of the Sun.

Fire, as in *actual* fire, can result in an abundance of new growth. The Empress wears a robe decorated with red pomegranates symbolizing the outgoing, active energy of the seed, denoting fertility as an aspect of new growth.

Yellow, as the color of enlightenment and therefore a connection to the divine, is also a common element in these three cards: the King's crown, the orb on the staff, the collar of the Empress's robe, and the sun and sunflowers on the Sun card. All the major arcana cards, in fact, include yellow, even the card for the Devil, whose beard is yellow.

**Empress Dynamics:**
Creating
Interacting
Supporting

## Chapter Six

### Four and the Emperor

*The power to manifest was given by the Divine so the creative mind, by original thinking, could discover for itself the power of change.*

**Four – Physical Manifestation, Three-Dimensional Form**

Examples of four are everywhere within the Duality: the four elements—earth, air, fire, water; the four directions—north, south, east, west; the sequence of progression—idea, seed, growth, maturity; and even the physical body—head, torso, arms, legs. There are also four directions in relation to the body—up, down, left, right.

Four represents energy that has been altered so it can take solid form in the Duality. Some non-solids become solid when the molecules within vibrate at a slow enough rate. The rate of vibration for conversion to a solid varies with the type of molecules. As the rate of vibration slows down, energy becomes denser, making it more solid. Four provides a stable framework for energy physically manifesting in three dimensions.

The cube represents the number four in three dimensions. The cube and the square symbolize truth because they have the same dimensional qualities no matter which way you look at them.

Let's see what the numerology of the word "four" tells us.

Chart Forty-one
Four

| 6 | 15 | 21 | 18 = 60/6 |
|---|----|----|-----------|
| F | O  | U  | R         |
| 6 | 6  | 3  | 9 = 24/6  |

\* Four key words: *manifestation, foundation, physical.*

\* Translation of esoteric numbers 6, 0, 6:
The Harmony (6) of physical manifestation is a Reflection (0) of our Vision (6).

\* Translation of root numbers 2, 4, 6:
The Dual (2) nature of our Physical (4) dimension leads us to ever-expanding Awareness (6) and vision.

The definition of vision in the *Merriam Webster's Collegiate*

*Dictionary: Tenth Edition* is "the conceiving of and discernment of some thing." In this case, it would be the conceiving of and discernment of the spiritual. Translating the number six as vision and using this definition, 6, 0, 6 (full numbers of "four") is interpreted as: Manifestation is harmoniously expressed by the conceiving and discernment of our spiritual intelligence, knowledge, and awareness.

The nature of physical reality allows us to see what we create. Because of Duality's matrix, we have the opportunity to manifest our own concepts and designs using divine energy. The Duality promotes the perception of spiritual insight and understanding of what divinity is within our reality and how it manifests.

Pythagoras was a Greek mathematician and philosopher who started a school of math and metaphysics at Croton in southern Italy around 530 B.C. Pythagoras studied with the ancient Egyptians learning about numbers and the nature of the universe. The tetractys illustrates an important idea about the foundational properties of the number four.

Chart Forty-two
Tetractys

```
      •
     • •
    • • •
   • • • •
```

The number four is the basis of the tetractys, which is a mathematical idea and a metaphysical symbol. The properties of the tetractys were taught in the Pythagorean school of mysteries. The word tetractys is from the Greek word *tettares* meaning four. The pattern of dots of the tetractys illustrates the mathematical equation of $1 + 2 + 3 + 4 = 10$. Ten is the number of perfection because the digits of ten added together lead back to the divine ($1 + 0 = 1$). Divine energy takes four steps to create the Duality. Because the equation illustrated by the tetractys adds to ten (divine perfection), ten contains the four steps of creation.

The number four can be represented in three-dimensional space as point, line, plane, with a fourth point added in space. This three-dimensional diagram is the simplest three-dimensional form, the tetrahedron. A tetrahedron is a figure with four triangular faces, one of which is the triangular base.

## Chart Forty-three
## Tetractys

| 20 | 5 | 20 | 18 | 1 | 3 | 20 | 25 | 19 = 131/5 |
|----|---|----|----|---|---|----|----|------------|
| T  | E | T  | R  | A | C | T  | Y  | S          |
| 2  | 5 | 2  | 9  | 1 | 3 | 2  | 7  | 1 = 32/5   |

\* Translation of esoteric numbers 1, 3, 1, 5:
The ability to manifest was given by the Divine (1) so the Creative (3) mind, by Original (1) thinking, could discover for itself the power of Change (5).

\* Translation of root numbers 3, 2, 5:
Creativity (3) within the Duality (2) always denotes Change (5).

The root numbers of "tetractys" show that creativity and change are synonymous.

**The Emperor – Conscious Creation within the Duality**
The Emperor is the fourth card of creation. He is the archetype of physical manifestation, as distinct from an imagined form that never becomes tangible. The Emperor completes the components necessary for making what is created physically manifest within the Duality. The archetypes of creation include the potential of zero, the outward expression of one, the differentiation and duality of two, the creative impetus and support matrix of three, and the ability to manifest energy within three dimensions represented by the four. The Emperor is the master of all four elements working harmoniously together. He blends the energy of the three previous archetypes to his own in order to create his world.

## Chart Forty-four
## Emperor

| 5 | 13 | 16 | 5 | 18 | 15 | 18 = 90/9 |
|---|----|----|---|----|----|-----------|
| E | M  | P  | E | R  | O  | R         |
| 5 | 4  | 7  | 5 | 9  | 6  | 9 = 45/9  |

\* Conversion of esoteric numbers 9, 0, 9 into letters:
9 = I, 0 = O, 9 = I.

\* Translation of letters I, O, I:
The Emperor is the Initiation (I) Of (O) an Individual (I) spirit into

the physical.

* Conversion of root numbers 4, 5, 9 to letters:
4 = D, 5 = E, 9 = I.

* Translation of letters D, E, I:
This archetype is Divine (D) Energy's (E) Initiation (I) into consciousness and solid matter.

* Translation of root numbers 4, 5, 9:
The Emperor's energy provides the Foundation (4) for Man (5) by the Initiation (9) of spirit's consciousness manifesting within the Duality.

    The Emperor represents the initiation of spirit into a field of manifestation. Learning about and fully experiencing the Duality requires spirit to create a body and to express creations physically in three-dimensional space. Having a body creates self-identity.
    Self-identity includes ego. The ego's basic function is to provide a survival instinct for the body. Ego also defines our individual concept of "I am." Survival instinct is necessary because spirit does not equate existence solely with the physical. Spirit defines concepts of existence beyond the ego identity. The initiation of spirit into physical existence allows spirit and the divine to experience infinite variety and the uniqueness of individuality. As spirit learns about itself by what it creates, so does the divine.

Chart Forty-five
Initiation

| 9 | 14 | 9 | 20 | 9 | 1 | 20 | 9 | 15 | 14 = 120/3 |
|---|----|---|----|---|---|----|---|----|------------|
| I | N  | I | T  | I | A | T  | I | O  | N          |
| 9 | 5  | 9 | 2  | 9 | 1 | 2  | 9 | 6  | 5 = 57/12/3 |

* Translation of full numbers 1, 2, 0, 3:
The Divine (1) gives Us (2) the opportunity to work with the Unlimited Potential (0) of individual Creative (3) consciousness.

* Translation of root numbers 5, 7, 1, 2, 3:
Man (5) contains the Intelligence (7) of Divine (1) consciousness while in the Duality (2), where there is an innate impetus toward Self-Expression (3).

* Conversion of root numbers 5, 7, 1, 2, 3 into letters:
5 = E, 7 = G, 1 = A, 2 = B, 3 = C.

* Translation of letters E, G, A, B, C:
The Emperor (E) Gives (G) All (A) the Building (B) blocks necessary for conscious Creation (C) in physical form within the duality matrix.

Let's take a look at the numbers for "physical manifestation" next. Because Chart Forty-six could not fit on the same lines, numbers that are in italics are added together, and numbers in bold are added together.

### Chart Forty-six
### Physical Manifestation

|    |    |    |    | *93* |    |    |    |
|----|----|----|----|----|----|----|----|
| 16 | 8  | 25 | 19 | 9  | 3  | 1  | 12 |
| P  | H  | Y  | S  | I  | C  | A  | L  |
| 7  | 8  | 7  | 1  | 9  | 3  | 1  | 3  |
|    |    |    |    | **39** |    |    |    |

*93* + *146* = *239*

|    |    |    |    |    |    | *146* |    |    |    |    |    |
|----|----|----|----|----|----|----|----|----|----|----|----|
| 13 | 1 | 14 | 9 | 6 | 5 | 19 | 20 | 1 | 20 | 9 | 15 | 14 = *239/14/5* |
| M  | A | N  | I | F | E | S  | T  | A | T  | I | O  | N |
| 4  | 1 | 5  | 9 | 6 | 5 | 1  | 2  | 1 | 2  | 9 | 6  | 5 = **95/14/5** |
|    |   |    |   |   |   |    | **56** |   |   |   |   |   |

**39 + 56 = 95**

* Translation of full numbers 2, 3, 9, 1, 4, 5:
We (2) Create (3) Compassion (9) by the Divine (1) Service (4) of Man (5) helping others.

* Translation of root numbers 9, 5, 1, 4, 5:
Compassion (9) Changes (5) the Individual (1), providing a Foundation (4) for greater Personal Change (5).

Notice that "physical manifestation" has a karmic full and root number of 14/5. This karmic number warns that spirit manifesting itself in the physical can have negative consequences.

Because the interpretation of the phrase "physical manifestation" talks about compassion, let's look at the numerology of this word next.

Chart Forty-seven
Compassion

| 3 | 15 | 13 | 16 | 1 | 19 | 19 | 9 | 15 | 14 = 124/7 |
|---|----|----|----|---|----|----|---|----|------------|
| C | O  | M  | P  | A | S  | S  | I | O  | N          |
| 3 | 6  | 4  | 7  | 1 | 1  | 1  | 9 | 6  | 5 = 43/7   |

\* Translation of full numbers 1, 2, 4, 7:
The Divine (1) Reflection (2) has a Foundation (4) of Spirituality (7).

\* Translation of root numbers 4, 3, 7:
Compassion is the Foundation (4) of Creation (3) within a Spiritual (7) context.

**Translation Review**

The Harmony of physical manifestation is a Reflection of our Vision. The Dual nature of our Physical dimension leads us to ever-expanding Awareness and vision. The ability to manifest was given by the Divine so the Creative mind, by Original thinking, could discover for itself the power of Change. Creativity within the Duality always denotes Change.

The Emperor is the Initiation Of an Individual spirit into the physical. This archetype is Divine Energy's Initiation into consciousness and solid matter. The Emperor's energy provides the Foundation for Man by the Initiation of spirit's consciousness manifesting within the Duality. The Divine gives Us the opportunity to work with the Unlimited Potential of individual Creative consciousness.

Man contains the Intelligence of Divine consciousness while in the Duality, where there is an innate impetus toward Self-Expression. The Emperor Gives All the Building blocks necessary for conscious Creation in physical form within the duality matrix.

We Create Compassion by the Divine Service of Man helping others. Compassion Changes the Individual, providing a Foundation for greater Personal Change. The Divine Reflection has a Foundation of Spirituality. Compassion is the Foundation of Creation within a Spiritual context.

## Applying the Revealed Information

### Acquired Meanings – New Meanings Revealed by Numerology
Spirit consciousness in physical form, foundation, the power of conscious creation, truth, development, ego, sense of self-identity, spirit creating physical form.

### Relevant Questions
What is important for me to manifest in my life? What foundation do I need for this manifestation? What is my spiritual connection to what I have manifested? What are the basic components of …? What are my four steps of creation?

### Practical Application
Reading: the Emperor, the Page of Swords, the Ten of Cups, the King of Pentacles.

Note that the Emperor and the King of Pentacles are the first and last cards of the spread. The King of Pentacles is the energy of the Emperor manifesting in everyday life. The King shows a heightened ability for manifestation. What and how the manifestations take place are important considerations. The creation and development of the querent's life is in the querent's hands. The Page of Swords, looking back toward the Emperor, indicates that a well thought-out approach and careful consideration of goals is important. A more mature approach to balance youthful enthusiasm is needed. The Page, who is looking toward the Emperor, can also indicate the seeking out of experienced advice.

The Ten of Cups suggests that there is an emotional component to the act of manifestation which includes gratitude and joy. Perhaps attachment to what is manifested has an effect on the quality of reality we manifest.

The stream crossing the background in the Ten of Cups speaks of the continuum, connecting us to the divine and what we manifest. Thankfulness and appreciation for what we have also connects us to the divine.

The last card, the King of Pentacles, shows a man sitting on a throne, with abundant plant life around him. His eyes seem to be closed. His left hand rests on a pentacle, and in his right hand he holds a scepter with a globe at the top. This indicates the querent has some power or authority over his or her physical surroundings. The surroundings are an integral part of the king. The closed eyes reflect an attitude of non-attachment. The querent should not overly identify with the 'things of life,' but appreciate them for what they are: the innate, natural abundance of divine creative consciousness within the Duality.

The pentacle is an object of magic and suggests that control may be somewhat dependent on forces active behind what is obvious. The yellow background, as the color of enlightenment, suggests that everyone, through his or her higher knowledge, has a certain innate understanding of how to manifest what he or she wants.

**Just a Thought**

The process of personal creation within the Duality is a recapitulation of universal creation embodied in the first four archetypes: the Magician, the High Priestess, the Empress, and the Emperor. I thought it might be interesting to ask the cards, "What are the four steps of *personal* creation?" I am basing this inquiry on the number four because the Emperor is the number four and represents the attributes of the number four in numerology. The cards randomly pulled were the Ten of Wands, the Hierophant, the King of Pentacles, and the Eight of Pentacles. Each card in the reading represents one step.

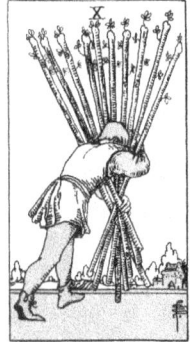   

The first card, the Ten of Wands, shows the first step of personal creation is connecting to the divine. Ten is the number of the divine. Ten indicates a connection between personal consciousness (1) and divine consciousness (10).

The suit of Wands is associated with the element of fire. Fire, and therefore Wands, represents pure spirit. While fire can be destructive, it promotes creation. When we create, we draw on our connection to divine consciousness and our own creative impetus. The connection between divine creativity and personal creativity is active and responsive.

The second card is the Hierophant. This archetype promotes the evolution of consciousness and spiritual growth. He directs outwardly flowing energy inward again for evaluation. The second step of creation has three considerations: evaluate on a deeper level what we create, how we interact with what we create, and how what we create interacts with the world. Personal creativity promotes spiritual growth when the Hierophant encourages us to examine our connection to what we create.

The third card is the King of Pentacles. The King of Pentacles sits with his eyes closed. The third step of creation is to create not only what we need, but also what reflects abundance on a deeper level. Creating our life isn't about what we see and therefore desire; I see this, therefore I want it. It is about creating true abundance.

The last card is the Eight of Pentacles. This card shows a relationship between our creative energy and how we focus it to bring something into our reality. A man sits on a bench repeatedly creating the same thing. His effort is focused and intense.

Eight is the number of power and a circulating and a reflecting energy. Eight is also four, doubled. Four is the number of physical creation. Creativity leads to more creativity. The intensity of focus is the way we tap into our conscious and unconscious ability to create and manifest. The fourth step of creation is intensity and focus.

* The Four Steps of Creation:

1. Connecting the divine act of creation and our personal act of creation.

2. Considering the spiritual connection between self and what we create.

3. Creating what reflects abundance on a deeper level.

4. Directing intensity and focus.

The four steps of creation lead to the expansion of our ability to manifest the reality we want.

**Emperor Dynamics:**
Empowering
Manifesting
Promoting
Stabilizing

**Summary of the First Five Cards**
The archetypes of the Fool, the Magician, the High Priestess, the Empress, and the Emperor can be summarized as follows: The unlimited potential (the Fool) of the divine (the Magician) reflects (the High Priestess) itself to produce an energy matrix (the Empress) that results in the creation of a physically manifested universe (the Emperor).

# Chapter Seven

## Commentary: The Four Archetypes of Creation

The Magician (1), High Priestess (2), Empress (3), and Emperor (4) form a very powerful group dynamic. They represent the first four steps taken by the divine toward manifestation. In this instance, I am using the word manifestation to apply, in a broad sense, to the creating of the duality matrix. The duality matrix is the energy grid our universe is built on.

The Magician, archetype of the divine, made a reflection of itself. At the same time, basic units of energy were created. These basic units of energy form our four elements of Earth, Air, Fire, Water. These four elements are represented in the Rider-Waite tarot as Pentacles, Swords, Wands, Cups.

The High Priestess is the archetype of the divine reflection. She promotes the illusion of polarity and the dynamic characteristics of duality. Once the Magician created a reflection of itself by outwardly expressing energy, the dynamics of duality was a result. The dynamics of duality include all the characteristics of dualism, one of which creates the appearance of polarity within the duality matrix.

Polarity expresses sometimes as the positive and negative charge within electricity, sometimes as the positive and negative within magnetism. The same polarity also expresses as opposite ends of the color spectrum; for example, yellow and violet. Another polarity expressed within dualism is active and passive. The High Priestess is the guardian of the lemniscate—the Magician's symbol of the Duality—and of outward flowing energy returning to its source.

The Empress, archetype of the creative matrix, is the innate result of interacting energy (1 + 2 = 3), the original divine energy (1) interacting with its reflection (2). This interaction created the matrix on which the duality of our universe is expressed. The dynamics of the duality matrix allow spirit to create energy patterns that can become solid manifestations.

The Emperor, archetype of physical manifestations within the duality matrix, represents spirit's ability to form structures of energy. These structures of energy can become solid within the Duality. The structures created reflect the nature of the spirit's consciousness. What is created reflects this consciousness because the duality matrix is innately interactive and reflective in nature.

The analogy of the mirror is helpful here. Nothing appears in the mirror that is not in the field of reflection. But the refection of the Divine in the Duality includes interactions of the elements within the duality matrix. The result is a reflection with changes. Changes arise from interactions between what is reflected and the dynamics of the duality matrix. (Reflection dynamic, Chapter Three, page 28.)

## Chapter Eight

### Five and the Hierophant

*The Divine made the Duality a place for expression within the material dimension as a reflection of self.*

**Five – Change and the Creativity of Man within the Duality**
Five is the result of adding odd and even numbers (1 + 4, 2 + 3). It contains a mix of energies. Three, a component of five, represents creativity. Five represents change. When we create, change occurs. Change is inherent within creativity. Change, as a foundation of physical manifestation within the Duality, creates variety and abundance.

Five, as the center between one and ten, is a balance point. Five also represents the balance between the physical and the divine (10). To review, we now have the numbers one, two, three, four, and five.

* Translation of numbers 1, 2, 3, 4, 5:
The Divine (1) made the Duality (2) a place for Expression (3) within the Physical (4) dimension made abundant by Change (5).

The dynamics of change provide the necessary diversity for our survival. A series of these changes brought about life as we know it. Fifteen, (1 + 2 + 3 + 4 + 5 = 15) as three times five, is the Creative (3) matrix multiplying variations of creativity to help bring about Change (5).

Five, as one plus four, is the divine (1) creating a physical (4) dimension. The physical dimension includes our planet and physical life. It takes four emanations of the divine to create physical life. The representation of the four divine emanations that create life on earth are the components of life: carbon, oxygen, nitrogen, and hydrogen (Chapter Three, page 33).

Five has both masculine and feminine energy: one, the masculine energy, plus four (1 + 4 = 5), or two, the feminine energy, plus three (2 + 3 = 5). Five can perpetuate itself through multiplication. If you multiply five times another number with five as the last digit, it produces a higher number with five as the last digit (5 x 5 = 25, 5 x 25 = 125, etc.). Five is unique in its ability to reproduce itself, just as male and female reproduce themselves. Five is a re-generator, just as male and female represent the principle of reproduction. Five also represents the human body because of the five senses.

## Chart Forty-eight
## Five

|   |   |   |   |
|---|---|---|---|
| 6 | 9 | 22 | 5 = 42/6 |
| F | I | V  | E        |
| 6 | 9 | 4  | 5 = 24/6 |

* Five key words: *re-generation, change, expansiveness, freedom, man.*

* Translation of full numbers 4, 2, 6:
When the Foundation (4) of the Duality (2) is centered around Vision (6), we remain grounded in spirituality.

* Translation of root numbers 2, 4, 6:
The Dual (2) nature of physical existence provides a Foundation (4) which promotes Vision (6).

* Conversion of full numbers 4, 2, 6 into letters:
4 = D, 2 = B, 6 = F.

* Translation of letters D, B, F:
Divinity (D) Brings (B) spirituality into this Foundation (F).

* Conversion of 2, 4, 6 into letters:
2 = B, 4 = D, 6 = F.

* Translation of B, D, F:
Divinity also Brings (B) a sense of Devotion (D) and Faith (F) to spirituality.

Five is the number of man, and the root number of "five" is six, the number of family. Within the word "five" is Man's Family (6) or the family of man. Creating a family can bring a sense of devotion. Following is the numerology of devotion.

## Chart Forty-nine
## Devotion

| 4 | 5 | 22 | 15 | 20 | 9 | 15 | 14 = 104/5 |
|---|---|----|----|----|---|----|------------|
| D | E | V  | O  | T  | I | O  | N          |
| 4 | 5 | 4  | 6  | 2  | 9 | 6  | 5 = 41/5   |

* Translation of full numbers 1, 0, 4, 5:
The Divine (1) is Reflected (0) within the Duality as the Foundation (4) of Man's (5) life.

* Translation of root numbers 4, 1, 5:
This Foundation (4) of Divine (1) energy brings Balance (5) in all things.

The Pentagram is a common geometric representation of the number five.

## Chart Fifty
## Pentagram

| 16 | 5 | 14 | 20 | 1 | 7 | 18 | 1 | 13 = 95/14/5 |
|---|---|---|---|---|---|---|---|---|
| P | E | N | T | A | G | R | A | M |
| 7 | 5 | 5 | 2 | 1 | 7 | 9 | 1 | 4 = 41/5 |

* Translation of full numbers 9, 5, 1, 4, 5:
Integrity (9) comes first when Man (5) uses Divine (1) energy to bring about Fundamental (4) Change (5).

If integrity is not considered, then karmic consequences may take effect, hence the 14/5 karmic number.

* Conversion of full numbers 9, 5, 1, 4, 5 into letters:
9 = I, 5 = E, 1 = A, 4 = D, 5 = E.

* Translation of I, E, A, D, E:
A pentagram is an Integrated (I) Energy (E) form often used as A (A) Diagram (D) in Energy (E) manipulation or magic.

* Translation of karmic number 1, 4, 5 on esoteric level:
Using a pentagram only when the Individual (1) is Served (4) abuses Personal Freedom (5).

* Translation of equation 1 + 4 = 5:
The Divine (1) and the Four (4) aspects of the human existence—spiritual, emotional, mental, and physical—are an ever-Changing (5) experience within the Duality.

## The Hierophant – Mentor of Spiritual Growth

At the bottom of the Hierophant card there are two crossed keys. The archetypal energy of the Hierophant, like a skeleton key, unlocks the mysteries of our spiritual nature and how our deeper understanding is reflected in our personal life. This archetype centers us in our spiritual nature. He also directs our attention to energy that has been sent outward, bringing our focus inward again to consider the effects of our energy on our environment. The Hierophant promotes the evolution of consciousness and leads the way to spiritual knowledge, insight, and understanding. The consideration of the effects of our outward-directed energy helps bring about and maintain an alignment of spirit, subconscious, and conscious.

The Hierophant is the archetypal teacher of the principle of reflection, which states two properties: your environment reflects your personal spiritual energy; what you put out is what you get back. The principle of reflection is due to the innate reflective quality of the duality matrix.

The Hierophant, as card number five, represents the way of balance. Midway between the Magician and the Wheel of Fortune, the Hierophant promotes a re-balancing of self. Discovering and following the way of balance promotes opportunities for positive change, as we move toward inevitable change brought about by the Wheel of Fortune.

Chart Fifty-one
Hierophant

| 8 | 9 | 5 | 18 | 15 | 16 | 8 | 1 | 14 | 20 = 114/6 |
|---|---|---|----|----|----|---|---|----|------------|
| H | I | E | R  | O  | P  | H | A | N  | T |
| 8 | 9 | 5 | 9  | 6  | 7  | 8 | 1 | 5  | 2 = 60/6 |

\* Translation of full numbers 11, 4, 6:
The Hierophant translates Spiritual (11) energy in the Physical (4) by Vision (6).

\* Alternate translation of 11, 4, 6:
The Hierophant's Spiritual Understanding (11) and insight is a Foundation (4) of our Vision (6).

The Hierophant acts as a frequency modulator, modulating our spiritual as well as our physical vibrations so that spiritual emanations can be translated into something we can understand. He comes after the Emperor because an adjustment of vibration is not necessary until spirit has manifested within the physical.

* Conversion into letters of full numbers 11, 4, 6:
11 = K, 4 = D, 6 = F.

* Translation of letters K, D, F:
The Hierophant is the spiritual Knowledge (K) of the Divine (D) that serves as a Foundation (F) for personal conduct.

* Conversion into letters of root numbers 6, 0, 6:
6 = F, 0 = O, 6 = X.

* Translation of letters F, O, X:
When one abuses a position of authority, they become the F (6), O (0), X (6) or the FOX in the henhouse.

* Translation of root numbers 6, 0, 6:
The abuse of position may be because of a distorted Idealistic (6) view of Potential (0) that seeks recognition through Responsibility (6) to boost the ego's sense of power.

Keys have always been an important symbol, whether literal or metaphorical. The keys on this card are skeleton keys. Skeleton keys have the special ability to unlock any warded lock. A warded lock is one that is protected by obstructions inside the lock. In magic, a warded lock is one that has been protected by a single or multiple spells to strengthen it. Following is the numerology of "key".

Chart Fifty-two
Key

| 11 | 5 | 25 = 41/5 |
| K | E | Y |
| 11 | 5 | 7 = 23/5 |

* Translation of full numbers 4, 1, 5:
A key allows Foundational (4) elements to interact so One (1) can bring about Change (5) on a spiritual level, where all change begins.

* Translation of root numbers 2, 3, 5:
Within the Duality (2) the key to what we Create (3) is reflected by our Expanding (5) spiritual nature.

It is not surprising that the root number of "key" is five, the number of change. Once a key is inserted into a lock, it causes changes inside the lock that lock or unlock it. Metaphorically a key can change a person's perception and understanding. A mentor can also do this.

Chart Fifty-three
Mentor

| 13 | 5 | 14 | 20 | 15 | 18 | = 85/13/4 |
|----|---|----|----|----|----|-----------|
| M  | E | N  | T  | O  | R  |           |
| 4  | 5 | 5  | 2  | 6  | 9  | = 31/4    |

The full numbers of "mentor" include the karmic numbers of 13/4. Being a mentor includes the responsibility of working hard to lay the proper foundation of guidance. The individual who does not express guidance appropriately pays the consequence.

* Translation of full numbers 8, 5, 1, 3, 4:
A Powerful (8) Person (5) whose Ego (1) Expresses (3) inappropriately will be reminded of a Fundamental (4) principle of karma.

* Translation of root numbers 3, 1, 4:
How we Express (3) the Self (1) is a Fundamental (4) responsibility.

**Translation Review**

When the Foundation of the Duality is centered around Vision, we remain grounded in spirituality. The Dual nature of physical existence provides a Foundation which promotes Vision. Divinity Brings spirituality into this Foundation. Divinity also Brings a sense of Devotion and Faith to spirituality.

The Divine is Reflected within the Duality as the Foundation of Man's life. This Foundation of Divine energy brings Balance in all things. Integrity comes first when Man uses Divine energy to bring about Fundamental Change.

A pentagram is an Integrated Energy form often used as A Diagram in Energy manipulation or magic. Using a Pentagram only when the Individual is Served abuses Personal Freedom. The Divine and the Four aspects of the human existence—spiritual, emotional, mental and physical—are an ever-Changing experience within the Duality.

The Hierophant translates Spiritual energy in the Physical by Vision.

The Hierophant's Spiritual Understanding and insight is a Foundation of our Vision. The Hierophant is the spiritual Knowledge of the Divine that serves as a Foundation for personal conduct.

When one abuses a position of authority, they become the FOX in the henhouse. The abuse of position may be because of a distorted Idealistic view of Potential that seeks recognition through Responsibility to boost the ego's sense of power.

A key allows Foundation elements to interact so One can bring about Change on a spiritual level, where all change begins. Within the Duality the key to what we Create is reflected by our Expanding spiritual nature.

A Powerful Person whose Ego Expresses inappropriately will be reminded of a Fundamental principle of karma. How we Express the Self is a Fundamental responsibility.

**Applying the Revealed Information**

**Acquired Meanings – New Meanings Revealed by Numerology**
Man, five senses, change, the dynamic interaction between differing energies, spirit within matter, perpetuation of change, devotion, alignment of spirit and consciousness, teacher of universal principles, the middle way of balance, bridge between the spiritual and material world, redirected energy or awareness, transmutation of spiritual energy.

**Relevant Questions**
What should the changes I make be focused on? How do I keep my spirit and consciousness aligned? What is perpetuating this situation? In what area am I balanced or unbalanced? How do I transmute this negative energy? What is my personal bridge between the spiritual and material? What area of my life needs my devotion?

**Practical Application**

Reading: the Nine of Wands, the Nine of Swords, the Hierophant.

Sometimes the result of our actions is knowable, sometimes not. The Nine of Wands indicates a mindfulness of actions taken and how we react. The Nine of Swords shows the result of thoughts or fears keeping the querent awake at night. The Hierophant suggests that balance is regained through alignment of action with spirit.

The Hierophant indicates the querent needs a change. The two nines—the number of ending in numerology—show a cycle has ended. The end of a cycle brings inevitable change. Where the querent's actions have taken him or her and where he or she would like to be suggest a re-evaluation. Positive choices become more apparent with the process of re-evaluation. Seeking a middle ground is suggested by the Hierophant. Change is coming, so the question is, "What reaction to the changes serves the querent best?"

Sometimes it adds meaning to a reading to find the core number. The core number of a reading is reached by adding the numbers of the cards together and reducing the resulting number to a single digit. In this case, we add $9 + 9 + 5 = 23$. Next, add the single digits of the result 23, $2 + 3 = 5$. Five is the core number of this reading, which shows change is the focus of this reading. Taking a pro-active approach allows the querent to evaluate his or her situation and choices. By embracing change, the querent can make the most of the opportunities that are available.

**Just a Thought**

I see the Hierophant as not only an interpreter of spiritual messages, but also of spiritual concepts. We are always gaining new understanding of our spirit self, as well as the connection to what we manifest in our reality.

The paradoxes of life in a dualistic reality hold the key to important revelations. The Hierophant embraces paradox as a way to gain spiritual knowledge, growth, and new understanding.

**Hierophant Dynamics:**
Tuning
Re-aligning
Unlocking
Redirecting

## Chapter Nine

### Six and the Lovers

*The vision of spirit manifests abundance by the emanation of unconditional love expressed by divine potential.*

### Six – The Spiritual Vision of the Divine

The numbers one through four lay the foundation for physical manifestation. The number five signals a moment of change and a redirection of divine energy. The numbers six through nine represent divine spiritual concepts.

The sum of six through nine is thirty, 6 + 7 + 8 + 9 = 30. A key word of three is expression. The sum of these numbers is the expression of divine potential. The numbers 6, 7, 8, 9 express divine potential (potential is introduced by the 0 after the 3) in specific ways according to their attributes.

* Translation of numbers 6, 7, 8, 9, 3, 0:
The Vision (6) of Spirit (7) embraces Power (8) by the emanation of Unconditional Love (9) Expressed (3) by divine Potential (0).

The geometric three-dimensional symbol for the number six, a six-pointed star or hexagram, consists of interlaced upward- and downward-pointing triangles. The upward-pointing triangle represents male energy. The downward-pointing triangle represents female energy. The hexagram represents the blending of masculine and feminine principles. The upward-pointing triangle also represents spiritually expressed energy, the downward-pointing triangle, physically expressed energy. Looking at the numbers of the word "six", we have the following chart.

Chart Fifty-four
Six

| 19 | 9 | 24 = 52/7 |
|----|---|-----------|
| S  | I | X         |
| 1  | 9 | 6 = 16/7  |

* Six key words: *vision, harmony, beauty.*

* Translation of full numbers 5, 2, 7:
Changes (5) within the Duality (2) are made on a Spiritual (7)

level first.

* Translation of root numbers 1, 6, 7:
When the Ego (1) Harmonizes (6) with spirit, Spiritual (7) integrity is maintained.

* Translation of karmic root numbers 1, 6, 7:
Ego (1) that is not in harmony with spirit can ignore Vision (6), distancing itself from the Spiritual (7), seeing itself as special, different, and separate.

* Conversion of full numbers 5, 2, 7 into letters:
5 = E, 2 = B, 7 = G.

* Translation of letters E, B, G:
Every (E) spirit physically manifesting has a Body (B) by divine Grace (G).

* Conversion of root numbers 16, 7 into letters:
16 = P, 7 = G.

* Translation of letters P, G:
The human body requires Parental (P) Guidance (G).

Six represents procreation because it is the sum of two threes, the number of creativity. Two threes (corresponding to the letter "C") are interpreted as Creative (C) Consciousness (C) innately expressing itself. Six also consists of five plus one: five, the number of man, plus one more. Man needs one "other" being to bring another physical body into the world. To create a traditional family, we usually think of a man and a woman forming the core relationship, which may include having children, the creation of a body that has both Form and Function (key words of 6).

Let's look at the numerology of the words "male" and "female". Notice that "male" has 13 (a karmic number) on the mundane level, which is the reflection of 31 on the esoteric level.

### Chart Fifty-five
### Male

| 13 | 1 | 12 | 5 = 31/4 |
|----|---|----|----------|
| M  | A | L  | E        |
| 4  | 1 | 3  | 5 = 13/4 |

\* Translation of full numbers 3, 1, 4:
Male describes energy that is Creative (3), Aggressive (1), outgoing, and able to co-create a Physical (4) body.

\* Translation of root numbers 1, 3, 4 as karmic numbers 13/4:
When the Individual (1) ego comes first and Creativity (3) is misused, the result is Limitation (4) and hard work.

Male has the karmic number 13/4. The karmic numbers indicate an unbalanced expression of energy where consequences cannot be avoided. The numbers of male suggest that the male human has to do a lot of work (4). If the work is avoided, there will be consequences. The word "aggressive" also has the karmic root number of 13/4.

Chart Fifty-six
Female

| 6 | 5 | 13 | 1 | 12 | 5 = 42/6 |
|---|---|----|---|----|----------|
| F | E | M  | A | L  | E        |
| 6 | 5 | 4  | 1 | 3  | 5 = 24/6 |

\* Translation of full numbers 4, 2, 6:
Female describes receptive energy using the Physical (4) laws of the Duality (2) to Procreate (6).

\* Translation of root numbers 2, 4, 6:
Cooperatively (2) Working (4) together, it is possible for male and female to create a Vision (6) they share.

Add the root number of male (4) to the root number of female (6) and we have the equation 4 + 6 = 10/1. The equation describes two basic energies, male and female, co-creating a body that contains divine potential. "Soul" also has a root number of four, which shows the soul is able to take physical form by incarnating into a physical body. Let's take a look at the word "conception", as in to conceive a child.

Chart Fifty-seven
Conception

| 3 | 15 | 14 | 3 | 5 | 16 | 20 | 9 | 15 | 14 = 114/6 |
|---|----|----|---|---|----|----|---|----|------------|
| C | O  | N  | C | E | P  | T  | I | O  | N          |
| 3 | 6  | 5  | 3 | 5 | 7  | 2  | 9 | 6  | 5 = 51/6   |

\* Translation of full numbers 1, 1, 4, 6:
The Divine (1) recreates Itself (1) in Form (4) resulting in something Beautiful (6).

\* Translation of root numbers 5, 1, 6:
Man (5) and woman blend Individual (1) traits to create a Family (6).

\* Conversion of root numbers 5, 1, 6 into letters:
5 = N, 1 = A, 6 = F.

\* Translation of letters N, A, F:
The result of blending traits is Not (N) Always (A) Foreseeable (F).

## The Lovers – Co-Creators and the Illusion of Gender Identity

The illusion of gender identity comes from the world of the High Priestess, where the Duality is a reflection of divine energy. She personifies the continuum, which includes the gender polarities of maleness and femaleness. The Lovers are one of many expressions of dualism generated by the High Priestess.

The Lovers archetype is the representation within the Duality of the foundation principle of one plus two creating three (Chapter Five: Three and the Empress). The Lovers archetype also embodies the basic illusion of male and female as opposites within the Duality. Divine energy is undifferentiated. As such, it contains the potential for maleness and femaleness, but energy cannot express gender in this differentiated form until after the polarizing effect of the High Priestess. Therefore gender only exists within the Duality.

The Lovers archetype embodies the energy of the divine heart, which reveals truth. We see by the root number seven of "heart" (Chart Fifty-eight) that our hearts are connected to spirit, and thus the divine. Perhaps this is why we say, "In your heart, you know it's true," whatever "it" is. The word "true" has a full number of nineteen, which reduces to ten. Ten shows truth is divine in nature. The Divine emanation of love reveals the truth.

### Chart Fifty-eight
### Heart

| 8 | 5 | 1 | 18 | 20 = 52/7 |
|---|---|---|----|-----------|
| H | E | A | R  | T         |
| 8 | 5 | 1 | 9  | 2 = 25/7  |

* Translation of full numbers 5, 2, 7:
Freedom (5) and change within the Duality (2) are in part about learning to follow the heart's Spiritual (7) conscience.

* Translation of root numbers 2, 5, 7:
The Duality (2) matrix interacts with Man's (5) manifested connection to the Spiritual (7).

There are possible spiritual ramifications when we don't follow the truth in our hearts.

The Lovers archetype also includes the concept of human love. Here is the numerology of "love".

### Chart Fifty-nine
### Love

| 12 | 15 | 22 | 5 = 54/9 |
|----|----|----|----------|
| L  | O  | V  | E        |
| 3  | 6  | 4  | 5 = 18/9 |

* Translation of full numbers 5, 4, 9:
Life (5) has a Foundation (4) in Unconditional Love (9).

* Translation of root numbers 1, 8, 9:
Divine (1) Power (8) is contained in Unconditional Love (9).

* Conversion of root numbers 1, 8, 9 into letters:
1 = A, 8 = H, 9 = I.

* Translation of letters A, H, I:
This is why Love is A (1), H (8) I (9); Love is A HI, or high.

Love can give us that euphoric feeling. Let's look at the numbers in the word "lover", which also has a root of nine.

## Chart Sixty
### Lover

| 12 | 15 | 22 | 5 | 18 = 72/9 |
|----|----|----|---|-----------|
| L  | O  | V  | E | R         |
| 3  | 6  | 4  | 5 | 9 = 27/9  |

\* Conversion of full numbers 7, 2, 9 into letters:
7 = G, 2 = B, 9 = I.

\* Translation of letters G, B, I:
The divine promotes Growth (G) by Balancing (B) us in spiritual Illumination (I) (understanding).

\* Translation of root numbers 2, 7, 9:
The Duality's (2) lessons of Spirituality (7) can lead us back to and center us in Unconditional Love (9).

## Chart Sixty-one
### Lovers

| 12 | 15 | 22 | 5 | 18 | 19 = 91/10/1 |
|----|----|----|---|----|--------------|
| L  | O  | V  | E | R  | S            |
| 3  | 6  | 4  | 5 | 9  | 1 = 28/10/1  |

\* Translation of full numbers 9, 1, 1, 0, 1:
Unconditional Love (9) of the Divine (1) is Reflected (0) within the Individual (1).

We all have the capacity for unconditional love by virtue of the divine. "Lovers" is representative of an energy that is created in divine perfection (10). A loving act embodies the potential of divine perfection.

\* Conversion of full numbers 9, 1, 1, 0, 1 into letters:
9 = I, 1 = A, 1 = A, 0 = O, 1 = A.

\* Translation of letters I, A, A, O, A:
Intrinsic (I) unconditional love is An (A) Aspect (A) Of (O) All (A) of us.

\* Translation of root numbers 2, 8, 1, 0, 1:
The Duality (2) is given Power (8) by the Divine (1) through the

divine's Reflection (0) of its Self (1).

\* Alternate translation of 2, 8, 10, 1:
The Duality's (2) Power (8) can be seen as a Divine (10) extension of the One (1).

**Translation Review**

The Vision of Spirit embraces Power by the emanation of Unconditional Love Expressed by divine Potential. Changes within the Duality are made on a Spiritual level first. When the Ego Harmonizes with spirit, Spiritual integrity is maintained. Ego that is not in harmony with spirit can ignore Vision, distancing itself from the Spiritual, seeing itself as special, different, and separate.

Every spirit physically manifesting has a Body by divine Grace. The human body requires Parental Guidance.

Male describes energy that is Creative, Aggressive, outgoing, and able to co-create a Physical body. When the Individual ego comes first and Creativity is misused, the result is Limitation and hard work. Female describes receptive energy using the Physical laws of the Duality to Procreate. Cooperatively Working together, it is possible for male and female to create a Vision they share.

The Divine recreates Itself in Form resulting in something Beautiful. Man and woman blend Individual traits to create a Family. The result of blending energy is Not Always Foreseeable.

Freedom and change within the Duality are in part about learning to follow the heart's Spiritual conscience. The Duality matrix interacts with Man's manifested connection to the Spiritual. Life has a Foundation in Unconditional Love. Divine Power is contained in Unconditional Love. This is why Love is A High. The divine promotes Growth by Balancing us in spiritual Illumination.

The Duality's lessons of Spirituality can lead us back to and center us in Unconditional Love. Unconditional Love of the Divine is Reflected within the Individual. Intrinsic unconditional love is An Aspect Of All of us. The Duality is given Power by the Divine through the divine's Reflection of its Self. Duality's Power can be seen as a Divine extension of the One.

**Applying the Revealed Information**

**Acquired Meanings – New Meanings Revealed by Numerology**

Higher love, expansive energy, aggressive, receptive, open, the harmony and beauty of form, procreation, the blending of energies, co-creators, male/female, form and function, attraction, the illusion of opposites.

**Relevant Questions**
What is love centered around for me? How does love expand me? What energies can love bring together for me? What is it possible for me to co-create through love? What will love open me up to? How is love most often expressed within my relationships? How can I trust myself to love?

**Practical Application**
Reading: the Ace of Swords, the Lovers, the Nine of Cups.

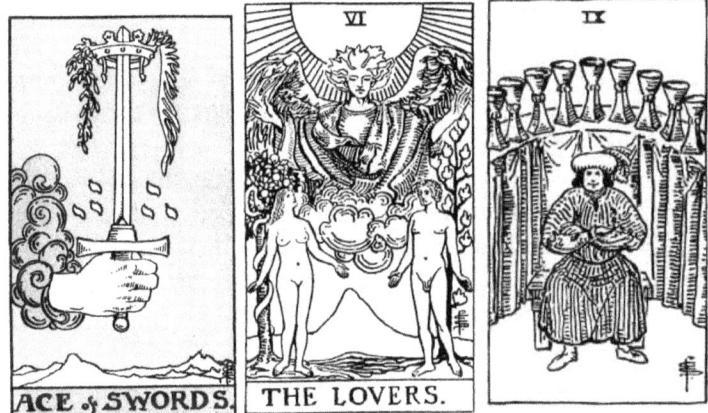

The querent is encouraged to think about things in a new way, expanding his or her concepts about love and relationships. On a higher level, the energy of the Lovers archetype is in part about looking beyond perceived differences—differences that sometimes are only in our minds. These cards suggest that embracing new attitudes about relationships can lead the querent to a more emotionally fulfilling experience.

The integrity and wisdom taught by emotional experiences can give the querent a broader and deeper perspective of understanding in his or her relationships.

**Just a Thought**
The numbers of this reading add to seven ($1 + 6 + 9 = 16$, $1 + 6 = 7$), the number of spirituality. The overall vibration of this reading has roots in the spiritual. Life can open you up to a less judgmental, more co-creative, harmonious, and beautifully cooperative experience when we approach life from a place of spirituality. Spirituality can bring one to a point of view that is more expansive. It resolves and incorporates apparent opposites. Spirituality is the expression of the divine's unconditional love, projected

into all of the Duality. We all become more by the vibration of unconditional love.

The attraction of male and female is a reflection of another basic principle within the Duality: opposites attract. If one extreme is expressed as male and the other extreme expressed as female, it would seem these are the extremes of sexually expressed energy. As discussed under the High Priestess, what we see as polarities is a continuum of energy that appears as such because it is seen from a limited point of view. The basic attraction of opposites on a larger scale is also a universal law. This law reveals that as opposite ends attract and meet each other, they join to form one continuous circle. This is the ultimate way in which two becomes one again. This circular motion of energy is demonstrated in many different ways within the Duality.

The archetypal energy of The Lovers, in the esoteric sense, is the illusion of relationship with another person. Love is not the illusion in the Duality. "Other" is the illusion.

"Love" and "lover" have a root vibration of nine, the number of unconditional love. Also, as the number of completion, nine would imply that unconditional love is the completion or ending. Unconditional love is the ultimate fulfillment for us, and perhaps the divine's ultimate fulfillment is to lead us back to unconditional love.

**Lovers Dynamics:**
Opening
Expanding
Procreating
Co-creating

# Chapter Ten

## Seven and the Chariot

*When man uses his vision, it brings a deeper understanding of the Duality.*

### Seven – Spirit and the Physical Connection

Seven represents the connection between spirit and consciousness. Spirit expresses in the physical by the higher self, subconscious, and conscious. Seven, as two plus five, has intuitive roots as represented by the High Priestess (2) that can bring about Change (5) which originates from spirit. Seven, as three plus four, is the Support Matrix (3), the basic energy structure that supports Form (4). The word "form" has a root number of seven, showing that form originates from spirit and the divine. Here is the numerology of the word "seven".

Chart Sixty-two
Seven

| 19 | 5 | 22 | 5 | 14 = 65/11 |
|----|---|----|---|------------|
| S  | E | V  | E | N          |
| 1  | 5 | 4  | 5 | 5 = 20/2   |

* Seven key words: *spirit, spirituality, trust, intelligence.*

* Translation of full numbers 6, 5, 11:
Vision (6) is given to Man (5) by spiritual Knowing (11).

* Conversion of numbers 6, 5, 11 into letters:
6 = F, 5 = E, 11 = K.

* Translation of letters F, E, K:
Spirit Focuses (F) on and Embraces (E) spiritual Knowledge (K).

* Conversion of root numbers 2, 0, 2 into letters:
2 = B, 0 = O, 2 = B.

* Translation of letters B, O, B:
Without spiritual knowledge, the Beauty (B) (the innate natural state of spirit) of spiritual expression gets Out (O) of Balance (B).

\* Translation of root numbers 2, 0, 2:
True Balance (2) Reflects (0) Balance (2).

The word "balance" has a root number of two. Staying in a balanced state results in this state being reflected back to us. Spirit stays balanced when focused on divine will. Let's look at "divine will" next.

### Chart Sixty-three
### Divine Will

```
            63                              56
4    9   22   9   14   5      23   9   12   12 = 119/11
D    I   V    I   N    E      W    I   L    L
4    9   4    9   5    5      5    9   3    3 = 56/11
            36                              20
```

\* Conversion of full numbers 1, 19, 11:
1 = A, 19 = S, 11 = K.

\* Translation of letters A, S, K; or ASK:
All you have to do is ASK.

Ask and you shall receive. There is an intrinsic aspect of the divine that responds when we ask for something.

\* Translation of full numbers 11, 9, 11:
The truth of 'ask and you shall receive' requires Spiritual Insight (11), Wisdom (9), and Understanding (11).

\* Translation of root numbers 5, 6, 11:
When Man (5) uses his Vision (6), it brings a deeper Understanding (11) of the Duality.

There is divine will, and there is personal will attached to ego. Let's look at the word "ego" next.

### Chart Sixty-four
### Ego

```
5      7     15 = 27/9
E      G     O
5      7      6 = 18/9
```

\* Translation of full numbers 2, 7, 9:
When We (2) forget our Spiritual (7) origin, we seem to lose our connection to the Divine (9).

\* Translation of root numbers 1, 8, 9:
If an Individual (1) gives too much Power (8) to ego, they lose their spiritual Integrity and Wisdom (9).

Losing our connection to the divine is impossible, but we may seem to lose our connection when we forget our spiritual nature. The invisible emanation of divine energy is an innate part of us and all that is.

The divine gives us free choice, which we exercise by using personal will. Let's take a look at phrase "personal will".

Chart Sixty-five
Personal Will

|     |   |    |    | 100 |    |   |    | 56 |    |              |
|-----|---|----|----|-----|----|---|----|----|----|--------------|
| 16  | 5 | 18 | 19 | 15  | 14 | 1 | 12 | 23 | 9  | 12 | 12 = 156/12/3 |
| P   | E | R  | S  | O   | N  | A | L  | W  | I  | L  | L            |
| 7   | 5 | 9  | 1  | 6   | 5  | 1 | 3  | 5  | 9  | 3  | 3 = 57/12/3  |
|     |   |    |    | 37  |    |   |    | 20 |    |              |

\* Conversion of full numbers into letters:
15 = O, 6 = F, 12 = L, 3 = C.

\* Translation of letters O, F, L, C:
When personal will and divine will are one, they emanate Openly (O) Flowing (F) Love (L) leading to the highest expression of Consciousness (C).

\* Translation of full numbers 1, 5, 6, 1, 2, 3:
The Divine (1) gave Man (5) Vision (6) so that Individuals (1) could Cooperate (2) Creatively (3).

\* Translation of root numbers 5, 7, 1, 2, 3:
When Man's (5) Spirituality (7) is focused on the Divine (1) within the Duality (2), he Expresses (3) great beauty.

\* Conversion of root numbers into letters:
5 = E, 7 = G, 12 = L, 3 = C.

\* Translation of letters E, G, L, C:
Ego (E) Gregariously (G) Looks (L) outward for Confirmation (C); spirit looks inward for confirmation.

### The Chariot – Divine Will, Human Will, and the Ego

The Chariot is the archetype of divine will and its relationship to human will. Human will is represented by the black and white sphinxes lying down in front of the chariot. The human faces show personal will is exerted over animal instinct. The animal bodies represent the mind attached to the baser instincts and ego.

The charioteer represents divine will. The eight-pointed star represents the divine on the charioteer's crown, more specifically the divine cosmic order. The charioteer's placing above the sphinxes implies divine will has influence on human will. Looking at the card, it is hard to tell if the chariot can be moved, but the wheels imply movement. The charioteer aligns himself with divine will to guide the mind, personal will, and ego. The chariot itself represents any vehicle of spiritual understanding.

Chart Sixty-six
Chariot

| 3 | 8 | 1 | 18 | 9 | 15 | 20 = 74/11 |
|---|---|---|----|---|----|-----------|
| C | H | A | R  | I | O  | T |
| 3 | 8 | 1 | 9  | 9 | 6  | 2 = 38/11 |

\* Translation of full numbers 7, 4, 11:
Aligning with divine will and Trust (7), we embrace one of the Foundations (4) of Spiritual Understanding (11), which is truth.

\* Conversion of full numbers 7, 4, 11 into letters:
7 = G, 4 = D, 11 = K.

\* Translation of letters G, D, K:
Spiritual Growth (G) happens with Dedication (D) to spiritual Knowledge (K) and understanding.

\* Translation of root numbers 3, 8, 11:
The Expression (3) of divine Power (8) channeled through the Light (11) of spirit can bring one into harmony with divine will.

\* Conversion of root numbers 3, 8, 11 into letters:
3 = C, 8 = H, 11 = K.

> \* Translation of letters C, H, K:
> Communication (C) through speech Has (H) Knowledge (K) beyond what is heard.

Light, another word that reduces to an eleven, is a divine emanation. The "light" of spirit contains and transmits divine knowledge. Eleven is translated as spiritual understanding, but is also the number of spiritual illumination. The illumination of spiritual truth.

Whatever meaning we take from words is only part of the meaning we absorb. Our higher self also receives inherent messages that are embedded within the sound vibrations.

Important Points:

> \* The words "seven", "divine will", and "chariot" all have a full number of eleven on the esoteric level.
>
> \* These words are related by the number eleven.
>
> \* These words focus on spiritual truth and a way to understand that truth.
>
> \* The Chariot archetype represents the dichotomy between divine will and human will.

**Translation Review**

Vision is given to Man by spiritual Knowing. Spirit Focuses on and Embraces spiritual Knowledge. Without spiritual knowledge, the Beauty of spiritual expression gets Out of Balance. True Balance Reflects Balance. All you have to do is ASK. The truth of 'ask and you shall receive' requires Spiritual Insight, Wisdom, and Understanding. When Man uses his Vision, it brings a deeper Understanding of the Duality. When We forget our Spiritual origin, we seem to lose our connection to the Divine. If an Individual gives too much Power to ego, they lose their spiritual Integrity and Wisdom.

When personal will and divine will are one, they emanate Openly Flowing Love leading to the highest expression of Consciousness. The Divine gave Man Vision so that Individuals could Cooperate Creatively. When Man's Spirituality is focused on the Divine within the Duality, he Expresses great beauty. Ego Gregariously Looks outward for Confirmation; spirit looks inward for confirmation. Aligning with divine will and Trust, we Embrace one of the Foundations of Spiritual

Understanding, which is truth. Spiritual Growth happens with Dedication to spiritual Knowledge and understanding. The Expression of divine Power channeled through the Light of spirit can bring one into harmony with divine will. Communication through speech Has Knowledge beyond what is heard.

**Applying the Revealed Information**

**Acquired Meanings – New Meanings Revealed by Numerology**
Spiritual knowing, divine will, personal will, spiritual intelligence, discernment, surrender, the hidden message, progress on a deeper level.

**Relevant Questions**
How do I recognize my connection to the divine? What hidden message is in what is being read or said? What is the best way for me to access my spiritual knowledge? In what way is my spiritual intelligence different from my intellectual intelligence? How do I learn to trust divine will? What is the best way to keep my ego in balance with my higher self?

**Practical Application**
Reading: the Chariot, the Queen of Cups, the Seven of Cups, the Knight of Wands.

The querent has the opportunity for a deeper understanding of the relationship between divine will and personal will. Following the flow of his or her emotions may also lead to a deeper understanding as well a deeper connection to the divine. The Seven of Cups indicates the querent is pursuing too many dreams, not connecting to the one dream that resonates on a deeper level. The querent may be missing the true opportunity by not listening to the inner voice of the higher self that connects him or her to divine will. Trust, openness, and surrender to divine will allows the querent to embrace his or her passion for what he or she undertakes. If the querent's heart and mind are aligned, he or she will know what needs to be done and have the will to proceed on the chosen course.

**Just a Thought**

The sphinx is a symbol of wisdom and secrets. They guard temples and the mysteries within. The black and white sphinxes, implied motion (where are we going spiritually), divine direction, and the charioteer are all about man's relationship to the divine. The card is also about how we reconcile the relationship between our personal will, ego, and divine will, and how that relationship influences our personal reality.

In the reading, the Queen of Cups has her back to the dreams represented by the Seven of Cups. She stares intently at her ornate cup that has angels on each side. The Queen of Cups also faces the Chariot. The Queen stays aligned with her spiritual awareness and divine will by focusing on her deeper emotions and sensitivity. She listens to the truth within her heart. The Knight of Wands—wands representing spiritual energy and fire—is riding toward the dreams. Staying focused in the energy of spirit can ultimately lead you to your passion and the fulfillment of your dreams.

**Chariot Dynamics:**
Progressing
Surrendering
Knowing
Trusting

## Chapter Eleven

### Eight and Strength

*Duality's creative consciousness plays within the freedom of self-expression.*

### Eight – Power within the Duality

Our glyph for eight (8) represents the expression of personal energy within the Duality. Eight is the number of power as raw energy, how energy functions, and how we manipulate it in the Duality. The glyph shows the dynamic of our outgoing and returning energy, self-contained and always circulating.

When we use our personal energy to create a complex structure within the Duality, we use the energy of eight. The dynamic nature of eight lends itself to building. The complexity of eight is reflected on a molecular level as well as on a larger scale. As discussed in Chapter Three (page 34), the element carbon has four electrons but seeks a total of eight. To this end, carbon bonds and shares with other elements, building more complex molecular chains. Eight's energy dynamic mimics the ability of carbon to create a more complex physical prototype, or model, of energy in the duality matrix. Because of this model, we see that eight builds on chains of four.

Four, physical manifestation and the beginning of form, is half of eight. Four, as a basic building block of structure, expands into chains. Present day astrologer Lubomir Dimitrov (http://lubomir.name) describes the relationship between four and eight. Paraphrasing his ideas, he states that the number eight, made up of 4 + 4, builds on what four has brought into physical manifestation. We see this in the numerology of the word "eight", which has a root number of four. Structures of the four at the energetic level tend to be very rigid and inflexible, whereas structures of the eight contain greater complexity, flexibility, and detail.

Starting with the word "eight", let's look at the numerology.

Chart Sixty-seven
Eight

| 5 | 9 | 7 | 8 | 20 = 49/13/4 |
| E | I | G | H | T |
| 5 | 9 | 7 | 8 | 2 = 31/4 |

\* Eight key words: *power, dynamic, continual, reflective.*

\* Translation of full numbers 4, 9, 1, 3, 4:
By the Foundational (4) model of an Ideal (9) coming from the Divine (1), there is Created (3) the basic Form (4) for all physically manifesting energy.

\* Conversion of full numbers 4, 9, 13, 4 into letters:
4 = D, 9 = I, 13 = M, 4 = D.

\* Translation of letters D, I, M, D:
The Duality (D) Is (I) continually Manifesting (M) energy in very Dynamic (D) ways.

\* Translation of root numbers 3, 1, 4:
The Creative (3) consciousness of an Individual (1) has the ability to Manifest (4) energy influenced by his spiritual uniqueness.

Our glyph for eight is the representation of our method of manifesting energy within the Duality. Our method of manifestation is basically the same as the divine's. As in the case of the divine, our energy constructs can also become ever more complex due to the mechanics of reflection, as described by the lemniscate.

Coincidentally the word "model" also reduces to a four. Therefore, "model" and "eight" are related. Here is the numerology.

Chart Sixty-eight
Model

| 13 | 15 | 4 | 5 | 12 = 49/13/4 |
|----|----|---|---|--------------|
| M  | O  | D | E | L            |
| 4  | 6  | 4 | 5 | 3 = 22 (4)   |

\* Translation of full numbers 4, 9, 1, 3, 4:
A Model (4) is the prototype of an energy pattern being Initiated (9) into the Duality by the Divine's (1) Creativity (3) potentially expressed in Form (4).

\* Translation of root numbers 22, 4:
Model is the Master Plan (22) at the energetic level that provides a Foundation (4) for what is being created.

As architects and builders of our reality, we take a divine model and translate it into our personal plan for bringing an energy template into the physical.

Let's look at the numerology of "energy".

Chart Sixty-nine
Energy

| 5 | 14 | 5 | 18 | 7 | 25 = 74/11 |
|---|----|---|----|---|------------|
| E | N  | E | R  | G | Y          |
| 5 | 5  | 5 | 9  | 7 | 7 = 38/11  |

\* Translation of full numbers 7, 4, 11:
A Spiritual (7) energy and a physical Foundation (4) of our reality is Light (11).

\* Translation of root numbers 3, 8, 11:
From this Dimension (3) we see some of the Energy (8) dynamic that emanates from the divine as actual Light (11).

The word "light" has a root number of eleven. Much of the energy of our universe is seen as light or an absence of light.

**Strength – Power within the Context of Our Personal Reality**

Strength of spirit is a reflection of divine power. Accepting responsibility for the reality we create expresses strength. Creating personal reality expresses power. Expressing spiritual strength gives us knowledge about the way spirit and consciousness interact. The interactive and reflective nature of the Duality helps us understand the relationship between strength, power, and creativity.

Creativity and responsibility go hand in hand. The word "creativity" has a root number of six. A key word for the number six is responsibility. Our creative choices and the way we make them teach us about inner strength and personal power.

Next is the numerology of "Strength".

Chart Seventy
Strength

| 19 | 20 | 18 | 5 | 14 | 7 | 20 | 8 = 111/3    |
|----|----|----|---|----|---|----|--------------|
| S  | T  | R  | E | N  | G | T  | H            |
| 1  | 2  | 9  | 5 | 5  | 7 | 2  | 8 = 39/12/3  |

The numbers 111/3 can be translated as two different groups of numbers.

* Translation of full numbers 1, 11, 3:
Divinity (1) Illuminates (11) the truth about our ability to Create (3) our personal reality when we are ready to accept that truth.

* Translation of alternative group of full numbers 11, 1, 3:
The Spiritual Understanding (11) of an Individual's (1) ability to Create (3) one's personal reality is important.

* Conversion of full numbers into letters:
11 = K, 1 = A, 3 = C.

* Translation of letters K, A, C:
Taking responsibility for what we create gives us Knowledge (K) About (A) Creative (C) consciousness.

* Translation of root numbers 3, 9, 1, 2, 3:
Creativity (3) combined with the Compassion (9) of an Individual (1) encourages Cooperation (2) in creative Expression (3).

* Conversion of root numbers into letters:
3 = C, 9 = I, 1 = A, 2 = B, 3 = C.

* Translation of letters C, I, A, B, C:
Creativity (C) Is (I) About (A) Being (B) more Consciously (C) aware.

Everything we create has a personal spiritual connection.
On the Strength card, a woman stands by the head of a lion. Five is the number of freedom, change, and the constructive use of personal freedom. Here is the numerology of "lion".

### Chart Seventy-one
### Lion

| 12 | 9 | 15 | 14 = 50/5 |
|----|---|----|-----------|
| L  | I | O  | N         |
| 3  | 9 | 6  | 5 = 23/5  |

* Translation of full numbers 5, 0, 5:
Coming from a place of true strength, our use of Personal Freedom

(5) is a Reflection (0) of Divine intention and a Key (5) to our reality.

* Translation of root numbers 2, 3, 5:
Our (2) Creative (3) consciousness plays with the Freedom (5) of self-expression and the changes we make in how we express ourselves.

The lemniscate on the Strength card implies there is a connection between strength and divine energy. There is nothing stronger than energy. It is indestructible. When we tap into our personal connection to divine energy, we are also infinitely strong and indestructible. Pamela Coleman Smith's illustration of the Strength card shows a woman standing beside a lion with her left hand on the lion's face and her right hand under the lion's chin. It is obvious that physical strength is not going to subdue the lion, and yet he appears acquiescent. The white blouse the woman wears represents the purity of her connection to the divine and her complete faith in that connection. In the face of her faith and connection to divine energy, she has no fear and can overcome all obstacles with the strength of her spirit and connection to the divine.

**Translation Review**
By the Foundation model of an Ideal coming from the Divine, there is Created the basic Form for all physically manifesting energy. The Duality Is continually Manifesting energy in very Dynamic ways. The Creative consciousness of an Individual has the ability to Manifest energy influenced by his spiritual uniqueness.

A Model is a prototype of an energy pattern being Initiated into the Duality by the Divine's Creativity potentially expressed in Form. Model is the Master Plan at an energetic level that provides a Foundation for what is being created.

A Spiritual energy and physical Foundation of our reality is Light. From this Dimension we see some of the Energy dynamic that emanates from the divine as actual Light.

Divinity Illuminates the truth about our ability to Create our personal reality when we are ready to accept that truth. The Spiritual Understanding of an Individual's ability to Create one's personal reality is important. Taking responsibility for what we create gives us Knowledge About Creative consciousness. Creativity combined with the Compassion of an Individual encourages Cooperation in creative Expression. Creativity Is About Being more Consciously aware.

Coming from a place of true strength, our use of Personal Freedom is a

Reflection of Divine intention and a Key to our reality. Our Creative consciousness plays with the Freedom of self-expression and the changes we make in how we express ourselves.

**Applying the Revealed Information**

**Acquired Meanings – New Meanings Revealed by Numerology**

Power within form, dynamic energy, self contained, sophisticated manifestation, individually unique creation, perpetual motion, our ability to accept truth, inner strength, freedom of self-expression.

**Relevant Questions**

What truth am I seeking? What will help me understand this truth? How does my inner strength serve me? What is perpetuating the energy I am currently stuck in? How will expressing my unique creativity enhance my life experience? What inner strength is my best asset at this time?

**Practical Application**

Reading: the Two of Pentacles, the Eight of Swords, Strength, the Four of Wands.

A lemniscate connects the two pentacles that are being juggled by a young man in the Two of Pentacles. The querent is trying to balance different aspects of his or her everyday life. The things the querent is trying to balance are connected in some way. By seeing things as distinctly separate, the mind keeps us trapped in separateness, limiting our choices of solution. The key is the querent's ability to recognize connections. It takes strength, especially in a negative mindset, to embrace truth, which allows change as a positive thoughtful process. Accepting the truth of a situation is an important component to personal growth and gives the querent the ability to recognize the choices he or she has. In doing so, the result is his or her ability to create a foundation for a reality that is more fulfilling.

**Just a Thought**
This reading shows a relationship between the Eight of Swords and the eighth archetype, Strength, linked by the number eight. All of the eights in the minor arcana refer to different kinds of strength: in the Eight of Swords, strength is needed to move beyond thoughts that create loops of repression and stagnation; the Eight of Wands shows the strength to carry through with a plan of action; the Eight of Pentacles shows the strength to stay focused on the task at hand; and the Eight of Cups shows the strength to carry on despite emotional difficulties.

The Two of Pentacles and the Strength card are visually connected by the lemniscate illustrated on both cards. We strengthen our ability to handle a situation with lack of fear and a better understanding of the connection between things. We are no longer caught in the juggling act between illusion and truth when we see the relationship between things.

As divine energy emanates into the Duality, some of it is translated by the dynamics within the duality matrix as light.

**Strength Dynamics:**
Revealing
Empowering
Sustaining
Liberating

# Chapter Twelve

## Nine and the Hermit

*When we express ourselves in harmonious ways, the beauty of that vibration is reflected back to us within the Duality.*

### Nine – Unconditional Love, Completion of a Cycle

In numerology, nine is the last number at the end of a cycle of numbers. Nine is the number of humanity and philanthropy. The Old Testament says there were nine generations between Adam and Noah, and between Noah and Abraham. Nine represents the completion of a cycle of generations and as well as other cycles. Here is the numerology of the word "nine".

Chart Seventy-two
Nine

| 14 | 9 | 14 | 5 = 42/6 |
|----|---|----|----------|
| N  | I | N  | E        |
| 5  | 9 | 5  | 5 = 24/6 |

* Nine key words: *unconditional love, ending, altruistic, faithful, generous.*

* Translation of full numbers 4, 2, 6:
A Basic Pattern (4) of manifestation within the Duality (2) provides Function within Form (6).

* Translation of root numbers 2, 4, 6:
The Duality (2) matrix enables spirit to bring patterns into Solid Form (4), which reflect Beauty (6) and harmony.

The root number of "nine", 24, is a mirrored reflection of the full number 42. The mirroring of full and root numbers raises the question: how does the mundane mirror the spiritual? The divine projected himself outward to see his creation, therefore we project our creations outward to see what we have created. The patterns we create for possible manifestation are imprinted with our balanced—as well as unbalanced—energy.

Let's look at the numerology of the word "balance" next.

## Chart Seventy-three
## Balance

| 2 | 1 | 12 | 1 | 14 | 3 | 5 = 38/11 |
|---|---|----|---|----|---|-----------|
| B | A | L  | A | N  | C | E         |
| 2 | 1 | 3  | 1 | 5  | 3 | 5 = 20/2  |

\* Translation of full numbers 3, 8, 11:
Creativity (3), when expressed within the physical, is one of the most Powerful (8) and Spiritually Revealing (11) energies.

\* Translation of root numbers 2, 0, 2:
The Beauty (2) of harmonious expression is Reflected (0) back to us by the Duality (2).

"Beauty" has a root number of 2.

## Hermit – Teacher and Guide to Spirit

The Hermit is a guide to our deepest inner nature. His eyes are closed because he uses other senses to navigate inner landscapes. The yellow wand represents his personal connection to the divine spirit within. Here is the numerology of "Hermit".

## Chart Seventy-four
## Hermit

| 8 | 5 | 18 | 13 | 9 | 20 = 73/10/1 |
|---|---|----|----|---|--------------|
| H | E | R  | M  | I | T            |
| 8 | 5 | 9  | 4  | 9 | 2 = 37/10/1  |

\* Translation of full numbers 7, 3, 1, 0, 1:
The Spiritual (7) nature of Creative consciousness (3) given to us by the Divine (1) is Reflected (0) within each Individual (1).

\* Translation of root numbers 3, 7, 1, 0, 1:
The Hermit guides us to understand and creatively Express (3) our inner Spiritual (7) nature as a part of the Divine (1) Reflection (0) within an Individual (1).

The Hermit helps us reconnect with our inner self to promote further personal and spiritual growth. We search inwardly to better understand our true nature, allowing us to bring all parts of self into a more cohesive whole.

The Hermit's lantern has a six-pointed star, or hexagram, enclosed within it. This geometric shape is formed by two overlapping equilateral triangles; one pointing up, one pointing down. The two triangles represent the masculine aspect of spiritual fire and the feminine aspect of physical earth. Two triangles made up of three points each have a total of six points. Six represents fertility; as Shirley Blackwell Lawrence pointed out in *The Secret Science of Numerology*, the glyph for "6" has a womb in the enclosed circle at the bottom of the glyph. The union of these triangles symbolically represents fertility in the Duality, as well as in spirit. The formation of the hexagram symbolizes balance, fertility, and duality (represented by the male and female symbolism of the triangles). The archetype of the Hermit guides us to balance and unify our spiritual and physical nature. Here is the numerology of "hexagram".

Chart Seventy-five
Hexagram

| 8 | 5 | 24 | 1 | 7 | 18 | 1 | 13 = 77/14/5 |
|---|---|----|---|---|----|---|--------------|
| H | E | X  | A | G | R  | A | M            |
| 8 | 5 | 6  | 1 | 7 | 9  | 1 | 4 = 41/5     |

\* Translation of full numbers 7, 7, 1, 4, 5:
The Spiritual (7) nature of Earth (7) embodies the Divine (1) Foundation (4) of Change (5).

\* Translation of root numbers 4, 1, 5:
The Foundation (4) of change facilitates the Individual's (1) ability to reconcile apparent differences by Devotion (5) to spiritual understanding.

Interestingly, "hexagram" has a full number of seventy-seven, the number of Christ consciousness. This geometric figure is also the pattern of blending the spiritual and physical, a physical representation of a divine pattern of wholeness. Having learned from our inner Hermit, the Wheel of Fortune (the next card) turns as we go forward with inner harmony, faith, confidence, and trust in our relationship to the divine. Also, the word "harmony" and the phrase "inner nature" both reduce to a four, the number of physical manifestation, foundation, process, and work. Harmony as a process is constantly at work.

Harmony is the natural state of our divine inner nature. Let's look at "harmony" next.

Chart Seventy-six
Harmony

| 8 | 1 | 18 | 13 | 15 | 14 | 25 = 94/13/4 |
|---|---|----|----|----|----|--------------|
| H | A | R  | M  | O  | N  | Y            |
| 8 | 1 | 9  | 4  | 6  | 5  | 7 = 40/4     |

\* Translation of full numbers 9, 4, 1, 3, 4:
Unconditional Love (9), as a Foundation (4) of Divine (1) Expression (3), emanates throughout the Physical (4) world.

\* Translation of root numbers 4, 0, 4:
The Foundation (4) of unconditional love and the ways we respond to it are Reflected (0) in the Processes (4) of our personal lives.

The numerology of harmony shows that unconditional love and the ways it interacts with our reality is one of the primary ways divine energy expresses itself to us and through us. We may not be able to express unconditional love on a conscious level, but any time we hold the vibration of love, we express it outwardly to others in all the things we do. We influence our personal reality positively, and the reality of others, by giving and accepting love. We also interact with others by this vibration in positive ways that we may not be consciously aware of. Unconditional love on a deep inner level is within all of us and a part of all we do. Unconditional love is a vibration we respond to continuously. It is a part of our inner nature. The unconditional love that the Divine expresses to us takes many forms in our reality and is an inherent part of us. Unconditional love is always at work in the background as an emanation of the divine, changing, uplifting, and transforming all that is. It has the power to transform us, bringing forth our divine nature.

The lantern and the staff stand out on this card. Notice that the Hermit's staff is yellow, as is the star in the lantern. The light of the Hermit's divine inner nature shines brightly within the staff. This inner light supports the Hermit no matter where he is and can show others the way as well. Let's look at the numerology of the word "staff".

Chart Seventy-seven
Staff

| 19 | 20 | 1 | 6 | 6 = 52/7 |
|----|----|---|---|----------|
| S  | T  | A | F | F        |
| 1  | 2  | 1 | 6 | 6 = 16/7 |

\* Translation of full numbers 5, 2, 7:
Man (5) Reflects (2) the nature of self in symbols of Spirit (7) and by his spiritual intellect.

\* Alternate translation of full numbers 5, 2, 7:
Man's (5) Dual (2) nature becomes one within divine love and Spirituality (7).

\* Translation of root numbers 1, 6, 7:
The Individual (1) is supported by the Vision (6) and harmony of Spirit (7).

Similarly, our inner nature reflects the divine nature of unconditional love.

### Chart Seventy-eight
### Inner Nature

```
                  60                            79
 9    14    14    5    18      14    1    20    21    18    5 = 139/13/4
 I    N     N     E    R       N     A    T     U     R     E
 9    5     5     5    9       5     1    2     3     9     5 = 13/4
            6 (33)                   7 (25)
```

\* Translation of full numbers 1, 3, 9, 1, 3, 4:
The Divine (1) Expresses (3) Unconditional Love (9) to the Individual (1) through Creativity (3), which is part of the Process (4) of personal transformation within the Duality.

Let's look at the karmic root number 13/4 of "inner nature".

\* Translation of root numbers 1, 3, 4 :
If One (1) insists on Expressing (3) negatively, impeding the Work (4) of positive transformation, the work seems never-ending.

\* Conversion of root numbers 1, 3, 4 into letters:
1 = A, 3 = C, 4 = D.

\* Translation of letters A, C, D:
To discover the inner nature of something is to see the Always (A) Changing (C) Dynamics (D) within it.

Hermit, as the ninth card, is the ending of the first cycle of archetypes. Our world has many cycles: cycles of nature, cycles of growth and decay, and cycles of birth and death, to name a few. Here is the numerology of "cycle".

Chart Seventy-nine
Cycle

| 3 | 25 | 3 | 12 | 5 = 48/12/3 |
|---|----|---|----|-------------|
| C | Y  | C | L  | E           |
| 3 | 7  | 3 | 3  | 5 = 21/3    |

* Translation of full numbers 4, 8, 1, 2, 3:
The Processes (4) of divine energy and Power (8) are Individually (1) Balanced (2) to aid our self-Expression (3).

* Translation of root numbers 2, 1, 3;
The Duality (2) is an interactive grid for Individual (1) self-Expression (3).

Divine processes, such as change, creativity, and spirituality, help us to express ourselves appropriately within the Duality. These processes of divine energy reflect our individual divine nature and personal spiritual growth.

The Duality is created by the divine for the purpose of self-expression and co-creation. The Duality is a grid of energy, which is calibrated to us to suit our individual creative needs. The properties of physics within the Duality are a part of what makes this possible.

The Hermit, representing the end of a cycle of creation, manifestation, and spirit development, is placed before the Wheel of Fortune because the Wheel of Fortune is a transition to the next cycle on a higher level.

**Translation Review**

A Basic Pattern of manifestation within the Duality provides Function within Form. The Duality matrix enables spirit to bring patterns into Solid Form, which reflect Beauty and harmony. Creativity, when expressed within the physical, is one of the most Powerful and Spiritually Revealing energies. The Beauty of harmonious expression is Reflected back to us by the Duality. The Spiritual nature of Creative consciousness given to us by the Divine is Reflected within each Individual.

The Hermit guides us to understand and creatively Express our inner Spiritual nature as a part of the Divine Reflection within an Individual. The

Spiritual nature of Earth embodies the Divine Foundation of Change. The Foundation of change facilitates the Individual's ability to reconcile apparent differences by Devotion to spiritual understanding.

Unconditional Love, as a Foundation of Divine Expression, emanates throughout the Physical world. The Foundation of unconditional love and the ways we respond to it are Reflected in the Processes of our personal lives. Man Reflects the nature of self in the symbols of Spirit and by his spiritual intellect. Man's Dual nature becomes one within divine love and Spirituality. The Individual is supported by the Vision and harmony of Spirit. The Divine Expresses Unconditional Love to the Individual through Creativity, which is a part of the Process of personal transformation within the Duality. If One insists on Expressing negatively, impeding the Work of positive transformation, the work seems never-ending.

To discover the inner nature of something is to see the Always Changing Dynamics within it. The Processes of divine energy and Power are Individually Balanced to aid our self-Expression. The Duality is an interactive grid for Individual self-Expression.

**Applying the Revealed Information**

**Acquired Meanings – New Meanings Revealed by Numerology**
The end of a cycle, unconditional love, selflessness, discovery of our true inner nature, expression of the divine within, spiritual assessment, transformative qualities of spiritual growth, our inner spiritual teacher.

**Relevant Questions**
What is the best way for me to access my inner self? How will this inward search help me? How will it affect my outer world? What is the most effective way for me to deepen my connection to my inner spiritual teacher? What is the nature of this connection for me? What energy has been dominant around me lately? What cycle is ending for me? What energy will be taking its place?

## Practical Application

Reading: the High Priestess, the Six of Wands, the Hermit, the Eight of Pentacles.

The High Priestess, as we saw before, is about the dual nature of our world, intuition, and paradox. She indicates the querent has made an intuitive connection leading to deeper understanding. The understanding could be on a subconscious or conscious level. The querent now projects a self-confidence that is recognized by others, an inner victory at the very least. The querent will continue to see the goals he or she diligently works toward (Eight of Pentacles) manifest by focusing his or her intent and connecting with the inner self for guidance and wisdom (Hermit).

## Just a Thought

When the Hermit comes up in a reading, it indicates the present would be a good time to deepen the connection to the deepest part of ourselves. Or it may be reminding you that the connection to your higher self and guidance is always there as an innate part of who you are. In any case, the energy is getting ready to shift—sometimes in small ways, sometimes in more obvious ways—as we move on to the next card: the Wheel of Fortune.

## Hermit Dynamics:
Teaching
Centering
Guiding
Revealing

# The Second Group of Nine – Wheel of Fortune through the Moon

## Chapter Thirteen

### Ten and the Wheel of Fortune

*Change and karma help balance humanity, as we gain spiritual understanding and live it in our lives.*

### Ten – Expression of Spirit at a Higher Level

Zero after a single digit raises the vibration of the digit so it expresses at its fuller potential, as stated previously. This concept came to me in the book *The Life You Were Born To Live* by Dan Millman. According to Mr. Millman, zero represents the vibration of higher purpose and potential. Ten is the first number of transition in the tarot's major arcana. Numerically, ten is transitioning from single-digit numbers to double-digit numbers. Ten is also a transition from one level to the next within the major arcana, which will be explained more fully under the Wheel of Fortune. Let's look at the numerology of "transition" first.

Chart Eighty
Transition

| 20 | 18 | 1 | 14 | 19 | 9 | 20 | 9 | 15 | 14 | = 139/13/4 |
|----|----|---|----|----|---|----|---|----|----|-----------|
| T  | R  | A | N  | S  | I | T  | I | O  | N  |           |
| 2  | 9  | 1 | 5  | 1  | 9 | 2  | 9 | 6  | 5  | = 49/13/4 |

\* Translation of full numbers 1, 3, 9, 1, 3, 4:
The Divine (1) Creates (3) Endings (9) and transitions so the Individual (1) can Create (3) Foundations (4) for new beginnings.

\* Translation of root numbers 4, 9, 1, 3, 4:
Transition (4) and Ending (9) help the Individual (1) embrace the Cycle (3) of impermanence in the Physical (4) world.

Where the number one in general can refer to an individual person or the ego, adding a zero after one, as in ten, refers to divine perfection, divine potential, or the divine within the individual. Here is the numerology of "ten".

Chart Eighty-one
Ten

| 20 | 5 | 14 = 39/12/3 |
|----|---|--------------|
| T  | E | N            |
| 2  | 5 | 5 = 12/3     |

* Ten key words: *divine potential, divine perfection, divinity within us.*

* Translation of full numbers 3, 9, 1, 2, 3:
Creativity (3) passing through the emanation of Unconditional Love (9) from the Divine (1) gives Balance (2) to what is Created (3).

Divine unconditional love is a part of all that is created. The numbers 1, 2, 3 on the mundane level of "ten" show divine potential as the building blocks (1 = A, 2 = B, 3 = C; ABCs) of what the divine creates.

*The Secret Science of Numerology* by Shirley Blackwell Lawrence states that when the numbers one through ten are added together, their total is fifty-five. Ms. Lawrence calls fifty-five the number of intelligence because the word "intelligence" has a full number of fifty-five. Fifty-five can also be called the number of higher intelligence because in the Hebrew tradition, there are ten globes on the Tree of Life; five on the upper half and five on the lower half can be seen as 5, 5 or fifty-five. The Tree of Life is the symbol of the esoteric knowledge, or higher learning, of Judaism. Let's look at the numerology of the word "higher"—another word with the full number fifty-five on the esoteric level.

Chart Eighty-two
Higher

| 8 | 9 | 7 | 8 | 5 | 18 = 55/10 |
|---|---|---|---|---|------------|
| H | I | G | H | E | R          |
| 8 | 9 | 7 | 8 | 5 | 9 = 46/10/1 |

* Translation of full numbers 55, 10:
There is a Higher Intelligence (55) behind Divine Perfection (10).

* Translation of root numbers 4, 6, 1, 0, 1:
The Work (4) we do on the spiritual level helps us stay in Harmony (6) with the Divine (10) and our higher Self (1).

\* Alternate translation of 4, 6, 10, 1:
The Foundation (4) of Vision (6) is a part of Divine Potential (10) within an Individual (1).

The Wheel of Fortune implies new beginnings by change. When we go through a transition, we begin again. Let's look at the numerology of "begin".

Chart Eighty-three
Begin

| 2 | 5 | 7 | 9 | 14 | = 37/10 |
|---|---|---|---|----|---------|
| B | E | G | I | N  |         |
| 2 | 5 | 7 | 9 | 5  | = 28/10/1 |

\* Translation of full numbers 3, 7, 1, 0:
The Expression (3) of truth within Spirituality (7) is a part of Divine Potential (10).

\* Translation of root numbers 2, 8, 10, 1:
The Duality (2) contains the Power (8) of Divine Potential (10) expressed by the Individual (1) and all other life forms.

The word "beginning", however, reduces to a nine, the number of ending. Within all beginnings, there is an ending. All endings contain a beginning, creating cycles of transition.

**Wheel of Fortune – The Karmic Energy of Change**

The Wheel of Fortune is the first card of transition. After the Wheel of Fortune, spiritual intelligence is expressed at a more sophisticated level. During this transition, personal spiritual energy balances itself. The circular shape of a wheel implies movement; movement implies change. Change helps us grow spiritually. You could call the Wheel of Fortune the card of divine engagement, the divine engaging changes.

The Wheel of Fortune brings us opportunities to re-align ourselves with divine direction emotionally, spiritually, and psychologically. The nature of change may be less important than how we react and respond to change. Imagine the Wheel of Fortune as a spinning vortex. The more you stay in the eye of the vortex, or your spiritual center, the longer you remain stable and balanced. Stability and balance facilitate transition.

The nature of the change that is indicated by the Wheel of Fortune is karmic. Many belief systems define karma as the result of good or bad actions. Karma can also be thought of as life providing us with many opportunities to make better choices. Spirit experiences constant feedback due to karma—the result of our choices—and the interactive reflective nature of the Duality matrix.

As the tenth card, the Wheel of Fortune (10) is associated with the Magician (1) because ten reduces to a one (1 + 0 = 1). Change brought about by the Wheel allows the Magician to focus divine energy in a specific way to bring about greater personal spiritual growth and balance.

In a reading where the Wheel of Fortune appears indicating change is inevitable, the Magician may be implied. An implied card is one that is not actually drawn, but the reading suggests another card's influence can be intuited. The meanings of the drawn cards, in context or content, can bring the dynamics of the implied card to mind. When the higher number of a major arcana card reduces to the lower number of a major arcana card, it is up to the reader of the cards to determine if the lower-numbered card is pertinent to the reading.

If the Magician is implied, whether by number association as in this case or by reading dynamics, the Magician can be used to facilitate the results of change. For example, let's look at a reading in which the following cards are drawn: the King of Wands, the Wheel of Fortune, and the Two of Swords. The King of Wands is a decisive man of action, but circumstances are about to change (the Wheel) making decisions difficult (Two of Swords). Ten's reduction to one implies the Magician's association with the Wheel (the tenth card). The Magician's card shows the four suits on his table. He has the energy of all the suits to work with. Focusing on the implied influence of the Magician, the King of Wands might also choose to work with the energy of the four suits. Taking the suits individually and considering how they would facilitate a decision (what each suit would base a decision on) can help bring an answer into focus. Using the different approaches of the suits can make decisions clearer. For example, Cups would base a decision on what feels right. Pentacles would base a decision on a practicality. Swords would base a decision on careful consideration and planning. Taking the Magician—the card implied by the numerology—into consideration can help that process.

Here is the numerology of "Wheel of Fortune".

## Chart Eighty-four
## Wheel of Fortune

```
        53              21                    99
23   8   5   5  12   15  6    6  15 18   20  21  14   5 = 173/11
W    H   E   E   L    O  F    F   O   R   T   U   N   E
5    8   5   5   3    6  6    6   6   9   2   3   5   5 = 20/2
         8 (26)          3                9 (36)
```

* Translation of full numbers 1, 7, 3, 11:
Divinity (1), using change and karma, passes on Knowledge (7) Expressed (3) as Spiritual Concepts (11).

* Translation of root numbers 2, 0, 2:
The Balancing (2) effect of which is reflected (0) within the Duality (2) as well as the individual.

* Conversion of full numbers 5, 3 (53), 2, 1 (21), 9, 9 (99) into letters:
5 = E, 3 = C, 2 = B, 1 = A, 9 = I, 9 = I.

* Translation of E, C, B, A, I, I:
Every (E) Consciousness (C) that is Brought (B) into An (A) Incarnation (I) has the potential to Initiate (I) karma.

Any living thing that has consciousness can also have karma. Let's look at the numerology of "change" next.

## Chart Eighty-five
## Change

```
     3    8    1    14    7     5 = 38/11
     C    H    A    N     G     E
     3    8    1    5     7     5 = 29/11
```

* Translation of full numbers 3, 8, 11:
Change, a fundamental Expression (3) of divinity and Karma (8), promotes the reflective properties of the Duality and Spiritual Understanding (11).

* Translation of root numbers 2, 9, 11:
Change and Karma help Balance (2) Humanity (9) as we gain

Spiritual Understanding (11) and live it in our lives.

\* Conversion of full numbers 3, 8, 11 into letters:
3 = C, 8 = H, 11 = K.

\* Translation of C, H, K:
Change creates Checks (C, H, K) and balances.

\* Conversion of root numbers 2, 9, 11 into letters:
2 = B, 9 = I, 11 = K.

\* Translation of B, I, K:
Before (B) Intellectual (I) Knowledge (K), there is spiritual knowing.

The powerful dynamics of change help us gain spiritual understanding. The Wheel of Fortune promotes spiritual growth by cycles of karma and change. Here is the numerology of "karma".

### Chart Eighty-six
### Karma

| 11 | 1 | 18 | 13 | 1 | = 44/8 |
|----|---|----|----|---|--------|
| K  | A | R  | M  | A |        |
| 11 | 1 | 9  | 4  | 1 | = 26/8 |

\* Translation of full numbers 4, 4, 8:
In the Duality, karma is one of the Foundational (4) Processes (4) of divine Energy (8).

\* Translation of root numbers 2, 6, 8:
Personal Will (2) and acceptance of Responsibility (6) facilitate learning from the Cycles (8) of karma and change.

The Wheel implies movement, so next is the numerology of "movement".

Chart Eighty-seven
Movement

| 13 | 15 | 22 | 5 | 13 | 5 | 14 | 20 = 107/8 |
| M | O | V | E | M | E | N | T |
| 4 | 6 | 22 | 5 | 4 | 5 | 5 | 2 = 53/8 |

\* Translation of full numbers 10, 7, 8:
Divine Perfection (10) and Spiritual Intelligence (7) are innate Powers (8) expressed within the movement of the Wheel.

\* Translation of root numbers 5, 3, 8:
Man (5) Expresses (3) himself by the spiritual understanding of his personal Power (8).

\* Conversion of root numbers 5, 3, 8 into letters:
5 = E, 3 = C, 8 = H.

\* Translation of E, C, H:
Everything (E) CHanges (C, H).

The perfection of the divine forever moves spirit toward its own realization of perfection by the dynamics of change and karma. The more a person understands his spiritual nature, the more it influences his karma and the way he express his personal power. Movement implies change, change implies movement, and so the Wheel of Fortune turns.

**Translation Review**

The Divine Creates Endings and transitions so the Individual can Create Foundations for new beginnings. Transition and Ending help the Individual embrace the Cycle of impermanence in the Physical world.

Creativity passing through the emanation of Unconditional Love from the Divine gives Balance to what is Created. There is a Higher Intelligence behind Divine Perfection. The Work we do on the spiritual level helps us stay in Harmony with the Divine and our higher Self.

The Foundation of Vision is a part of Divine Potential within an Individual. The Expression of truth within Spirituality is a part of Divine Potential. The Duality contains the Power of Divine Potential expressed by the Individual and all other life forms.

Divinity, using change and karma, passes on Knowledge Expressed as Spiritual Concepts. The Balancing effect of which is reflected within the Duality as well as the individual. Every Consciousness that is Brought into

An Incarnation has the potential to Initiate karma. Change, a fundamental Expression of divinity and Karma, promotes the reflective properties of the Duality and Spiritual Understanding. Change and Karma help Balance Humanity as we gain Spiritual Understanding and live it in our lives. Change creates Checks and balances.

Before Intellectual Knowledge, there is spiritual knowing. In the Duality, karma is one of the Foundational Processes of divine Energy. Personal Will and acceptance of Responsibility facilitate learning from the Cycles of karma and change. Divine Perfection and Spiritual Intelligence are innate Powers expressed within the movement of the Wheel. Man Expresses himself by the spiritual understanding of his personal Power. Everything Changes.

**Applying the Revealed Information**

**Acquired Meanings – New Meanings Revealed by Numerology**
Higher purpose, divine perfection, work done on a spiritual level, a beginning on a new level, the challenges of change and karma, re-balancing of personal spiritual energy, understanding of personal power, spiritual lessons, spiritual knowing.

**Relevant Questions**
What negative karmic energy do I need to balance? What spiritual insight can I gain from this? What higher purpose is change serving in my life? What new level am I beginning? What can I take to a higher level? What spiritual lessons do I need to focus on? How can I become more open to change?

**Practical Application**
Reading: the Ten of Swords, the Wheel of Fortune, the Ten of Cups.

Notice these cards are all tens. Three tens equal thirty, which is creativity taken to a new level. In the Ten of Swords, the querent's thoughts and emotions impact him or her as no one else's can. The Wheel of Fortune brings movement and therefore cycles of change and karma. Change cannot be stopped by personal feelings, fears, anger, or anxiety, however these things affect the querent's perception or reaction to change. When we allow negative feelings to affect what we create, the results are negative as well. The challenge is to be open to change. By doing that, we allow ourselves to be inspired by our creativity, and we nurture a more positive, shared reality in our personal life and in our community.

**Just a Thought**

The core vibration of the sample reading is thirty. These three cards tell us change is an expression of creativity on a higher level. Change is an opportunity, the outcome of which will impact us on many levels. Change is inevitably unavoidable. How we handle change is an indicator of spiritual maturity.

A second thought: the Wheel indicates a shift. In a reading where you have a major arcana card that is directly after the Wheel, that card can indicate context for the change.

Example: the Wheel of Fortune followed by the Hanged Man.

The Hanged Man, as the context, is about a change (the Wheel) happening specifically in outlook or perspective (the Hanged Man). Any minor arcana card, that comes after the Wheel and Hanged Man tells about the content of the new perspective.

Example: the Wheel of Fortune, the Hanged Man, the Four of

Pentacles.

The Four of Pentacles indicates the new perspective is about the handling of money, practical aspects of life, or domestic concerns.

Change (Wheel of Fortune) in perspective (Hanged Man) about the way money is dealt with (Four of Pentacles).

**Wheel of Fortune Dynamics:**
Challenging
Changing
Divine Re-balancing
Adapting

## Chapter Fourteen

### Eleven and Justice

*When we have spiritual maturity, truth brings power from the Divine to humanity through vision and acceptance.*

### Eleven – Spiritual Values and Understanding

Continuing with the double-digit numbers, eleven is next. From this point on, the numbers reflect a level of spiritual maturity and start with the number one. One, as the first digit of this next number group, puts the emphasis on the individual expressing at a higher level. As two ones, 1, 1, eleven is the divine (1) expressing as inspiration within an individual (1).

The first number of the second cycle of nine tells us the card numbers eleven through nineteen are steps taken toward ending the illusion of duality. Eleven, as nine plus two, is the end (9) of duality (2) as a result of spiritual understanding. As ten plus one, eleven is divine potential (10) within an individual (1) that understands the spiritual (11) teachings of duality. Divine potential is within an individual, as the individual expresses divine potential. Let's see what "eleven" can tell us.

Chart Eighty-eight
Eleven

| 5 | 12 | 5 | 22 | 5 | 14 = 63/9 |
|---|----|---|----|---|-----------|
| E | L  | E | V  | E | N         |
| 5 | 3  | 5 | 22 | 5 | 5 = 45/9  |

* Eleven key words: *spiritual understanding, illumination, visionary.*

* Translation of full numbers 6, 3, 9:
The spiritual teachings of our Vision (6) that we understand and Express (3) promote Integrity and Wisdom (9), helping us to spiritually mature.

* Translation of root numbers 4, 5, 9:
The Processes (4) of Man's (5) spiritual maturing can bring an End (9) to duality and karma.

The word "duality" also has a full number of eleven. The Duality, considered in its entirety as a living entity, has awareness and spiritual intelligence. The Duality's spiritual intelligence supports and promotes vision, which can bring an end to the cycle of karma. We incur less karma as we spiritually mature. Let's take a look at the word "mature" next.

## Chart Eighty-nine
## Mature

| 13 | 1 | 20 | 21 | 18 | 5 = 78/15/6 |
|----|---|----|----|----|-------------|
| M  | A | T  | U  | R  | E           |
| 4  | 1 | 2  | 3  | 9  | 5 = 24/6    |

\* Translation of full numbers 7, 8, 1, 5, 6:
Truth (7) brings Power (8) from the Divine (1) to Man (5) by Vision (6) and acceptance as we gain spiritual maturity.

\* Translation of root numbers 2, 4, 6:
We (2) maintain Stability (4) by the process of maturing spiritually and accepting Responsibility (6) for that process.

We become more spiritually mature by our ability to discern spiritual truth and by accepting that truth for what it is.

Eleven, the number of spiritual knowledge or light ("light" has a root number of eleven), includes the embracing of spiritual principles and spiritual insight. Following is the numerology of the word "light".

## Chart Ninety
## Light

| 12 | 9 | 7 | 8 | 20 = 56/11 |
|----|---|---|---|------------|
| L  | I | G | H | T          |
| 3  | 9 | 7 | 8 | 2 = 29/11  |

\* Translation of full numbers 5, 6, 11:
Man's (5) Vision (6) (our ability to conceive of and discern spiritual insight) is perceived as Light (11).

\* Translation of root numbers 2, 9, 11:
The Duality (2) is bathed in the emanation of Unconditional Love (9) by Light (11).

When we say some one has "seen the light," perhaps on a deeper level it means the person has spiritual insight. Divine unconditional love is seen in the Duality as light.

## Justice – The Archetype of Recompense

The card Justice is about understanding recompense within a spiritual context. The higher concept of recompense engages growth and spiritual balance. The archetype of Justice plays out the dynamic of recompense to reveal the higher concepts of justice.

Justice is "served" when we reach an understanding of non-judgment. Recompense for achieving non-judgment comes in the form of restored balance, understanding, and personal growth. As a result, a person steps into the light of higher spiritual understanding.

A higher understanding of justice requires non-judgment. A higher vision of justice requires an unbiased point of view. There is recompense to living in a state of non-judgment. By non-judgment, we experience a greater sense of totality. The divine creates without judgment.

Realizing non-judgment within a spiritual context is the key to understanding justice and recompense. Judgment slows growth on many levels. Non-judgment promotes growth. Non-judgment is facilitated and promoted by the interactive, reflective nature of the duality matrix. Unconditional love carries and promotes the message of non-judgment throughout the Duality.

Eleven is the higher vibration of two (11, $1 + 1 = 2$). Justice (card eleven) relates to the High Priestess (card two) because both express archetypal aspects of the number two. The archetype of Justice reveals judgment. Judgment implies a polarity. The High Priestess embodies the connection between polarities, but until we accept the existence of connections where there appear to be none, non-judgment may be elusive. The High Priestess, as the continuum, is at the core of non-judgment. Accepting the connection between all things promotes non-judgment. The possibility that connections exist results in the unlimited potential of non-judgment.

Judging in thought, feeling, or action creates a spiritual imbalance activating the archetypal energy of Justice. Justice promotes non-judgment as a result of reflection. The innate nature of the Duality promotes many ways of understanding by reflecting our balance or imbalance back to us for personal assessment.

The scales of Justice remain balanced when we maintain neutrality and hold to an unbiased point of view. Justice helps reveal the connections within the continuum, and as a result, we come closer to experiencing the unity of all that is.

Next, we have the numerology of "Justice".

## Chart Ninety-one
### Justice

| 10 | 21 | 19 | 20 | 9 | 3 | 5 = 87/15/6 |
|----|----|----|----|----|---|-------------|
| J  | U  | S  | T  | I  | C | E           |
| 1  | 3  | 1  | 2  | 9  | 3 | 5 = 24/6    |

\* Translation of full numbers 8, 7, 1, 5, 6:
Part of the Power (8) of Spiritual Intelligence (7) given from the Divine (1) to Man (5) is seen within us as our Vision (6).

\* Translation of root numbers 2, 4, 6:
The re-Balancing (2) continues within the archetypal Foundation (4) of Justice as we accept Responsibility (6) for our actions and spiritual growth.

The focus of recompense is understanding in a spiritual context, rather than a mundane context. Monetary compensation is currently common as recompense, but the archetype of Justice asks us to consider other options that embrace a deeper spiritual understanding. Let's take a look at the numerology of "recompense".

## Chart Ninety-two
### Recompense

| 18 | 5 | 3 | 15 | 13 | 16 | 5 | 14 | 19 | 5 = 113/5 |
|----|---|---|----|----|----|---|----|----|-----------|
| R  | E | C | O  | M  | P  | E | N  | S  | E         |
| 9  | 5 | 3 | 6  | 4  | 7  | 5 | 5  | 1  | 5 = 50/5  |

\* Translation of full numbers 11, 3, 5:
Spiritual Insights (11) Expressed (3) within a physical context can bring about personal positive Change (5).

\* Conversion of full numbers to letters:
A = 1, M = 13, E = 5.

\* Translation of letters A, M, E; AME or AIM:
If we Aim for a higher understanding of justice, we step forward in our personal journey of spiritual maturity.

\* Translation of root numbers 5, 0, 5:
By the archetype of Justice, the higher nature of Man (5) can be

Reflected (0) in Changes (5) he makes as well as his words.

Recompense (50) is activated by the universal principle of change and Justice. The full number fifty on the mundane level shows that greater potential, invoked by the zero, accompanies the change. As a universal principle, recompense embraces balance, understanding, and the non-judgmental expression of our higher spiritual nature. Justice and recompense bring about profound spiritual change.

We can be freed in different ways by embracing the spiritual concepts of the archetype of Justice. The act of non-judgment results in more options and choices when we maintain neutrality. Suspending judgment can also free us from karma. The act of judgment narrows options and invites reaction to any action taken, often a negative action. The result is that we remain trapped in a cycle of karma. By aspiring to the higher expression of justice, we come closer to realizing the freedom non-judgment brings.

The Justice card shows a figure seated while holding scales in his left hand. The karmic number fourteen that appears in the word "scales" suggests these scales measure karma. All change results in karma and promotes spiritual growth, but not all change results in positive karma. Following is the numerology of "scales".

### Chart Ninety-three
### Scales

| 19 | 3 | 1 | 12 | 5 | 19 = 59/14/5 |
|----|---|---|----|---|--------------|
| S  | C | A | L  | E | S            |
| 1  | 3 | 1 | 3  | 5 | 1 = 14/5     |

* Translation of full numbers 5, 9, 1, 4, 5:
Man's (5) ideas and expression of justice handled with integrity and Wisdom (9) are a part of One's (1) Process (4) of spiritual maturity, which can lead to greater Freedom (5).

The scales also symbolize the balancing of energy within us as we initiate and react to change in our lives. The word scales brings to mind balance, which we will take another look at next.

### Chart Nine-four
### Balance

| 2 | 1 | 12 | 1 | 14 | 3 | 5 = 38/11 |
|---|---|----|---|----|---|-----------|
| B | A | L  | A | N  | C | E         |
| 2 | 1 | 3  | 1 | 5  | 3 | 5 = 20/2  |

\* Translation of full numbers 3, 8, 11:
Balance is an Expression (3) of Power (8) within the context of Spiritual Understanding (11).

\* Translation of root numbers 2, 0, 2:
Our spiritual Balance (2), or lack of it, is reflected (0) back to us within the Duality (2).

Remaining balanced promotes our sense of spiritual power. Balance—or a lack of balance—is reflected back to us by the duality matrix. Justice also brings to mind the words "right" and "wrong," which imply judgment.

### Chart Ninety-five
### Right

| 18 | 9 | 7 | 8 | 20 = 62/8 |
|----|---|---|---|-----------|
| R  | I | G | H | T         |
| 9  | 9 | 7 | 8 | 2 = 35/8  |

\* Translation of full numbers 6, 2, 8:
Right Vision (6) gives Us (2) true spiritual Power (8).

\* Translation of root numbers 3, 5, 8:
Self-Expression (3) demonstrating positive Change (5) results in our Power (8) being reflected back to us.

### Chart Ninety-six
### Wrong

| 23 | 18 | 15 | 14 | 7 = 77/14/5 |
|----|----|----|----|-------------|
| W  | R  | O  | N  | G           |
| 5  | 9  | 6  | 5  | 7 = 32/5    |

\* Translation of full numbers 77, 14, 5:
Christ Consciousness (77), as a pattern of the divine within,

imprints us with the knowledge of how an Individual (1) should use knowledge of right and wrong as a Foundation (4) of Change (5).

* Translation of root numbers 3, 2, 5:
Our Expression (3) of Balance (2) affects our spiritual power and Personal Freedom (5).

The figure of Justice holds a sword in his right hand. The sixteen of "sword" warns of a potential for negative karma. Sword is an anagram for words. The sword on the Justice card is a symbol for words that are just. Words spoken unjustly can result in negative karma.

Chart Ninety-seven<br>Sword

| 19 | 23 | 15 | 18 | 4 = 79/16/7 |
|----|----|----|----|-------------|
| S  | W  | O  | R  | D           |
| 1  | 5  | 6  | 9  | 4 = 25/7    |

* Translation of full numbers 7, 9, 1, 6, 7:
When Spiritual (7) Integrity (9) is disregarded and One (1) denies Responsibility (6) for their words, there are Spiritual (7) consequences.

* Conversion of root numbers 2, 5, 7 to letters:
2 = B, 5 = E, 7 = G.

* Translation of letters B, E, G; BEG:
Aggressively used words (and swords) can lead us to BEG for mercy.

* Translation of root numbers 2, 5, 7:
Balanced expression within the Duality (2) is reflected in positive Changes (5) and shows Spiritual (7) maturity.

## Translation Review

The spiritual teachings of our Vision that we understand and Express promote Integrity and Wisdom, helping us to spiritually mature. The Processes of Man's spiritual maturing can bring an End to duality and karma. Truth brings Power from the Divine to Man by Vision and acceptance as we gain spiritual maturity. We maintain Stability by the process of maturing spiritually and accepting Responsibility for that process. Man's Vision is perceived as Light. The Duality is bathed in the emanation of Unconditional Love by Light.

Part of the Power of Spiritual Intelligence given from the Divine to Man is seen within us as our Vision. The re-Balancing continues within the archetypal Foundation of Justice as we accept Responsibility for our actions and spiritual growth. Spiritual Insights Expressed within a physical context can bring about personal positive Change. If we Aim for a higher understanding of justice, we step forward in our personal journey of spiritual maturity. By the archetype of Justice, the higher nature of Man can be Reflected in Changes he makes as well as his words. Man's ideas and expression of justice handled with integrity and Wisdom are a part of One's Process of spiritual maturity, which can lead to greater Freedom.

Balance is an Expression of Power within the context of Spiritual Understanding. Our spiritual Balance, or lack of it, is reflected back to us within the Duality. Right Vision gives Us true spiritual Power. Self-Expression demonstrating positive Change results in our Power being reflected back to us. Christ Consciousness, as a pattern of the divine within, imprints us with the knowledge of how an Individual should use knowledge of right and wrong as a Foundation of Change. Our Expression of Balance affects our spiritual power and Personal Freedom.

When Spiritual Integrity is disregarded and One denies Responsibility for their words, there are Spiritual consequences. Aggressively used words can lead us to BEG for mercy. Balanced expression within the Duality is reflected in positive Changes and shows Spiritual maturity.

The words associated with eleven and the Justice archetype show us that:

* Our understanding of justice and recompense is expanded by change, spiritual growth, and maturity.

* Working through personal karma can lead us to spiritual freedom and perhaps release us from the cycle of reincarnation.

* Words we speak can result in negative karmic consequences.

* Change and balance result in positive karma.

* Right vision brings us true power.

* We are bathed in divine unconditional love perceived as light.

## Applying the Revealed Information

### Acquired Meanings – New Meanings Revealed by Numerology

Spiritual maturity, divinity within the individual, spiritual understanding and principles, divine light, accepting individual responsibility for our own spiritual growth, the higher meanings of justice, recompense, balance as a spiritual concept.

### Relevant Questions

What principle of Justice is at work in my life at this time? How does Justice function on a spiritual level? How is balance manifesting in my life? How am I reflecting the divinity within me? What approach will help me to become more spiritually mature?

### Practical Application

Reading: the Knight of Pentacles, Justice, the Queen of Pentacles.

The Knight of Pentacles indicates the querent is observing the practical aspects of a situation while waiting to see what develops. The Knight looks toward Justice to evaluate his own judgment. Whatever the situation and whatever action the querent decides to take, the spiritual principle of non-judgment is engaged. The querent needs accept responsibility for his or her part in the situation while looking for a greater understanding and meaning within the content of his or her daily life. By embracing the spiritual concepts of Justice and the insights provided by his or her life situation, the querent is likely to see the positive effects as he or she creates ways to manifest material security and abundance (Queen of Pentacles).

**Just a Thought**

The Knight in this reading is in the process of taking care of the everyday practical aspects of life while acquiring what is needed. Being responsible for the way he engages the practical side of life keeps the scales balanced. The Queen of Pentacles speaks of the more creative, nurturing side of his personality. She is more aware of the deeper rhythms and cycles of life, and the abundance of nature. This awareness also helps to keep the scales balanced. The Knight must embrace his respect for nature and use of natural resources wisely. Applying a higher meaning to Justice and recompense can bring us a better understanding of their dynamics in the natural processes of our life.

**Justice Dynamics:**
Accepting
Balancing
Maturing

## Chapter Fifteen

### Twelve and the Hanged Man

*Change within the Duality expands our vision and bring us more fully into the light.*

### Twelve – Creativity on a New Level

Twelve is divinity expressing as duality. Twelve is comprised of the number one, as in divinity, and the number two, the reflection of divinity. Divinity reflects itself as the Duality and in many different ways within the Duality. In numerology, the number twelve contains the natural progression of one, two, three (1 + 2 = 3). Twelve represents Divinity (1) that Reflects (2) itself in order to Create (3). This equation also represents the great diversity within the divine.

Chart Ninety-eight
Twelve

| 20 | 23 | 5 | 12 | 22 | 5 = 87/15/6 |
|----|----|---|----|----|-------------|
| T  | W  | E | L  | V  | E           |
| 2  | 5  | 5 | 3  | 22 | 5 = 42/6    |

\* Translation of full numbers 8, 7, 1, 5, 6:
The Power (8) and Spiritual Intelligence (7) of the Divine (1) bring Variety (5) and Beauty (6) into form.

\* Translation of root numbers 4, 2, 6:
A Foundational (4) nature of the Duality (2) is to express beauty and Function (6) in form.

Divine creative energy is innately beautiful. The creative impulse of the divine is infinite, undeniable, and multitudinous. Following is the numerology of "creative".

Chart Ninety-nine
Creative

| 3 | 18 | 5 | 1 | 20 | 9 | 22 | 5 = 83/11 |
|---|----|---|---|----|---|----|-----------|
| C | R  | E | A | T  | I | V  | E         |
| 3 | 9  | 5 | 1 | 2  | 9 | 22 | 5 = 56/11 |

\* Translation of full numbers 8, 3, 11:
The Power (8) of creative Expression (3) is Spiritual (11) in nature.

\* Translation of root numbers 5, 6, 11:
Change (5) within the Duality expands our Vision (6) and brings us more fully into the Light (11).

Creativity, as change, brings us greater understanding of the nature of spirit and therefore ourselves. As we spiritually mature, we expand our ability to see beauty in everything and our ability to be the creators of beauty within the Duality.

Chart One Hundred
Beauty

| 2 | 5 | 1 | 21 | 20 | 25 = 74/11 |
|---|---|---|----|----|------------|
| B | E | A | U  | T  | Y          |
| 2 | 5 | 1 | 3  | 2  | 7 = 20/2   |

\* Translation of full numbers 7, 4, 11:
The beauty we see by our Spiritual (7) insight is a Work (4) in progress related to our Spiritual Understanding (11).

\* Translation of root numbers 2, 0, 2:
Beauty (2) is Reflected (0) throughout the Duality (2).

Both "beauty" and "duality" have a root number of two. Beauty and duality are synonymous. There is nothing created that is not beautiful. We may not see the beauty with our physical eyes, but our spiritual nature sees it and responds to it, regardless of how things appear.

## Hanged Man – The Expansion of Perspective; The Third Archetype of Paradox

What is a paradox? The *Webster's Collegiate Dictionary* defines it as "a statement that seems contradictory yet can still be true." The Hanged Man is the third archetype of paradox. The first archetype of paradox is the Fool: the nothingness of zero containing all potential. The second archetype of paradox is the High Priestess: divine reflection, two that is one. The third archetype of paradox is the Hanged Man: clarity from reversal.

The image of the Hanged Man shows a person suspended by one leg in an inverted position. This archetype is about seeing things from a different perspective, e.g., upside down. His reversed position allows him to see from a divine point of view. The Hanged Man, by changing perspective, exposes the inherent problems of point of view.

The resolution of paradox integrates two apparent opposites, which also resolve the illusion of diversity, revealing the underlying unity. The many forms of the one, as in the divine, is the primary paradox.

The Hanged Man archetype initiates the expansion of creative thinking, which embraces a different perspective that develops new understanding. He encourages the mind to search for the resolution of a paradox. In searching for the resolution of a paradox, the mind must embrace new ways of thinking. New ways of thinking require the individual to become mentally creative. The resolving of paradox—the reconciliation of apparent opposites—demonstrates an expanded creativity of the mind.

While the High Priestess and the Hanged Man dissolve illusions of separateness, the Hanged Man and the Empress, by the number three, express different aspect of creativity.

The High Priestess and the Hanged Man dissolve illusions of separateness within their contexts. The High Priestess dissolves illusions of separateness by revealing connections between different forms of energy. The Hanged Man dissolves illusions of separateness by engaging mental creativity to resolve coinciding contradiction.

The Hanged Man (12/3) and the Empress (3) both express aspects of the number three. The creative matrix of the Empress (3) provides the foundation for the Hanged Man (12/3). The Hanged Man expresses the creative energy of three expanded within the context of the mind, where as the Empress provides the matrix for expression.

The Hanged Man is the creativity of the expanded mind that sees diversity as the expression of divinity and self.

The Duality innately contains paradox. Paradox is also created in part by the restrictions of our personal perspectives. The truth of a paradox as an illusion of perspective is symbolized by the Hanged Man. As an archetype, he expands our awareness by expanding the mind, potentially to resolve paradox.

The full number forty on the mundane level shows the Hanged Man takes our perception of the physical to a higher understanding.

## Chart One Hundred One
## Hanged Man

```
              39                          28
 8   1  14   7   5   4    13   1  14 = 67/13
 H   A   N   G   E   D     M   A   N
 8   1   5   7   5   4     4   1   5 = 40/4
              30                          10
```

\* Translation of full numbers 6, 7, 1, 3, 4:
The Form and Function (6) of Paradox (7) reflect the Divine's (1) Creative (3) diversity.

\* Translation of root numbers 4, 0, 4:
The Foundation (4) of paradox within the Duality is Reflected (0) as a Foundation (4) for spiritual understanding.

    The legs of the Hanged Man are positioned in a reflected and inverted number four. Hanged Man, paradox, and foundation (4) are linked to each other by the concepts and numbers of the Hanged Man. The physical world expresses paradox, as suggested by the root number four of "Hanged Man". Paradox contains characteristics of dualism. Dualism is the conceptual division of something into two opposing or contrasting parts. There is no paradox without dualism. Paradox is a key to understanding and resolving duality. The root number seven of "paradox" (Chart One Hundred Two, page 133) reveals that it is a spiritual abstraction. Paradox is an abstract concept of the mind connected to spiritual understanding. Paradox is also a foundation principle within duality reiterated by the number four, and is a result of divine reflection.
    The Hanged Man archetype represents a perspective within expanded creative consciousness that is broad enough to assimilate all apparent contradictions and duality. Paradox, as a component of expanded consciousness, contains hidden spiritual truths. The dynamics within a paradox, or the paradox dynamic, is one in which the contradictory nature of something is emphasized. Spirit is asking us to engage our creative thinking when bringing our attention to the paradox dynamic. We may or may not be able to resolve the paradox, but sometimes the effort is enough to bring us sudden insight into our nature, the nature of divinity, or the nature of the Duality.

## Chart One Hundred Two
## Paradox

| 16 | 1 | 18 | 1 | 4 | 15 | 24 | = 79/16/7 |
|----|---|----|---|---|----|----|-----------|
| P  | A | R  | A | D | O  | X  |           |
| 7  | 1 | 9  | 1 | 4 | 6  | 6  | = 34/7    |

\* Translation of full numbers 7, 9, 1, 6, 7:
Spiritual Intelligence (7), as a tool for the Ascension (9) of an Individual (1), helps engage our Vision (6) leading to realizations about the truth of Paradox (7).

\* Translation of root numbers 3, 4, 7:
The divine Expression (3) of duality brings into the Physical (4) the Paradox (7) dynamic.

Seven, the number of spirituality and the root number of "paradox", shows there are spiritual messages and concepts within a paradox. The paradox dynamic is a unique expression of duality.

Despite the Hanged Man's inverted position, he sees with more clarity from this perspective. Expanding our awareness and seeing things from a different perspective can also bring us clarity. What exactly is that perspective? The root number of paradox suggests it is the perspective of spirit. Perspective helps determine what we believe about our reality. Let's look at "perspective" next.

## Chart One Hundred Three
## Perspective

| 16 | 5 | 8 | 19 | 16 | 5 | 3 | 20 | 9 | 22 | 5 | = 138/12/3 |
|----|---|---|----|----|---|---|----|---|----|---|------------|
| P  | E | R | S  | P  | E | C | T  | I | V  | E |            |
| 7  | 5 | 9 | 1  | 7  | 5 | 3 | 2  | 9 | 22 | 5 | = 75/12/3  |

\* Translation of full numbers 1, 3, 8, 1, 2, 3:
The Divine (1) constructs Creative (3) Power (8) so an Individual (1) within the Duality (2) can see what is Created (3) from different perspectives.

\* Translation of root numbers 7, 5, 1, 2, 3:
The Spiritual Intelligence (7) of Man (5) creates perspective when an Individual (1) spirit in the Duality (2) incarnates into a body.

Our spiritual intelligence creates perspective when spirit inhabits a physical body. Our spiritual intelligence is a part of divine creativity. Spiritual intelligence is also a part of the expanded mind.

**Translation Review**

The Power and Spiritual Intelligence of the Divine bring Variety and Beauty into form. A Foundational nature of the Duality is to express beauty and Function in form. The Power of creative Expression is Spiritual in nature. Change within the Duality expands our Vision and brings us more fully into the Light.

The beauty we see by our Spiritual insight is a Work in progress related to our Spiritual Understanding. Beauty is Reflected throughout the Duality. The Form and Function of Paradox reflects the Divine's Creative diversity. The Foundation of Paradox within the Duality is Reflected as a Foundation for spiritual understanding. Spiritual Intelligence, as a tool for the Ascension of an Individual, helps engage our Vision leading to realizations about the truth of Paradox. The divine Expression of duality brings into the Physical the Paradox dynamic.

The Divine constructs Creative Power so an Individual within the Duality can see what is Created from different perspectives. The Spiritual Intelligence of Man creates perspective when an Individual spirit in the Duality incarnates into a body.

**Applying the Revealed Information**

**Acquired Meanings – New Meanings Revealed by Numerology**

Creativity on a higher level, the beauty of all that is, creating diversity, higher perspective, expanding awareness, the meanings behind a paradox, the creativity of the expanded mind.

**Relevant Questions**

How can I take my creativity to a new level? What is the higher perspective in this situation? In what way will expanding my awareness of this situation change things? What paradox do I need to consider? What kind of mental or creative diversity would I especially benefit from?

**Practical Application**

Reading: the Fool, the Knight of Cups, the Hanged Man.

The Fool indicates the querent needs to give more consideration to an action or situation. There is, as yet, unrealized potential. Things may also be temporarily in stasis while forces are at work behind the scenes. Whatever the issue, it is likely to be emotionally engaging for the querent, as indicated by the Knight of Cups.

Delving into his or her emotional depths is important for the querent's personal growth. The Hanged Man shows a change of perspective from a higher awareness is needed. The Knight is riding toward the Hanged Man. This reading asks the querent to consider the possibilities and potential of the situation by seeing it from a more creative, diverse perspective. The process of investigating emotional issues may be uncomfortable, but the Hanged Man and the Fool show there is a greater potential for expanding the querent's personal awareness at this time.

**Just a Thought**

The archetype of the Hanged Man illustrates a truth about perspective. Sometimes a different perspective leads to a greater truth.

I decided to ask the tarot the following three questions:

"What is the paradox of perspective?"

"How does sensory input affect the paradox of perspective?"

"What is the overall result of the paradox of perspective?"

First question: What is the paradox of perspective?

The person in the Two of Pentacles tries to stay balanced while juggling two pentacles. More generally, a person juggles things in a physical world. The lemniscate in the Two of Pentacles shows there is a connection between two objects represented by the pentacles. From our perspective, we can't always see a connection, and two things can seem totally separate and unrelated. The paradox of perspective is that what appears to be many is in truth one.

Our ego, which promotes our individual sense of self, perpetuates the constant struggle of trying to find the truth between one perspective and another. Between different perspectives there is a truth, but because of our personal perspectives and ego identities, truth becomes difficult, if not impossible, to find.

In answer to the first question, "What is the paradox of perspective?" I drew the Two of Pentacles. The lemniscate in the Two of Pentacles implies that duality is an illusion. The illusion of duality significantly influences perspective in general. In addition, our individual perspective created by self-identity also influences perspective. We see everything in relationship to our physical bodies and who we are. Two people looking at the same object or situation see different versions due to their personal perspectives. If we accept that the appearance of reality is a matter of personal perspective—mine, yours, theirs—we are perpetually stuck trying to balance all the diverse perspectives to find the truth.

The waves shown in the background of the Two of Pentacles are an interesting evocation of the idea of a wavelength. We see our world through wavelengths of light. The physical limitations of the human eye and the mechanics and physics of light waves shape our visual perception, limiting our ability to see the truth of what the Duality is. The paradox of perspective is that personal perspective creates division where there is none; the one becomes many.

Second question: How does sensory input affect the paradox of perspective?

A knight rides a horse in a determined manner staring intently at a cup. The knight's attention on the cup indicates that his emotions are his primary focus. His emotions are activated by his sensory input and influence his perspective. Sensory input (what our senses tell us) creates fragmentation.

In answer to the second question, "How does sensory input affect the paradox of perspective?" I drew the Knight of Cups. The Knight confronts his emotional landscape. His sensory input impacts his emotions and therefore impacts his perspective. Sensory input adds another layer of separation from the truth within the paradox of perspective. Once we perceive something, our emotions qualify and emphasize the information our senses bring us. The stronger our emotional reaction to something, the more we separate it from everything else. Our emotional reactions fragment our reality.

We often get totally absorbed in our emotions, and we often get fixated on our strongest emotion at any given moment. Our emotions distort our perspective. Our emotions blind us to reality and the truth. Emotions create multiple versions of a single event, situation, or thing. For every person there is a unique version, which is an example of how sensory input coupled with emotion affect the paradox of perspective. Our sensory input and emotion create fragmentation, which enhances the dividing effect of personal perspective.

Third question: What is the overall result of the paradox of perspective?

A knight sits on a stationary horse intently staring at a pentacle. The knight's focus on the pentacle indicates his attention is primarily on his physical environment. He is grounded in what he sees, as are most people. We don't generally question what we see as anything more than what it seems. Because of perspective, two people may not agree on what they see even when they are looking at the same object.

"I see this from this position." Everyone sees a slightly different version because they are in different positions around an object, altering their perspective. Perspective divides duality into an infinite number of mini realities.

Our senses tell us about our environment. Sensory input means I experience this situation, person, or thing as a result of what my senses and emotions tell me about it. We get so absorbed in identifying with all the sensory information that we don't "see" past the illusion of duality. We get mesmerized by and absorbed in the deluge of sensory and emotional input. As a result, we all experience our own version of what we think reality is. We each think that what our senses and emotions tell us is the reality. Reality is shapeable. The processing of sensory input and individual perspective adds layers of fragmentation and division, making one seem like many. The overall result of the paradox of perspective is that the truth of unity is hidden.

The paradox of the Hanged Man pushes us to question our perspective and perceptions. Our ability to resolve a paradox of any kind requires an expansion of the way we contemplate, experience, and interact with the Duality.

**Hanged Man Dynamics:**
Engaging
Shifting
Expanding

## Chapter Sixteen

### Thirteen and Death

*Transformation is a process of vision and acceptance as the self cooperates within the laws of creativity.*

### Thirteen – Personal Transformational Change

Thirteen, as one and three, is the Divine's (1) Creative (3) impulse that brings energy into three dimensions. Thirteen is divinity (1) expressed as creation (3). Thirteen as the thirteenth major arcana card, Death, also represents the cycle of incarnation. Nine plus four, thirteen, is the end (9) of a cycle of physical manifestation (4). The number thirteen as a karmic number represents a cycle of hard work. Karmic thirteen indicates a person who focuses primarily on the selfish needs of the individual (negative 1) and puts frivolous things first (negative 3), while avoiding the work he or she is responsible for. To balance out the negatively expressed energy, there will seem to be twice as much work with few options. Spirit comes into the Duality to "work." The work involves understanding the nature of personal reality and creative consciousness.

Let's look at the numbers of the word "thirteen".

Chart One Hundred Four
Thirteen

| 20 | 8 | 9 | 18 | 20 | 5 | 5 | 14 = 99/18/9 |
|----|---|---|----|----|---|---|--------------|
| T  | H | I | R  | T  | E | E | N            |
| 2  | 8 | 9 | 9  | 2  | 5 | 5 | 5 = 45/9     |

* Translation of full numbers 99, 1, 8, 9:
Complete Fulfillment (99) of the Individual (1) releases the Power (8) of total transformation.

* Translation of root numbers 4, 5, 9:
When the Work (4) of Man (5) is Complete (9), he is released from the body.

Shirley Blackwell Lawrence in her book *The Secret Science of Numerology* calls the number ninety-nine the number of complete fulfillment. The meaning of complete fulfillment is assigned to the number ninety-nine because nine is the number of completion. Ninety-nine denotes the end of a cycle taking place on a higher level because ninety-nine is a master number. If you are complete, you may also have reached your fulfillment. Interestingly, the word "ascension" also has a full number of ninety-nine. Ascension is the result of complete fulfillment. Let's take a look at the numerology of "fulfillment".

## Chart One Hundred Five
### Fulfillment

| 6 | 21 | 12 | 6 | 9 | 12 | 12 | 13 | 5 | 14 | 20 = 130/4 |
|---|----|----|---|---|----|----|----|----|----|-----------|
| F | U  | L  | F | I | L  | L  | M  | E | N  | T         |
| 6 | 3  | 3  | 6 | 9 | 3  | 3  | 4  | 5 | 5  | 2 = 49/13/4 |

* Translation of full numbers 1, 3, 0, 4:
The Divine (1) Expresses (3) the potential for Perfection (0), which may be its ultimate Fulfillment (4).

* Translation of root numbers 4, 9, 1, 3, 4:
Fulfillment (4) can lead to Ascension (9) when the Individual (1) has completed Expressing (3) in a Physical (4) body.

Since death is a process all physical bodies go through, let's look at the numerology of the word "process".

## Chart One Hundred Six
### Process

| 16 | 18 | 15 | 3 | 5 | 19 | 19 = 95/14/5 |
|----|----|----|---|---|----|--------------|
| P  | R  | O  | C | E | S  | S            |
| 7  | 9  | 6  | 3 | 5 | 1  | 1 = 32/5     |

* Translation of 9, 5, 1, 4, 5:
The Completion (9) of an incarnational cycle brings Freedom (5) from physical form because it is part of the Divine's (1) Foundational (4) principle of Change (5).

* Translation of root numbers 3, 2, 5:
Self-Expression (3) within the Duality (2) promotes Change (5) in many forms.

When a person dies, they go through a transformation. Let's look at the numerology of the word "transformation".

Chart One Hundred Seven
Transformation

| 20 | 18 | 1 | 14 | 19 | 6 | 15 | 18 | 13 | 1 | 20 | 9 | 15 | 14 | = 183/12/3 |
|----|----|---|----|----|---|----|----|----|---|----|---|----|----|----|
| T | R | A | N | S | F | O | R | M | A | T | I | O | N | |
| 2 | 9 | 1 | 5 | 1 | 6 | 6 | 9 | 4 | 1 | 2 | 9 | 6 | 5 | = 66/12/3 |

* Translation of full numbers 1, 8, 3, 1, 2, 3:
The Divine (1) Continually (8) Creates (3) a Singular (1) Context (2) within self-Expression (3).

* Translation of root numbers 6, 6, 1, 2, 3:
Transformation, a process of Vision (6) and Acceptance (6), happens as the Individual (1) Cooperates (2) within the laws of Creativity (3).

Transformation happens when we conceive of and discern spiritual awareness and insight. While we may be able to conceive of a spiritual idea or teaching and recognize it for what it is, we also need to decide if we are going to accept it. Acceptance is a component of spiritual awareness and transformation.

**Death – The Transforming Dynamics of Ascension**
The word "ascension" (Chart One Hundred Eleven, page 145) has a full number of ninety-nine. A key word of ninety-nine is fulfillment due to its association with other related words that total nine. The spirit cannot ascend until it has accomplished fulfillment in the physical.

In the archetype Death (13/4), the individual (1) who has completed self-expression (3) finishes his or her cycle of manifestation (4) and is transformed back to a state of the un-manifested. The attributes of the number four connect the Emperor (the fourth card) and Death (the thirteenth card), 13/4. The Emperor, card number four, brings energy into physical manifestation, whereas Death, card thirteen, reflects the transitory nature of the physically manifested.

On the card, Death holds a black banner with a white rose. Here is the numerology of "rose".

## Chart One Hundred Eight
## Rose

| 18 | 15 | 19 | 5 = 57/12/3 |
|----|----|----|-------------|
| R  | O  | S  | E           |
| 9  | 6  | 1  | 5 = 21/3    |

\* Translation of full numbers 5, 7, 1, 2, 3:
Man's (5) Intellectual (7) pursuit of the spiritual is Individually (1) expressed in the Duality (2) as Creativity (3).

The root number of "rose" is three, the number of creativity. A white rose in particular can symbolize the purity (white) of creation (3). Typically, we think of death as the ending or destruction of something. Paradoxically, because the white rose appears on Death's banner, the purity of death can be seen as creation: the creation of a transformative process. Death is creation.

"Transformation" has a root number of three (Chart One Hundred Seven, page 142), as does "rose", so rose carries an association with transformation. White symbolizes purity; a rose symbolizes love. Therefore, the white rose is a symbol of a higher love associated with transformation. Within the context of the Death card, love as truth transforms and releases spirit from the physical so it can ascend (page 82). The dynamics of ascension include an adjustment of energy when spirit separates from the physical.

The particular style of the rose shown on Death's banner is the Tudor rose, which is the symbol of the Tudor dynasty of England. A Tudor rose is usually depicted as red in color. The white Tudor rose on Death's banner represents the purity of death. At the same time it evokes the dynastic rulers of a kingdom. Whereas Tudors ruled over a kingdom, Death rules over Duality.

The archetype of Death, taken as mortality, represents the spirit shedding the physical body. If the card is not seen as literal death, its placement before the Devil and the Tower refer to a profound shift in how a person sees his or her relationship to spirit, the divine, and physical reality. Near death experiences can bring about this shift, as well as other major events. The profound shift is often accompanied by a change in priorities regarding what is important in a person's life. Death transforms how we see life. Through the eyes of death, we see beyond the illusions of duality.

## Chart One Hundred Nine
### Death

| 4 | 5 | 1 | 20 | 8 = 38/11 |
|---|---|---|----|-----------|
| D | E | A | T  | H         |
| 4 | 5 | 1 | 2  | 8 = 20/2  |

\* Translation of full numbers 3, 8, 11:
The concept of Death Expresses (3) very Powerfully (8) within the context of Spiritual Understanding (11).

\* Translation of root numbers 2, 0, 2:
Balance (2) is Reflected (0) within spirit as a result of the Duality (2) matrix adjusting energy between the physical and non-physical during the process of death.

In actual death, we go through a re-balancing process of spiritual energy as spirit becomes non-corporeal again.

I added the full number of "death", eleven, to its root number of two, which equals 13/4. In essence, death is an Individually (1) Expressed (3) Process (4). Death re-adjusts personal energy as it merges back into spirit. As a process, death is the adjustment of energy expression between the physical and spiritual. The specific processes involved in death or near death experiences also allow us by reflection to examine our dual nature. Since death takes us beyond the physical, let's look at the numerology of "beyond" next.

## Chart One Hundred Ten
### Beyond

| 2 | 5 | 25 | 15 | 14 | 4 = 65/11 |
|---|---|----|----|----|-----------|
| B | E | Y  | O  | N  | D         |
| 2 | 5 | 7  | 6  | 5  | 4 = 29/11 |

\* Translation of 6, 5, 11:
The Beauty (6) of Death's process is that it promotes the Freedom (5) that Spiritual Understanding (11) brings.

\* Translation of 2, 9, 11:
The Duality (2) brings about Ascension (9) by facilitating Spiritual Understanding (11).

Notice that "Death" and "beyond" both have the full number eleven. Our physical bodies may end with death, but death as a process of change leads to spiritual insights about the physical world. The processes of death can also lead to greater understanding for those remaining. The process of death promotes the freedom from incarnation and karma by the realization of certain spiritual understandings. Since death can be considered an ascension, let's see what the numerology tells us about this word.

Chart One Hundred Eleven
Ascension

| 1 | 19 | 3 | 5 | 14 | 19 | 9 | 15 | 14 | = 99/18/9 |
|---|----|---|---|----|----|---|----|----|-----------|
| A | S  | C | E | N  | S  | I | O  | N  |           |
| 1 | 1  | 3 | 5 | 5  | 1  | 9 | 6  | 5  | = 36/9    |

* Translation of full numbers 99, 1, 8, 9:
When spirit has Fulfilled (99) the requirements of this incarnation, One (1) leaves the Material (8) behind, Ending (9) the current life.

* Translation of root numbers 3, 6, 9:
Ascension is the result Created (3) from a life of Vision (6) and acceptance that has physically Ended (9).

As we go through our lives, there are many mechanisms other than literal death that cause us to ascend in many ways on many levels. The archetype of Death embodies ascension dynamics as an act of love that transforms and reveals the truth of what we really are.

**Translation Review**
Complete Fulfillment of the Individual releases the Power of total transformation. When the Work of Man is Complete, he is released from the body. The Divine Expresses the potential for Perfection, which may be its ultimate fulfillment. Fulfillment can lead to Ascension when the Individual has completed Expressing in a Physical body. The Completion of an incarnational cycle brings Freedom from physical form because it is part of the Divine's Foundation principle of Change.

Self-Expression within the Duality promotes Change in many forms. The Divine Continually Creates a Singular Context within self-Expression.

Transformation, a process of Vision and Acceptance, happens as the Individual Cooperates within the laws of Creativity. Man's Intellectual pursuit of the spiritual is Individually expressed in the Duality as Creativity. The concept of Death Expresses very Powerfully within the context of Spiritual Understanding.

Balance is Reflected within spirit as a result of the Duality matrix adjusting energy between the physical and non-physical during the process of death. The Beauty of Death's process is that it promotes the Freedom that Spiritual Understanding brings. The Duality brings about Ascension by facilitating Spiritual Understanding.

When spirit has Fulfilled the requirements of this incarnation, One leaves the Material behind, Ending the current life. Ascension is the result Created from a life of Vision and acceptance that has physically Ended.

**Applying the Revealed Information**

**Acquired Meanings – New Meanings Revealed by Numerology**
Complete fulfillment, the end of a cycle, ascension, transformation, the process of adjusting to expression on another plane, the balancing of energy passing between corporeal and non-corporeal, the promotion of spiritual insight, a profound shift in the understanding of spirit, the divine and Duality.

**Relevant Questions**
How do my thoughts about death influence my approach to life? What is currently being transformed in my life? By considering things beyond what is manifested, what spiritual insights might come to light? What does fulfillment mean to me? What does the process of re-evaluating my life include for me? What defines my relationship with the divine?

**Practical Application**
Reading: Death, the Seven of Swords, the Emperor.

The querent is going to experience a major shift in his or her relationship to spirit, the divine, and the way he or she relates to their sovereignty. Death is riding toward the man in the Seven of Swords. The man is moving toward Death, but refuses to look at it. Refusing to think about the reality of death can create difficulties for the querent as well as others close to the querent. The man is moving away from the Emperor with eyes closed, indicating he needs to adjust his thoughts about life and how he manifests his personal reality. The Emperor understands that all he manifests is a part of something greater, a perspective the querent may not share. The querent is asked to re-evaluate what he or she has manifested in his or her life and think about what is truly important.

The transformation of a person happens on many different levels. Personal transformation can lead to insight and spiritual self-evaluation, the influence of thoughts on one's attitudes, and evaluation of what has been created.

**Just a Thought**

As a general statement about life and death, I find the practical application reading very interesting. The man in the Seven of Swords is someone going about life refusing to see (eyes are closed) or think about certain things. He is stuck between the proverbial rock and a hard place. Seven, as the number of the intellectual pursuit of spiritual knowledge, is stuck between Death, the card of transformation, and the Emperor, the card of physical manifestation. If you close your mind to what life is offering you, what will an inevitable experience of deep transformation be like for you? If you refuse to change, how does that influence your ability to manifest the life you want?

As I was looking at the rose on the flag I noticed that Death's skeleton is yellow, the color of enlightenment. Death is not only a pure energy, but it also brings out the enlightened spirit of the individual.

**Death Dynamics:**
Completing
Shifting
Ascending
Processing

# Chapter Seventeen

## Fourteen and Temperance

*The processes of balance take man to a higher level of self-completion, which is reflected in our self-expression.*

### Fourteen – The Foundational Nature of Change

Understanding is accomplished in many ways. As seven plus seven, fourteen is Spirit (7) understanding through the Intellectual (7) capacity of the mind. As nine plus five, fourteen tells us that after understanding has brought the Completion (9) of a level, Change (5) takes the Individual (1) to the Foundation (4) of the next level. Fourteen tells us the Divine (1) is the Foundation (4) of all that is. The number fourteen also tells us the Divine (1) provides the Foundation (4) of our universe.

Chart One Hundred Twelve
Fourteen

| 6 | 15 | 21 | 18 | 20 | 5 | 5 | 14 = 104/5 |
|---|----|----|----|----|---|---|---|
| F | O  | U  | R  | T  | E | E | N |
| 6 | 6  | 3  | 9  | 2  | 5 | 5 | 5 = 41/5 |

\* Translation of full numbers 1, 0, 4, 5:
Divinity (1) created the Boundaries (0), Limitations (4), and processes of the Duality for Man (5).

\* Translation of root numbers 4, 1, 5:
Processes (4) of an Individual (1) within the Duality include the Freedom (5) of personal choice.

The root number of "fourteen" is five. Five, as two plus three, is Polarity (2) within Creation (3). Polarity is the result of duality and perspective, as discussed under the High Priestess. Gradations within a continuum are part of the dynamic of change. Change is an integral part of the Duality's nature.

The Duality, as an interconnected system, has boundaries, limitations, and processes that influence anything existing within it. Let's take another look at the word "process".

## Chart One Hundred Thirteen
### Process

| 16 | 18 | 15 | 3 | 5 | 19 | 19 = 95/14/5 |
|---|---|---|---|---|---|---|
| P | R | O | C | E | S | S |
| 7 | 9 | 6 | 3 | 5 | 1 | 1 = 32/5 |

\* Translation of full numbers 9, 5, 1, 4, 5:
Process is the Initiation (9) of Changes (5) that start with a Divine (1) Construct (4). One such construct supports Man (5).

\* Translation of root numbers 3, 2, 5:
The Expressed (3) processes of Choice (2) educate man about the Changes (5) he makes.

It often seems to us that there are limits to our choices. Let's see what "limitation" tells us.

## Chart One Hundred Fourteen
### Limitation

| 12 | 9 | 13 | 9 | 20 | 1 | 20 | 9 | 15 | 14 = 122/5 |
|---|---|---|---|---|---|---|---|---|---|
| L | I | M | I | T | A | T | I | O | N |
| 3 | 9 | 4 | 9 | 2 | 1 | 2 | 9 | 6 | 5 = 50/5 |

\* Translation of full numbers 1, 2, 2, 5:
By limitation, the Divine (1) restricts or removes Choices (2) from Us (2) to promote the Process (5) of spiritual growth.

\* Translation of root numbers 5, 0, 5:
When man understands Limitation (5), his personal Boundaries (0) reflect better choices allowing more Freedom (5).

The two sevens of fourteen can also be seen as the Spirituality (7) of Nature (7).

## Chart One Hundred Fifteen
### Nature

| 14 | 1 | 20 | 21 | 18 | 5 = 79/16/7 |
|---|---|---|---|---|---|
| N | A | T | U | R | E |
| 5 | 1 | 2 | 3 | 9 | 5 = 25/7 |

The root number of "nature" is seven, therefore nature is aligned with spirit and intelligence.

> \* Translation of full numbers 7, 9, 1, 6, 7:
> The innate Intelligence (7) and Wisdom (9) of the Divine (1) works Harmoniously (6) within Nature (7).

> \* Translation of root numbers 2, 5, 7:
> Seeking Balance (2) in a relationship with the Divine, Man (5) develops his personal sense of Spirituality (7), which is a part of our basic nature.

The root number of "nature", 7, indicates the word "nature" includes the spiritual nature of everything that exists.

### Temperance – The Dynamics of Spiritual Energy and Change

Our definition of temperance includes making changes within ourselves that promote balance in action, thought, feeling, and spirit. "Temperance" has a root number of one (Chart One Hundred Sixteen, page 151), the number of beginning. Tempering energy that is out of balance makes new beginnings possible. Temperance is card fourteen, which reduces to a five, the number of change. Change is active in the tempering process.

Fire and water are usually associated with the process of tempering. The element of fire is represented on the Temperance card by the upward-pointing triangle on the breast of the angel's robe. A pool at the angel's feet is the element of water.

The card also shows the angel has a cup in each hand. Water is moving between the two cups. The water appears to be flowing almost sideways, defying gravity. The flowing water doesn't show direction. The inference is something that is not associated with physical life is occurring in a way that is unnatural; it is not physical, it is spiritual. Furthermore, the tempering process is unique to every individual.

Temperance is about the dynamics of spiritual energy. Not knowing which way the water flows and knowing change is an integral part of tempering, a question came to mind: "Does change bring about tempering, or does tempering bring about change?" Lack of directionality shows not only that both statements are true, but also both happen simultaneously. The question is unresolved; it cannot be answered, and that is the point. Temperance and change are part of an inevitable dance. The flowing water's lack of direction reflects tempering as a continuous process.

The two cups held by the angel can be considered as the Cup of Spirit, which I associate with the element of fire, and the Cup of Change, which is associated with the element of water. Fire and water are two elements closely associated with the tempering process. In this case, the way we interact with the Duality and our inner strength is constantly tempered. The focus of Temperance is inner personal balance, which is reflected by a life in balance. To restore balance, we become still in order to sense how to make changes that help us stay smoothly in the flow and rhythm of our lives.

The number of the card Temperance, card fourteen, reduces to a five (1 + 4 = 5), so it is related to the Hierophant, the fifth card. Change and tempering further the alignment process of the spirit activated in the Hierophant. Inner balance is the result of a tempering process. Our life experience tempers our way of being in the world. Tempering promotes balance and inner strength.

Flowing water represents the continuum of our spiritual unfolding. Temperance continues the promotion of spiritual growth specifically activated by change and the tempering process. Change, on all levels, is how the archetype of Temperance promotes balance.

The numbers of "Temperance" show us that the tempering process applies to the macrocosm, 100, as well as the microcosm, 10.

### Chart One Hundred Sixteen
### Temperance

| 20 | 5 | 13 | 16 | 5 | 18 | 1 | 14 | 3 | 5 = 100/1 |
|----|---|----|----|---|----|---|----|---|-----------|
| T  | E | M  | P  | E | R  | A | N  | C | E         |
| 2  | 5 | 4  | 7  | 5 | 9  | 1 | 5  | 3 | 5 = 46/10/1 |

* Translation of full numbers 1, 0, 0, 1:
Within the macrocosm and the microcosm, Divine (1) energy is Reflected (0) and Complete (0) within Itself (1).

* Translation of root numbers 4, 6, 1, 0, 1:
The Processes (4) of Balance (6) take man to a higher level of Self (1) Potential (0), which is reflected in our Self (1) expression and what we create.

The full number one hundred, consistent with the tradition of numerology, represents the macrocosm. The number ten on the mundane level represents the microcosm. Ten is a smaller component of one hundred. Our universe can also be seen as a part of a larger whole, which is the divine.

Spiritual energy promotes change by seeking balance. Some of our universal laws reflect the pursuit of balance as part of the macrocosm of existence. These laws influence all that exists at a basic level. Our laws of physics also reflect that energy seeks balance. Following is the numerology of "universal law".

Chart One Hundred Seventeen<br>Universal Law

```
                 157                    36
21  14  9  22  5  18  19  1  12    12  1    23 = 193/13/4
U   N   I  V   E  R   S   A  L     L   A    W
3   5   9  22  5  9   1   1  3     3   1    5 = 76/13/4
                 67                      9
```

    * Translation of full numbers 1, 9, 3, 1, 3, 4:
Growth (1), Free Will (9), and Change (5) within a Spiritual (7) context allow the Divine (1) to Create (3) Processes (4) that promote the tempering of spirit within the Duality.

    * Translation of root numbers 7, 6, 1, 3, 4:
The Spiritual (7) nature of Vision (6) shows the Individual (1) how to use Creative (3) Processes (4) within our reality to achieve temperance.

The root number of "universal law", four, show these laws are a foundation. These laws influence the spiritual as well as the physical. Universal law, which promotes balance, furthers the tempering process. Change is the mechanism that universal law, from a macrocosmic view, and temperance, from a microcosmic view, work through. Change makes it possible for the duality matrix to reflect back to us in a variety of ways the results of our individual expression and understanding. Change is an interactive process that gives us constant and instant feedback.

**Translation Review**
    Divinity created the Boundaries, Limitations, and processes of the Duality for Man. Processes of an Individual within the Duality include the Freedom of personal choice. Process is the Initiation of Changes that start with a Divine Construct. One such construct supports Man. The Expressed processes of Choice educate man about the Changes he makes. By limitation, the Divine restricts or removes Choices from Us to promote the Process of spiritual growth. When man understands Limitation, his personal Boundaries reflect better choices allowing more Freedom.

The innate Intelligence and Wisdom of the Divine works Harmoniously within Nature. Seeking Balance in a relationship with the Divine, Man develops his personal sense of Spirituality, which is a part of our basic nature.

Within the macrocosm and the microcosm, Divine energy is Reflected and Complete within Itself. The Processes of Balance take man to a higher level of Self Potential, which is reflected in our Self-expression and what we create. Growth, Free Will, and Change within a Spiritual context allow the Divine to Create Processes that promote the tempering of spirit within the Duality. The Spiritual nature of Vision shows the Individual how to use Creative Processes within our reality to achieve temperance.

## Applying the Revealed Information

### Acquired Meanings – New Meanings Revealed by Numerology

Understanding the spiritual, working within the nature of existence, the foundational nature of change, change that brings about spiritual growth, spiritual growth that brings about change, developing a personal sense of spirituality, the wisdom and intelligence of the Divine within spirit, the relationship between self and Higher Self, the processes of becoming balanced and whole.

### Relevant Questions

How is the nature of change active in my life? Where in my life is the wisdom and intelligence of the divine most obvious? What is the best way for me to promote the relationship between my self and my Higher Self? In what area of my life is temperance needed?

### Practical Application

Reading: the Eight of Cups, Temperance, the Seven of Cups, the King of Pentacles.

In the Eight of Cups, a person turns away from eight unevenly stacked cups. An emotionally difficult situation has made the querent retreat. The Moon is pictured eclipsing the sun. An eclipse minimizes light. The inference is that things are not seen clearly. The querent needs to look carefully at the situation by delving more deeply into his or her own emotional responses. Temperance suggests that a better understanding of the querent's emotional responses can bring balance to all aspects of his or her life. To remain in a balanced state in the ever-changing emotional landscape requires a connection to spirit and an acceptance of change. Remaining emotionally balanced allows the querent to know what is most important when many choices are available (Seven of Cups). The King of Pentacles shows it is possible for the querent to manifest the choices that are represented by the Seven of Cups. The best choice is made clearer by answering the question, "Which choice promotes balance and personal growth?"

**Just a Thought**

I have gained a different way to see the Eight of Cups after taking into consideration the new meanings of Temperance. The Sun and Moon are in a state of eclipse on the Eight of Cups. The time of an eclipse is often thought of as magical because it produces a state of "between-ness." It is neither fully light, nor fully dark. The idea of between-ness relates to the flowing liquid between the two cups held by the angel in Temperance. In a state of "in-between," in the stillness, it is possible to gain important insights.

An emotionally difficult situation causes us to search for a key to understanding. What brings understanding appears to be missing, symbolized by the gap between cups on the Eight of Cups. Taking time to enter an in-between state—using meditation, for example—can reveal the understanding we search for.

After writing this chapter, three questions regarding the relationship between spirit, change, and manifestation came to me as a possible reading. The reader may wish to do the following reading on their own.

* What is the relationship between spirit, change, and manifestation?

* What is the best way to stay centered in spirit during times of change?

* How does staying centered in spirit affect my ability to make the best change?

**Temperance Dynamics:**
Balancing
Tempering
Flowing
Moderating

## Chapter Eighteen

### Fifteen and the Devil

*The beauty of change is that it brings an endless variety of possible ways to gain spiritual understanding.*

### Fifteen – Diversity within Change

The one and five of fifteen reveal to us the Divine (1) energy of Change (5) as one of the driving forces within the Duality, life, and the universe. The root number of "fifteen", eleven, shows change is an integral part of spiritual understanding. The dynamics of change bring spiritual knowledge and understanding about our true nature. "Life" and "change", both with the root number five, are synonymous.

Chart One Hundred Eighteen<br>Fifteen

| 6 | 9 | 6 | 20 | 5 | 5 | 14 = 65/11 |
|---|---|---|----|---|---|-----------|
| F | I | F | T  | E | E | N         |
| 6 | 9 | 6 | 2  | 5 | 5 | 5 = 38/11 |

\* Translation of full numbers 6, 5, 11:
The Beauty (6) of change brings an endless Variety (5) of possible ways to gain Spiritual Understanding (11).

\* Translation of root numbers 3, 8, 11:
Creativity (3) expressed within the Material (8) world is a catalyst for Change (11).

The numbers one and five of fifteen can also be translated as the Divine (1) creating Life (5). As discussed in Chapter Eight (page 69), the number five is made up of male and female energy. In life, many organisms are hermaphrodites. Hermaphrodites are organisms that have both male and female reproductive organs. Some organisms can also change sexes. Sex, as in reproduction, is a key to life in the Duality.

The processes of change give us unlimited opportunities to make better decisions in our life. The experiences of change help us grow spiritually as well as personally.

Chart One Hundred Nineteen
Life

| 12 | 9 | 6 | 5 = 32/5 |
| L | I | F | E |
| 3 | 9 | 6 | 5 = 23/5 |

* Translation of full numbers 3, 2, 5:
The Creative (3), Cooperative (2) processes of basic components create Life (5) within matter.

"Matter" also has a root number of five. Matter has life within it.

* Translation of root numbers 2, 3, 5:
The Duality (2) is a holographic playground for Creating (3) Life (5).

The number fifteen is the sum of the first three basic energies represented in the numbers one, two, three, plus four (the number of foundation and manifestation) plus five (the number of life and change). This can be represented as the following equation: $1 + 2 + 3 + 4 + 5 = 15$. Fifteen is the spirit Self (1) manifesting in Matter (5), or the Divine (1) manifesting the Duality (2) to Create (3) the Foundation (4) for Life (5).

The word "dead" is another word with a root number of five (Chart Thirty-one, page 41), showing us that there is life in "dead", as in life after death. The five shows death is a process of change, in this case between life in matter and life in spirit.

Chart One Hundred Twenty
Matter

| 13 | 1 | 20 | 20 | 5 | 18 = 77/14/5 |
| M | A | T | T | E | R |
| 4 | 1 | 2 | 2 | 5 | 9 = 23/5 |

Matter has the karmic number 14/5 and the number of Christ consciousness ("Christ" = 77) on the esoteric level. Exist (Chart Thirty-nine, page 52) also has a full number of seventy-seven. The karmic number 14/5 shows changes that spirit makes while in matter can have karmic consequences. Therefore, to exist within matter, spirit needs a guide, such as Christ consciousness.

\* Translation of full numbers 7, 7, 1, 4, 5:
Spiritual (7) Intelligence (7) embodies the ideal of Christ consciousness. If One (1) dismisses this Ideal (4), there can be karmic consequences for spirit in Matter (5).

\* "Ideal" has a root number of four.

"Life" and "matter" have the same root numbers. Life and matter are related, as their root number of five shows. Matter expresses as a type of life. Contained within the complexity of the Duality, there can be matter without life, but not life in a physical construct without matter.

Diversity is a big part of life and carries the same 14/5 karmic warning. Getting caught up in diversity solely for the sake of experiencing something different can bring karmic consequences.

Chart One Hundred Twenty-one<br>Diversity

| 4 | 9 | 22 | 5 | 18 | 19 | 9 | 20 | 25 = 131/5 |
|---|---|----|---|----|----|---|----|-----------|
| D | I | V  | E | R  | S  | I | T  | Y |
| 4 | 9 | 22 | 5 | 9  | 1  | 9 | 2  | 7 = 68/14/5 |

\* Translation of full numbers 1, 3, 1, 5:
The Divine (1) Expresses (3) Itself (1) by creating changes, the result of which is Diversity (5).

\* Translation of root numbers 6, 8, 1, 4, 5:
Within the Duality, the Visionary (6) Power (8) of the Divine (1) is Processed (4) by the act of Change (5).

To try to resist or stop change goes against our very nature. As spiritual beings searching for truth, we need to embrace change. When we don't embrace change, the result may be the archetype of the Tower, which follows the Devil, giving us the push we need.

### Devil – The Dynamics within the Embodiment of Spirit

As spirit experiencing the Duality, we have the opportunity to accept responsibility for many things, for example taking responsibility for ourselves and our lives. The Devil keeps us on an ever-shortening chain when we deny responsibility that is ours (see the Devil card). If we don't engage self-discipline and we deny our responsibility, the Devil shows us the errors of our ways by the negative consequences of our actions.

The number six relates the Devil, the fifteenth card (1 + 5 = 6), to the Lovers, the sixth card. The man and woman in the Lovers who initially stood before an angel now stand before the devil. The dynamics of the Devil archetype remind the Lovers (and more generally the female and male) of their need to accept responsibility for their circumstances. When someone denies what they are responsible for, they also deny the understanding necessary to make positive change. The Devil archetype challenges us to take responsibility for the reality we create. The Devil also encourages us to examine how we use and express our ability to create.

Chart One Hundred Twenty-two<br>Devil

| 4 | 5 | 22 | 9 | 12 = 52/7 |
|---|---|----|---|-----------|
| D | E | V  | I | L         |
| 4 | 5 | 22 | 9 | 3 = 43/7  |

\* Translation of full numbers 5, 2, 7:
The Devil archetype promotes Change (5) and Cooperation (2) through the innate intelligence of Spirit (7).

\* Translation of root numbers 4, 3, 7:
The Processes (4) of Creativity (3) start on the level of Spirit (7).

We have the Devil to pay when we focus predominantly on the physical over the spiritual. The Devil card warns about self-centeredness in images of chains, fire, and an inverted pentagram. The Devil archetype draws attention to the inherent responsibilities that spirit acquires after incarnating into a human body. Actions that go against our spiritual nature can result in unforeseen consequences. The inverted pentagram above the Devil's head indicates that spirit is not the primary focus, the physical world is. It more specifically represents a predominantly ego-driven consciousness.

Since we are on the subject of the spirit that manifests, let's look at the numerology of the phrase "spirit manifestation".

## Chart One Hundred Twenty-three
## Spirit Manifestation

```
                    91
    19    16    9    18    9    20
    S     P     I    R     I    T
    1     7     9    9     9    2
                    37
```

$$91 + 146 = 237$$

```
                           146
13   1   14   9   6   5   19   20   1   20   9   15   14 = 237/12/3
M    A   N    I   F   E   S    T    A   T    I   O    N
4    1   5    9   6   5   1    2    1   2    9   6    5  = 93/12/3
                            56
```

**37 + 56 = 93**

\* Translation of full numbers 2, 3, 7, 1, 2, 3:
We (2) Express (3) ourselves as an aspect of divine Spirit (7) and as Individuals (1) that Cooperate (2) with the integrity of self-Expression (3).

\* Translation of root numbers 9, 3, 1, 2, 3:
Spirit manifesting within matter is an Initiation (9) into self-Expression (3) of the Individual (1) in Duality (2) for the purpose of Creating (3).

As such, Spirit (1) has to Cooperate (2) with the divine integrity of self-Expression (3). The number one refers to Spirit because the word "spirit" has a root number of one (3 + 7 = 10, 1 + 0 =1).

The Devil is an archetype of spirit because its root number is 7, meaning this archetype functions on the level of spirit first, then expresses in the physical world. The number seven shows there is a relationship between the Devil (root number seven) and the seventh major arcana card, the Chariot. Both archetypes encourage necessary changes, as spirit continues to grow by balancing ego and divine will. The divine may intercede through the archetype of the Devil when the dictates of ego dominate our will.

What happens when spirit gives into temptation? Let's look at the numbers.

### Chart One Hundred Twenty-four
### Temptation

| 20 | 5 | 13 | 16 | 20 | 1 | 20 | 9 | 15 | 14 | = 133/7 |
|----|---|----|----|----|---|----|---|----|----|---------|
| T  | E | M  | P  | T  | A | T  | I | O  | N  |         |
| 2  | 5 | 4  | 7  | 2  | 1 | 2  | 9 | 6  | 5  | = 43/7  |

* Translation of full numbers 1, 3, 3, 7:
Spirit (1) takes the inherent risk of Expressing (3) Creatively (3) within matter so that it can Study (7) its creations.

* Translation of root numbers 4, 3, 7:
If the Process (4) of self-Expression (3) leads spirit astray, then spirit has given into Temptation (7).

"Devil" and "temptation" both have a root number of seven. They teach important spiritual lessons at the core of their vibration. When you give into temptation, sometimes you are confronted by the devil.

Like the word "temptation", "flexibility" also has a root number of 7.

### Chart One Hundred Twenty-five
### Flexibility

| 6 | 12 | 5 | 24 | 9 | 2 | 9 | 12 | 9 | 20 | 25 =133/7 |
|---|----|---|----|----|---|---|----|----|----|-----------|
| F | L  | E | X  | I | B | I | L  | I  | T  | Y         |
| 6 | 3  | 5 | 6  | 9 | 2 | 9 | 3  | 9  | 2  | 7 = 61/7  |

* Translation of full numbers 1, 3, 3, 7:
As an Individual (1) Expresses (3) Creatively (3) within the Duality, he does so through Spirit (7) and divine energy.

* Translation of root numbers 6, 1, 7:
The Vision (6) of the Divine (1) is seen within the many forms of Spirit (7).

Spirit sees itself within all diversity. Unfortunately, diversity can tempt spirit into losing its flexibility of vision when it becomes enamored of one particular form.

* Alternative definition of flexibility: The ability to see spirit within everything.

The dynamics within the embodiment of spirit bring with it different opportunities for self-expression. Spirit's flexibility of vision is tested when ego narrows spirit's vision to focus on the physical. The narrowing of vision causes spirit to lose flexibility. Lack of flexibility leads to temptation; the ego pursuing its own ambitions.

**Translation Review**

The Beauty of change brings an endless Variety of possible ways to gain Spiritual Understanding. Creativity expressed within the Material world is a catalyst for Change. The Creative, Cooperative processes of basic components create Life within matter. The Duality is a holographic playground for Creating Life. Spiritual Intelligence embodies the ideal of Christ consciousness. If One dismisses this Ideal, there can be karmic consequences for spirit in Matter. The Divine Expresses Itself by creating changes, the result of which is Diversity. Within the Duality, the Visionary Power of the Divine is Processed by the act of Change. The Devil archetype promotes Change and Cooperation through the innate intelligence of Spirit. The Processes of Creativity start on the level of Spirit. We Express ourselves as an aspect of divine Spirit and as Individuals that Cooperate with the integrity of self-Expression.

Spirit manifesting within matter is the Initiation into self-Expression of the Individual in Duality for the purpose of Creating. As such, Spirit has to Cooperate with the divine integrity of self-Expression. Spirit takes the inherent risk of Expressing Creatively within matter so that it can Study its creations. If the Process of self-Expression leads spirit astray, then spirit has given into Temptation. As an Individual Expresses Creatively within the Duality, he does so through Spirit and divine energy. The Vision of the Divine is seen within the many forms of Spirit.

**Applying the Revealed Information**

**Acquired Meanings – New Meanings Revealed by Numerology**

The many ways in which we can gain spiritual understanding through change, creating change through creativity, basic components creating the foundation for all life, divine cooperation within creativity, spirit cooperating with the laws of change, the promotion of taking responsibility as co-creators, the true nature of spirit reflected in many spirit forms.

**Relevant Questions**

What changes are being asked of me at this time? What will happen if I make no changes? What basic energies do I need to employ to create a good foundation for my life? How can I use my creative abilities to bring about positive change? What spiritual understanding is behind the change/changes I am going through? What part does limitation play in my life? What are my responsibilities in this situation?

**Practical Application**
Reading: the Devil, the Ten of Cups, the Hierophant.

The Devil archetype promotes change as an avenue to understanding our spiritual nature. Satisfying all physical appetites and desires can lead the querent to the illusion of happiness, but true happiness depends on the querent also paying attention to the spiritual. The querent, by also taking responsibility for the good things in his or her life, acknowledges spirit. Everything the querent does promotes change, which brings opportunities for greater spiritual awareness and understanding about the nature of the Duality and the responsibility of co-creation.

Unconditional love, and appreciation for what we have, is promoted by relationships and what we learn from the changes we embrace. The lessons of the Hierophant encourage the querent to make changes, aligning spirit and consciousness to promote gratitude, spiritual insight, and balance.

**Just a Thought**
For spirit to manifest within matter, change occurs at a fundamental level. The full number of the word "spirit", seventy-seven, shows spirit needs to stay centered in divinity and Christ consciousness (77) after manifesting within matter. Staying centered in divinity requires not overly identifying with physical form or matter.

Adding the full numbers of the cards in the practical application, we get the root vibration which equals 30/3, the number of creativity. This reading tells us the best path is to embrace change and accept all the creative ways in which the Divine manifests, while acknowledging the spiritual nature of our physical existence.

**Devil Dynamics:**
Restricting
Compelling
Promoting
Expanding

# Chapter Nineteen

## Sixteen and the Tower

*Vision, initiated by the divine, guides spirit as it changes the dynamic of its reality.*

**Sixteen – The Dynamics of Change on a Personal Level**

In the number sixteen, as with all numbers in the teens, emphasis is placed on the one, or the individual. The innate impetus of the number six is to bring beauty and harmony into the different forms created. An individual has a choice about what to create. The changes made when creating may or may not promote beauty and harmony. They are, however, more likely to when the individual makes changes implemented through vision (the conceiving of and/or discernment of spiritual awareness and insight). Either way, the responsibility is placed on the individual.

The number six in sixteen can be broken down into three plus three. As such, it is the divine Individual (1) within Creative (3) Consciousness (3) (1, 3, 3). The one and the six also tell us an Individual (1) whose ability to conceive and discern spiritual concepts (6, vision) is guided by his or her Spiritual Intelligence (7), (1+ 6 = 7). Another word that describes the number six is responsibility. Sixteen warns that the Individual (1) should use his or her creative consciousness Responsibly (6) in order to avoid negative consequences.

Chart One Hundred Twenty-six
Sixteen

| 19 | 9 | 24 | 20 | 5 | 5 | 14 = 96/15/6 |
|----|---|----|----|---|---|--------------|
| S  | I | X  | T  | E | E | N            |
| 1  | 9 | 6  | 2  | 5 | 5 | 5 = 33/6     |

* Translation of full numbers 9, 6, 1, 5, 6:
The Integrity (9) and Beauty (6) of the Divine (1) within Man (5) is held in his innate Vision (6).

* Translation of root numbers 3, 3, 6:
This innate vision encourages Creative (3) Consciousness (3) to take Responsibility (6) for what it creates.

There are consequences when responsibility is denied. The numbers in the chart of "consequence" show us it is another founding principle of spirituality within the Duality.

Chart One Hundred Twenty-seven<br>Consequence

| 3 | 15 | 14 | 19 | 5 | 17 | 21 | 5 | 14 | 3 | 5 = 121/4 |
|---|----|----|----|---|----|----|---|----|---|-----------|
| C | O  | N  | S  | E | Q  | U  | E | N  | C | E         |
| 3 | 6  | 5  | 1  | 5 | 8  | 3  | 5 | 5  | 3 | 5 = 49/13/4 |

\* Translation of full numbers 1, 2, 1, 4:
The Individual (1) within the Duality (2) uses Divine (1) principles as his Foundation (4).

\* Translation of root numbers 4, 9, 1, 3, 4:
Consequence is a Foundation (4) principle for the Initiation (9) of an Individual (1) using Creative (3) Processes (4) within the Duality.

The 13/4 of "consequence" shows that the karmic consequences of shirking responsibility for our creations result in an unusual amount of hard work. Until we embrace the work and focus on the bigger picture instead of only concern for ourselves, limitation and hardship are the result.

The number sixteen broken down to four added four times (4 + 4 + 4 + 4) translates as: The individual has innate Processes (4) as part of a Foundation (4) for Materializing (4) Structures (4) within the Duality. Expressed on a personal biological level, an example of an innate process is cell division and the duplication of DNA strands, which form the foundations of our bodies. Let's look at "dynamic" next.

Chart One Hundred Twenty-eight<br>Dynamic

| 4 | 25 | 14 | 1 | 13 | 9 | 3 = 69/15/6 |
|---|----|----|---|----|---|-------------|
| D | Y  | N  | A | M  | I | C           |
| 4 | 7  | 5  | 1 | 4  | 9 | 3 = 33/6    |

\* Translation of full numbers 6, 9, 1, 5, 6:
Vision (6) Initiated (9) by the Divine (1) guides spirit as it Changes (5) the Dynamic (6) of its reality.

\* Translation of root numbers 3, 3, 6:
Spirit's power of Creative (3) Expression (3) is very Dynamic (6).

## Tower – Divine Nature and Negative Ego

The work of resolving negative aspects of ego is continued under the influence of this archetype. Resisting timely changes in our lives invokes the archetypal energy of the Tower. Considering the numerology of the sixteenth archetype, we observe one plus six equals seven (16, 1 + 6 = 7), translated as: Within the archetype of the Tower, the Individual (1) is seeking to restore the Harmony (6) of Spirit (7). Building walls around ourselves, signified by the Tower, expresses aspects of negative ego.

Change, as a process, cannot be stopped or avoided. Wrapped up in the symbolism of the Tower are words like control, defense, block, rigid, and status quo. Creating continual psychological resistance to change results in sudden and abrupt restructuring: the tower falls. Change inevitably causes structures, whether psychological or otherwise, to be temporary in real life. The temporary nature of structures includes structures of energy as well as physical buildings. The numerology of the word "Tower" has a root number of nine, the number of ending. Bringing about endings allows beginnings.

Chart One Hundred Twenty-nine
Tower

| 20 | 15 | 23 | 5 | 18 = 81/9 |
|----|----|----|---|-----------|
| T  | O  | W  | E | R         |
| 2  | 6  | 5  | 5 | 9 = 27/9  |

\* Translation of full numbers 8, 1, 9:
When the ego promotes a way of being that does not allow change, the Power (8) of the Divine (1) within us brings an End (9) to that way of being.

\* Translation of root numbers 2, 7, 9:
Making Choices (2) within a Spiritual (7) context allows Transitions (9) to be the most productive.

If our approach to life becomes rigid, we stifle our innate ability to adapt and change.

### Chart One Hundred Thirty
### Rigid

| 18 | 9 | 7 | 9 | 4 = 47/11 |
|----|---|---|---|-----------|
| R  | I | G | I | D         |
| 9  | 9 | 7 | 9 | 4 = 38/11 |

\* Translation of full numbers 4, 7, 11:
The Stability (4) of Spirit (7) depends on the breaking down of Rigid (11) behaviors and thoughts that resist change.

\* Translation of root numbers 3, 8, 1, 1:
The Creative (3) Power (8) of the Divine (1) cannot be stopped by an Individual (1).

### Chart One Hundred Thirty-one
### Control

| 3 | 15 | 14 | 20 | 18 | 15 | 12 = 97/16/7 |
|---|----|----|----|----|----|--------------|
| C | O  | N  | T  | R  | O  | L            |
| 3 | 6  | 5  | 2  | 9  | 6  | 3 = 34/7     |

\* Translation of full numbers 9, 7, 1, 6, 7:
An Unyielding (negative expression of 9) illusion of Control (7) blinds the Individual (1) to his Vision (6) and Spirituality (7).

The archetypal energy of the Tower is about bringing something to an end. An ego-driven life that is rigid or unyielding must end to allow for the possibility of positive change and personal growth. The energy of the Tower is an integral part of the Duality and the individual. This archetype is part of the dynamic of continuance and the propagation of existence.

Following is a list of words associated with all previous major arcana cards as aspects of divine nature: energy, free will, unconditional love, choice, creative consciousness, change, paradox, karma, and I am going to add curiosity, which I will get back to shortly. The concepts of the Tower are a part of divine nature. Esoterically, "divine nature" (7) and "spirit" (7) are synonymous.

## Chart One Hundred Thirty-two
## Divine Nature

```
         63                                    79
4   9   22   9   14   5    14   1   20   21   18   5 = 142/7
D   I   V    I   N    E    N    A   T    U    R    E
4   9   22   9   5    5    5    1   2    3    9    5 = 16/7
        9 (54)                        7 (25)
```

\* Translation of full numbers 1, 4, 2, 7:
Divine (1) nature creates the Process (4) of Choice (2) within the context of Spirituality (7).

\* Alternate Translation of full numbers:
Divine (1) nature also creates all Processes (4) of the Duality (2) within the context of Spirituality (7).

"Choice" has a root number of seven. One of seven's key words is spirituality. Choice needs the framework of spirituality. When choices are made outside the context of spirituality, there can be karmic consequences.

The words "divine" (9) and "love" (9) have a nine root number. "Nature" (7) and "compassion" (7) have a root number of seven. To have compassion is considered a part of divine nature. Therefore, to have a Divine (9) Nature (7) is to have Love (9) and Compassion (7). Nine plus seven equals sixteen. This shows the Tower, as the sixteenth card, acts with love and compassion within the divine nature of change. Seven also refers to intellectual curiosity. It is a part of our divine nature to be curious. Curiosity encourages us to explore possibilities and teaches us many things. Let's look at curiosity next.

## Chart One Hundred Thirty-three
## Curiosity

```
3   21   18   9   15   19   9   20   26 = 140/5
C   U    R    I   O    S    I   T    Y
3   3    9    9   6    1    9   2    7 = 49/5
```

\* Translation of curiosity full numbers 1, 4, 0, 5:
Divine (1) energy Builds (4) from Infinite Potential (0) materialized form, which is a result of Change (5).

* Translation of root numbers 4, 9, 5:
Building Structures (4) of Finite (9) existence is an innate aspect of Change (5) within the Duality.

The root number of "curiosity", 5, shows that when we are curious about something, it creates a Change (5). It creates a chemical change within our brains, which brings to mind what physicists say about trying to observe an experiment. We change the nature, and possibly the result, of the experiment by the act of observing. The act of observing has an effect on what is being observed. Being curious can change the nature of what we are curious about.

The two people on the Tower card are falling. The numbers of "fall" suggest the contrast between the world of the individual and the world of spirit. The number thirty-one, the full numbers of "fall", brings emphasis to the creativity of the divine as the primary focus. The number thirteen, the mundane full number of "fall", brings emphasis to the individual ego that creates. Creativity drives change. Negative ego believes it can deny both creativity and change. Conflict that arises from an individual ignoring spiritual guidance can bring a fall.

Chart One Hundred Thirty-four
Fall

| 6 | 1 | 12 | 12 = 31/4 |
|---|---|----|-----------|
| F | A | L  | L         |
| 6 | 1 | 3  | 3 = 13/4  |

* Translation of full numbers 3, 1, 4:
The innate Creativity (3) of Divine (1) energy is the Foundation (4) of all that is.

* Translation of root numbers 1, 3, 4:
The Ego (1) is sometimes promoted over all else. This Creates (3) discord, which unbalances our spiritual Foundation (4).

Note that the esoteric full number 31 and the mundane full number 13 mirror each other. On a spiritual level, we are divinely inspired, and what we create then reflects this inspiration. On a mundane level, if individual concerns are the only focus of creativity, the Tower's energy is engaged. We may fall.

Spirit seeks to restore balance, and as a result the stage is set for change. An imbalance occurs that cannot be ignored when the ego takes precedence over the creative expression of spirit. This is when lightning strikes and the dynamic of the Tower is engaged.

Chart One Hundred Thirty-five
Lightning

| 12 | 9 | 7 | 8 | 20 | 14 | 9 | 14 | 7 = 100/1 |
|----|---|---|---|----|----|---|----|-----------|
| L  | I | G | H | T  | N  | I | N  | G         |
| 3  | 9 | 7 | 8 | 2  | 5  | 9 | 5  | 7 = 55/10/1 |

\* Translation of esoteric numbers: 1, 0, 1:
Lightning (1) is an energetic reflection (0) of Divine (1) energy within this dimension.

\* Translation of root numbers 5, 5, 1, 0, 1:
When Man (5) allows Change (5) there are changes within the Individual (1) that Reflect (0) the flow of Divine (1) energy.

I did the numerology of the word "light" (Chart Ninety, page 120), which has the root number of eleven. The numbers told us that our "vision," as in our ability to conceive of and recognize spiritual concepts, is sometimes perceived as light in this physical dimension. When someone has an "ah ha" moment, we say they have seen the light. Lightning is a metaphor for the sudden flash of understanding. The lightning of the Tower is a symbol of the more intense form of our "vision."

Temperance (card fourteen), the Devil (card fifteen), and the Tower (card sixteen) are a group of archetypal energies that create an especially strong dynamic. The flow of energy starts with the previous card, Death (card thirteen) signifying an ending of some kind. Whenever there is an ending, there must be a beginning. Temperance promotes a re-balancing that facilitates the new beginning. If the changes made are inadequate, we may encounter the Devil. The Devil encourages us to take responsibility for the circumstances we find ourselves in. If we refuse to do that and become stuck, our Tower is struck by lightning, and we are unstuck.

Temperance suggests the opportunity for new beginning. The Devil uses restriction as motivation for change. The Tower's dynamics break down barriers to change, bringing an end to stagnation.

The root number of Temperance, one, suggests new beginnings. The root number of Devil, seven, suggests spiritual growth encouraged by restriction. The root number of Tower, nine, suggests an end to stagnation by breaking down barriers. In these three archetypes, you have the opportunity for a new beginning, a refocusing to reconsider choices, and the necessity of moving forward.

If we add the root numbers of Temperance, Devil, and Tower (1, 7, 9) the result is 17/8. The Individual (1) who accepts balance through Spirituality (7) can lessen the Power (8) of negative ego and fear. Fear often keeps us from change. The de-structuring energy of the Tower is less likely to be encountered when our negative ego is kept in balance.

The Tower, card 16, is related to the Chariot, card 7, because one plus six equals seven. The Chariot implies movement guided by the divine. When we ignore divine guidance, allowing only ego to guide us, the energy of the Tower may become activated. Remember, as discussed in Chapter Ten, the Chariot archetype is about the relationship between divine will, personal will, and ego. The Tower's dynamic is divine energy waking us up to certain realizations. The Tower coupled with the dynamics of the Chariot help us create a more balanced relationship between the divine and our individual spiritual nature.

**Translation Review**

The Integrity and Beauty of the Divine within Man is held in his innate Vision. This innate vision encourages Creative Consciousness to take Responsibility for what it creates.

The Individual within the Duality uses Divine principles as his Foundation. Consequence is a Foundation principle for the Initiation of an Individual using Creative Processes within the Duality. Vision Initiated by the Divine guides spirit as it Changes the Dynamic of its reality. Spirit's power of Creative Expression is very Dynamic.

When the ego promotes a way of being that does not allow change, the Power of the Divine within us brings an End to that way of being. Making Choices within a Spiritual context allows Transitions to be the most productive. The Stability of Spirit depends on the breaking down of Rigid behaviors and thoughts that resist change.

The Creative Power of the Divine cannot be stopped by an Individual. An Unyielding illusion of Control blinds the Individual to his Vision and Spirituality. Divine nature creates the Process of Choice within the context of Spirituality. Divine nature also creates all Processes of the Duality within the context of Spirituality. Divine energy Builds from Infinite Potential materialized form, which is a result of Change. Building Structures of Finite existence is an innate aspect of Change within the Duality. The innate Creativity of Divine energy is the Foundation of all that is.

The Ego is sometimes promoted over all else. This Creates discord, which unbalances our spiritual Foundation. Lightning is an energetic reflection of Divine energy within this dimension. When Man allows

Change, there are changes within the Individual that Reflect the flow of Divine energy.

**Applying the Revealed Information**

**Acquired Meanings – New Meanings Revealed by Numerology**
The dynamic flow of energy between the spiritual and the physical, vision within creative consciousness, the responsibility of what one creates, sense of self, separation, changing the dynamics of ego-driven consciousness, unblocking stagnated energy, allowing the flow of divine energy within.

**Relevant Questions**
What vision does spirit hold for me? In what way am I holding myself back from the divine flow of my life? Where is my energy expression blocked or stagnated? In what area do I need to review my responsibilities? In what area of my life do I need to implement change? What needs restructuring?

**Practical Application**
Reading: the Seven of Cups, Death, the Tower.

Changes in the querent's life are unavoidable. There is no more time for denial, dismissal, or avoidance. The querent blocks the flow of creative energy when he or she thinks about making personal changes, but never does. The blocking of creative energy also stifles the querent's communication with his or her higher self. The querent becomes stuck when he dismisses the inner guidance that allows him to understand and align with the changes that spirit and the divine compel him to make.

The seven of cups shows that the querent has several choices. The suit of cups indicates there is an emotional aspect to the choices. Making a good choice promotes personal growth, but only if the querent acts to make a change. The querent is separated from the flow of his or her life when he or she refuses to make changes and is unable to move forward. If the querent stifles necessary changes, an event that brings about change is inevitable and often emotionally stressful.

Death represents the energy of a transition because something is brought to an end. The transition is followed by the release of blocked, stagnated energy (the Tower). The release of blocked energy brings about necessary changes on a personal and spiritual level. This reading suggests that the querent find what change is needed so steps can be taken before a sudden, unexpected, life-changing event occurs.

**Tower Dynamics:**
Restructuring
Unblocking
Re-aligning

## Chapter Twenty

### Seventeen and the Star

*The Divine reflects spiritual wisdom within the Duality as a part of divine perfection within each individual.*

### Seventeen – The Growth of the Spiritual Mind

The seven of seventeen signals a concern with an innate awareness of spirit and a curiosity about what spirit is. Seven seeks to understand the spiritual and what it means on a personal level. The more we focus on our spiritual intelligence, the more we understand how it works within the context of our life. We search for what it means to us personally and how it functions in order to expand our knowledge and understanding of our nature, our spirit, and the divine.

Seventeen is Divine (1) Spirituality (7). Seven, as the number of intelligence or intellect, shows there is intelligence within divine spirituality. Seventeen represents the intelligence of the divine working through the conscious and subconscious mind. Seventeen also represents the intellectual capacity of the individual whose consciousness is more focused on the spiritual and how it works within the context of his or her life. Seventeen is also seven plus ten, the Intelligence (7) within Divine Perfection (10).

One plus seven equals eight. In numerology, eight is the number of power. We become powerful when we combine divine guidance with our spiritual intelligence. We can tap into the power of spirit and the mind to bring us to a deeper understanding of our divine nature. Let's look at the numerology of "seventeen".

### Chart One Hundred Thirty-six
### Seventeen

| 19 | 5 | 22 | 5 | 14 | 20 | 5 | 5 | 14 = 109 /10/1 |
|----|---|----|---|----|----|---|---|----------------|
| S  | E | V  | E | N  | T  | E | E | N              |
| 1  | 5 | 22 | 5 | 5  | 2  | 5 | 5 | 5 = 55/10/1    |

\* Translation of full numbers 1, 0, 9, 10, 1:
The Divine (1) Reflects (0) spiritual Wisdom (9) as a part of the Divine Perfection (10) within each Individual (1).

\* Translation of root numbers 55, 1, 0, 1:
Intelligence (55) taken to the next level, as a part of our Divine (1)

nature, is Reflected (0) within the Individual's (1) innate desire to expand his knowledge and understanding of spirituality.

As Shirley Blackwell Lawrence explains, fifty-five is the number of intelligence because there are ten globes on the tree of life. According to the Hebrew tradition, the ten globes contain all spiritual knowledge. If you add the numbers one through ten, the result is fifty-five, therefore the number fifty-five is the number of higher intelligence or intelligence applied to the understanding of the divine. The innate intelligence of spirit encourages us to pursue learning about our spiritual nature and divinity. Spiritual growth is an innate part of our personal journey.

Let's look at "growth" next.

Chart One Hundred Thirty-seven
Growth

| 7 | 18 | 15 | 23 | 20 | 8 = 91/10/1 |
|---|----|----|----|----|-------------|
| G | R  | O  | W  | T  | H           |
| 7 | 9  | 6  | 5  | 2  | 8 = 37/10/1 |

\* Translation of full numbers 9, 1, 10, 1:
Unconditional Love (9) is within us as Divine Potential (10) and part of an Individual's (1) spiritual intelligence.

\* Translation of root numbers 3, 7, 1, 0, 1:
Consciously (3) pursuing an awareness of Spirituality (7) leads One (1) to a better understanding of our true nature as we Reflect (0) upon the Divine (1) to promote growth.

As eight plus nine, seventeen is the Power (8) of Unconditional Love (9).

### Star – The Reconstruction of Self

The Star represents reconstruction of self on a deep level. After the upheaval of the Tower, there is often a re-ordering of priorities, leading to important changes.

The Star, as card seventeen, engages us more fully in an active, intellectual pursuit of the spiritual. Seventeen is one plus seven, which equals eight. Strength (card eight) and the Star (card seventeen) are connected by the number eight. Strength and the Star combine power within the context of spirituality, personal power, and personal strength to rebuild a reality that reflects personal and spiritual growth.

Strength and the Star are a powerful pair, especially when they appear in a spread which reflects important personal change. Strength and the Star show the use of spiritual power within the context of our personal reality (the Strength card) paired with the reconstruction of self (the Star card).

Two important symbols on the Star card are water and the eight-pointed star. "Water" has a root number of four. It is one of the primary foundations for life on earth. As such, water "feeds" our divine nature as well as our physical being. It flows and changes constantly, which we must also do, figuratively and literally.

The eight-pointed star is a universal symbol of balance, harmony, and cosmic order. After the Tower's lightning blast, the Star's archetypal energy promotes harmony and balance, allowing the individual to express his or her greater potential. Using the archetypal energy of the Star, we can realign with the flow of divine energy. The eight-pointed star crowning the Charioteer's head reminds us of the cosmic order of the divine.

Two of the most recognized star forms are the pentagram and the six-pointed star. The pentagram represents the human figure, the human as part of the cosmos. The six-pointed star represents the symbol of Fire as the downward-pointing triangle and Earth as the upward-pointing triangle interlaced; the transforming power of spiritual fire on Earth.

Let's look at the numerology of the word "Star".

### Chart One Hundred Thirty-eight
### Star

| 19 | 20 | 1 | 18 = 58/13/4 |
|----|----|----|--------------|
| S  | T  | A  | R            |
| 1  | 2  | 1  | 9 = 13/4     |

\* Translation of full numbers 5, 8, 1, 3, 4:
Changes (5) that are Powerful (8) allow the Divine (1) to Create (3) new Foundations (4).

\* Translation of root numbers 1, 3, 4:
We as Individuals (1) also Create (3) new Foundations (4) for ourselves when powerful changes occur.

The 13/4 of "Star" warns us to be careful of what kind of new foundations we create and how we create them. In order to create a more constructive, fulfilling life after our metaphorical tower has been struck by lightning, we need blueprints—a pattern we use to create a more flexible reality that allows for further growth. Flexible, in this context, refers to a life that is bound by fewer fears and limitations that we create for ourselves and spoken or unspoken rules that restrict our growth and positive expression. But where do the blueprints come from? Let's see what the numbers tell us.

Chart One Hundred Thirty-nine
Blueprints

| 2 | 12 | 21 | 5 | 16 | 18 | 9 | 14 | 20 | 19 = 136/10/1 |
|---|----|----|---|----|----|---|----|----|---------------|
| B | L  | U  | E | P  | R  | I | N  | T  | S             |
| 2 | 3  | 3  | 5 | 7  | 9  | 9 | 5  | 2  | 1 = 46/10/1   |

* Translation of full numbers 1, 3, 6, 10, 1:
The patterning of Divine (1) Creativity (3) expresses in the Harmony (6) and beauty of Divine Perfection (10) within the Individual (1).

* Translation of root numbers 4, 6, 10, 1:
Blueprints are a creative Process (4) resulting from the Beauty (6) within the Divine Perfection (10) of the higher Self (1).

* Alternate translation of root numbers 4, 6, 1, 0, 1:
Any Structure (4) our higher self creates is Beautiful (6) because it originates from a Divine (1) pattern which is Reflected (0) within the Individual (1) into what we create.

The esoteric level shows that the blueprints for anything constructed on the physical plane come from divine potential because the root number for "blueprints" is 10.

The word "power" has the full esoteric number of seventy-seven. Esoterically, power is associated with Christ consciousness, as represented by the number seventy-seven, as previously discussed in Chapter Five. There is a direct relationship between power and Christ consciousness. Christ consciousness is an aid that helps stop the abuse of power.

Chart One Hundred Forty
Power

| 16 | 15 | 23 | 5 | 18 = 77 (14/5) |
|----|----|----|---|----------------|
| P  | O  | W  | E | R              |
| 7  | 6  | 5  | 5 | 9 = 32/5       |

\* Conversion of full numbers 1, 4, 5 into Letters:
1 = A, 4 = D, 5 = E.

\* Translation of A, D, E:
Christ consciousness is an AID (ADE) to consciousness in the Duality.

\* Translation of root numbers 3, 2, 5:
Consciousness (3) tries to establish Balance (2) after Change (5).

\* Alternate translation of root numbers 3, 2, 5:
Consciousness (3) also tries to maintain Balance (2) as an expression of Power (5).

The word "matter" also has a full number of seventy-seven on the esoteric level (Chart One Hundred Twenty, page 157). Science has proven that there is tremendous power within matter.

The root number of "power" is five, whose key word is change. Change often promotes a better balance of energy, therefore is change synonymous with imbalance? If balance is only possible after change has taken place, and everything is always in a state of change, then is balance an illusion of ego consciousness?

**Translation Review**

The Divine Reflects Spiritual Wisdom as a part of the Divine Perfection within each Individual. Intelligence taken to the next level, as a part of our Divine nature, is Reflected within the Individual's innate desire to expand his knowledge and understanding of spirituality. Unconditional Love is within us as Divine Potential and part of an Individual's spiritual intelligence. Consciously pursuing an awareness of Spirituality leads One to a better understanding of our true nature as we Reflect upon the Divine to promote growth.

Changes that are Powerful allow the Divine to Create new Foundations. We as Individuals also Create new Foundations for ourselves when powerful changes occur. The patterning of Divine Creativity expresses in the Harmony and beauty of Divine Perfection within the Individual. Blueprints are a creative Process resulting from the Beauty within the Divine Perfection of the higher Self. Any Structure our higher self creates is Beautiful because it originates from a Divine pattern which is Reflected within the Individual into what we create.

Christ consciousness is an Aid to consciousness in the Duality. Consciousness tries to establish Balance after Change. Consciousness also tries to maintain Balance as an expression of Power.

**Applying the Revealed Information**

**Acquired Meanings – New Meanings Revealed by Numerology**
The intellectual pursuit of spiritual knowledge, contemplation of our relationship to spirit and the divine, the intelligence of divine perfection, restructuring of self, the creation of new foundations on a spiritual and physical level, the process of the divine creative plan, following the flow of divine energy.

**Relevant Questions**
What is my primary relationship to spirit and the divine? What form should my restructuring take? What will make the best foundations for me? How can I re-align with the flow of divine energy? What is the best way for me to nurture myself at this time?

**Practical Application**
Reading: the Page of Wands, the Star, the Hanged Man.

The querent's youthful energy, attitude, and open-mindedness aid his or her ability to "see" things differently. The querent's point of view will be reflected in his or her actions. The querent is entering a new phase of self-discovery. Staying in the flow of divine energy allows the restructuring of self (the Star) and one's life to occur more harmoniously. Life always has the potential to make us see ourselves and the world in new ways. New perspectives bring opportunities for expanded awareness about the true nature of self and the Duality.

**Just a Thought**
How would you interpret a reading of the Tower, the Star, and the Hanged Man?

**Star Dynamics:**
Evaluating
Releasing
Reconstructing

## Chapter Twenty-One

### Eighteen and the Moon

*Man's subconscious interprets spiritual communications from the divine, which change form within the dualistic mind.*

**Eighteen – The Power of Spirit on the Material Plane**
Eighteen, seen as eight plus ten, is the Power (8) of Divine Perfection (10). One is the Divine, and eight represents the continual flow of energy. Eighteen is the Divine's (1) Energy (8) dynamic. The numeral eight represents energy constantly circulating from the divine into the Duality and back again. The constantly circulating divine energy is reflected to create the Duality. This also explains the mirror effect of opposites within the Duality. Albert Einstein said, "Energy cannot be created or destroyed, it can only be changed from one form to another." Energy changes form as it circulates from the divine into the Duality and back again.

Energy also changes form within the Duality. As we gain understanding of how energy changes form within the Duality, we gain a better understanding of how all things are connected. Within the eight is four plus four, or the Process (4) and Foundation (4) of energy manipulation within the Duality. We manipulate energy whether we are consciously aware of it or not. Let's look at the numbers of "eighteen".

Chart One Hundred Forty-one
Eighteen

| 5 | 9 | 7 | 8 | 20 | 5 | 5 | 14 = 73/10/1 |
|---|---|---|---|----|---|---|--------------|
| E | I | G | H | T  | E | E | N            |
| 5 | 9 | 7 | 8 | 2  | 5 | 5 | 5 = 46/10/1  |

\* Translation of full numbers 7, 3, 1, 0, 1:
The powerful nature of Spirit's (7) Creative (3) Originality (1) is Reflected (0) from the Divine (1).

\* Translation of root numbers 4, 6, 1, 0, 1:
The Structures (4) of our Vision (6) are Reflected (0) from within the Individual (1) into the duality matrix.

Let's look at the word "structure" next. I left out the reduction of 145 as 10/1 in translation because 10/1 is translated as part of the root numbers.

## Chart One Hundred Forty-two
### Structure

| 19 | 20 | 18 | 21 | 3 | 20 | 21 | 18 | 5 | = 145 |
|----|----|----|----|---|----|----|----|---|-------|
| S  | T  | R  | U  | C | T  | U  | R  | E |       |
| 1  | 2  | 9  | 3  | 3 | 2  | 3  | 9  | 5 | = 37/10/1 |

\* Translation of full numbers 1, 4, 5:
Divinity (1) built into every Structure (4) the dynamic of Change (5).

\* Translation of root numbers 3, 7, 1:
Structures have a Creative Matrix (3) used by Spirit (7) to make Original (1) creations.

Structure in this context does not only refer to solid constructs. There are also structures created on an energetic level that never appear as solid. Change occurs to solid structures and energetic structures alike. One way we see the dynamic of change in action is through the constant, slow deterioration of objects. Change is rooted in the concepts of our spirituality because the word "change" has a root number of eleven, the number of spiritual understanding. Change brings us new spiritual insights. Three, in the root numbers, is the creative matrix. Inherent within the number three is one and two (refer to Chapter Five: Three and the Empress).

The word structure brought to mind the word construct. Wikipedia defines construct as "an ideal object, where the existence of the thing may be said to depend upon a subject's mind." We all manipulate and use energy to build constructs as an innate ability of spirit. The patterns that are constructed on the energetic level are sometimes physically manifested and sometimes not. All physically manifested structures are first created as energy patterns or constructs. The constructs may be mentally created or created by spirit. Following is the numerology of "construct".

## Chart One Hundred Forty-three
### Construct

| 3 | 15 | 14 | 19 | 20 | 18 | 21 | 3 | 20 | = 133/7 |
|---|----|----|----|----|----|----|---|----|---------|
| C | O  | N  | S  | T  | R  | U  | C | T  |         |
| 3 | 6  | 5  | 1  | 2  | 9  | 3  | 3 | 2  | = 34/7  |

\* Translation of full numbers 1, 3, 3, 7:
The Divine (1) empowered us with Creative (3) Consciousness (3)

so that Spirit (7) could build constructs within the Duality.

* Translation of root numbers 3, 4, 7:
Creative (3) consciousness Builds (4) some constructs within the Spiritual (7) context of the Duality.

**Moon – The Archetype of Personal Spiritual Symbolism**

One plus eight equals nine, which relates the Moon (18) to the Hermit (9). The Hermit encourages us to look more deeply into our inner landscape, while the Moon archetype gives us information about these landscapes by using symbols. The Moon archetype reflects these landscapes as a part of the universal mind and our personal language of symbols. Our quiet inner space, after emerging from the Hermit, expands in the archetype of the Moon into our landscape of symbols accessed by our dreams, visions, intuition, and meditation. The power of symbols lies in their ability to convey spiritual concepts.

The following quote is from *The Hidden Geometry of Life* by Karen L. French: "In the nineteenth century the discovery was made that there are fields within the underlying reality of the universe. The potential of the fields is realized when the forces within the fields interact. The potential of these fields is the dynamic of the geometric shapes that form our reality. Every human knows on the intuitive level about these dynamics and uses them through our mind's intent. Our mind's intent is represented in symbols and structures based on geometry."

The symbols and structures are the underlying foundation to our dreams represented by the Moon archetype. It is not necessary for us to know consciously what all the symbols and geometric structures are or what they mean. We use them instinctively as a part of our personal expression when we create. Here is the numerology of "Moon".

Chart One Hundred Forty-four
Moon

| 13 | 15 | 15 | 14 = 57/12/3 |
|----|----|----|--------------|
| M  | O  | O  | N            |
| 4  | 6  | 6  | 5 = 21/3     |

* Translation of full numbers 5, 7, 1, 2, 3:
At a deeper level, Man's (5) subconscious interprets the Spiritual (7) communications from the Divine (1), which change form within the Dualistic (2) Creative (3) mind.

* Translation of root numbers 2, 1, 3:
As We (2) work with symbols subconsciously, the conscious mind of the Individual (1) tries to interpret the Communication (3).

On the Moon card, small yellow drops appear between two pillars. Each drop represents the tenth letter of the Hebrew alphabet, Yod. The numerical value of "Yod" is ten. Yod represents a divine point of energy. As ten, it is the perfection of the divine. These Yods are placed in the field of blue, as opposed to the green of solid land, which separates the water from the blue field of symbols and dreams. The pillars mark the boundary between reality and the dream landscape. In the Duality, some symbols are translated into matter ranging from the simple to more complex forms. Life in its simplest form is believed to have originated in the ocean. The yellow road leads from the ocean back to the landscape of dream symbols, which originate from the divine.

Let's take a look at the word "symbol".

Chart One Hundred Forty-five
Symbol

| 19 | 25 | 13 | 2 | 15 | 12 = 86/14/5 |
|---|---|---|---|---|---|
| S | Y | M | B | O | L |
| 1 | 7 | 4 | 2 | 6 | 3 = 23/5 |

* Translation of full numbers 8, 6, 1, 4, 5:
The Powerful (8) Vision (6) of the Divine (1) Builds (4) Symbols (5) within the context of the Duality.

* Translation of root numbers 2, 3, 5:
Within the Duality (2), symbols are the Creative (3) basis of Man's (5) consciousness.

Symbols convey spiritual messages. The 14/5 of "symbol" tells us that: the Divine (1) Builds (4) the ability to Change (5) within symbols. The symbol's ability to change allows for endless variety. Symbols communicate to us by our conceiving and discernment of spiritual awareness and insight. Some of these messages are translated into our immediate reality; some are not. Symbols are an integral part of our life, whether received through dreams, meditation, intuition, or some other means. Since dreams are a part of the way the mind works, let's look at the numbers of the word "dreams".

## Chart One Hundred Forty-six
### Dreams

| 4 | 18 | 5 | 1 | 13 | 19 = 60/6 |
|---|----|---|---|----|-----------|
| D | R  | E | A | M  | S         |
| 4 | 9  | 5 | 1 | 4  | 1 = 24/6  |

\* Translation of full numbers 6, 0, 6:
Dreams (6) Reflect (0) Vision (6) back to us.

\* Translation of root numbers 2, 4, 6:
The Duality (2) interprets dream symbols when we build a reality as a part of our personal Process (4) of Vision (6).

We gain spiritual awareness through our dreams, which promotes change. The word "dream" has a root number of five, therefore a dream reflects the process of making changes.

Dreams are part of the subconscious. Let's take a look at the word "subconscious" next.

## Chart One Hundred Forty-seven
### Subconscious

| 19 | 21 | 2 | 3 | 15 | 14 | 19 | 3 | 9 | 15 | 21 | 19 = 160/7 |
|----|----|---|---|----|----|----|---|---|----|----|------------|
| S  | U  | B | C | O  | N  | S  | C | I | O  | U  | S          |
| 1  | 3  | 2 | 3 | 6  | 5  | 1  | 3 | 9 | 6  | 3  | 1 = 43/7   |

\* Translation of full numbers 1, 6, 0, 7:
The Divine (1) gives us Vision (6) to promote the Potential (0) of spirit, promoting growth of Spirit (7).

\* Translation of root numbers 4, 3, 7:
The subconscious perceives spiritual awareness and insights as fields of potential which may become mental Constructs (4) that are Expressed (3) as symbols within a Spiritual (7) context.

Our subconscious is linked to our spirit, so it makes sense to send messages through the subconscious. Spiritual content within the Duality takes place within a context that is created by the divine. Context is defined by the dictionary as "the interrelated conditions, such as environment, setting, framework, of an event." Divine context is not necessarily accessed directly by the conscious mind.

Chart One Hundred Forty-eight
Context

| 3 | 15 | 14 | 20 | 5 | 24 | 20 = 101/2 |
|---|----|----|----|---|----|-----------|
| C | O  | N  | T  | E | X  | T          |
| 3 | 6  | 5  | 2  | 5 | 6  | 2 = 29/11  |

\* Translation of full numbers 1, 0, 1, 2:
The Divine (1) Reflects (0) to the Individual (1) the context of creating within the Duality (2).

\* Translation of root numbers 2, 9, 11:
In the Duality (2) spirit is Initiated (9) into the context and content of Spiritual (11) symbolism.

When I think about the Moon archetype and its connection to the subconscious, I also think about the distortion that happens in the world of dreams. I found it interesting that the words "distort" and "distorted" both have a root number of six, the same as "dreams". Distortion seems to be an inherent part of the process of communication by dreams. Distortion happens when we try to bring the dream symbols into our conscious mind as a way of accessing and processing the information for interpretation.

**Translation Review**
The powerful nature of Spirit's Creative Originality is Reflected from the Divine. The Structures of our Vision are Reflected from the Individual into the duality matrix. Divinity built into every Structure the dynamic of Change. Structures have a Creative Matrix used by Spirit to make Original creations. The Divine empowered us with Creative Consciousness so that Spirit could build constructs within the Duality. Creative consciousness Builds some constructs within the Spiritual context of the Duality.

At a deeper level, Man's subconscious interprets the Spiritual communications from the Divine, which change form within the Dualistic Creative mind. As We work with symbols subconsciously, the conscious mind of the Individual tries to interpret the Communication. The Powerful Vision of the Divine Builds Symbols within the context of the Duality. Within the Duality, symbols are the Creative basis of Man's consciousness.

Dreams Reflect Vision back to us. The Duality interprets dream symbols when we build a reality as a part of our personal Process of Vision. The Divine gives us Vision to promote the Potential of spirit, promoting the growth of Spirit. The subconscious perceives spiritual awareness and insights as fields of potential which may become Constructs that are Expressed as symbols within a Spiritual context.

The Divine Reflects to the Individual the context of creating within the Duality. In the Duality spirit is Initiated into the context and content of Spiritual symbolism.

**Applying the Revealed Information**

**Acquired Meanings – New Meanings Revealed by Numerology**

The eternal cycle of energy, the spiritual nature of change, our personal language of symbols, distortion, the spiritual messages within symbols, structures and constructs we create, communication and understanding on a deeper level, the layers of meaning within symbols, communication on multiple levels.

**Relevant Questions**

How do I recognize what my personal symbols are on a conscious level? How can I use my personal symbols in a creative way? What is the spiritual message within this symbol? What meaning lies beneath the distortion? What is the core meaning of the symbol in this dream? What are some of the layers of meanings within this symbol centered around?

**Practical Application**

Reading: the Three of Pentacles, the Moon, the King of Wands.

In the Three of Pentacles, something is in the process of being created. What the querent creates has meanings on multiple levels that are associated with his or her personal language of symbols (the Moon).

Agreed upon meanings of certain symbols allows the creative process to be a group effort shared at a deeper level.

On a spiritual level, the querent understands how to use and interpret energy structures, constructs, and symbols because at that level, he or she has innate knowledge and command of them. Knowledge allows the querent to focus his or her intent and take actions that manifest the creations within his or her reality if that is the goal. The King of Wands shows that it takes a determined focus of energy and intention for the querent to bring his or her creation into form.

**Just a Thought**

One key to interpreting a spread is noticing which way the energy flows. In this reading, the King of Wands is looking at the Moon, showing that the energy of the court card is moving from right to left. If we accept that the King of Wands indicates the directional flow of energy, the cards can be read in reverse order from right to left.

The King of Wands commands the necessary focus of energy to bring the symbols of the Moon archetype into the field of manifestation. At the level of spirit, the querent wants to manifest something from within the matrix of symbols. Pentacles indicate something physical is being created. Whatever is manifested first takes form within the universal language of symbols. The symbols then coalesce into the duality matrix and our own personal language of symbols. Our symbols are interpreted, and the creative idea is shared with others, as shown in the Three of Pentacles.

The symbols may or may not manifest physically. They may remain an energy construct only. In this case, because of the presence of the Moon, I see the three pentacles more as a general symbolic representation than a literal physical creation. In the context of this reading, the act of creating—as well as what is created—has many layers of meanings, which are then interpreted by the individual within his or her personal language of symbols.

Self-expression is accomplished within the laws of divine creativity and the contextual matrix of spirituality, duality, and our personal language of symbols.

**Moon Dynamics:**
Dreaming
Distorting
Converting
Symbolizing

# The Last Group of Three – Sun, Judgement, and the World

# Chapter Twenty-Two

### Nineteen and the Sun

*In the blaze of divine light, ego and spirit blend. We are free again to fully embrace our true being of light and beauty.*

Keeping in mind that the Fool stands alone, the major arcana are divided into two rows of nine cards each, starting with the Magician, card one. This leaves three cards in the third and final row.

In numerology, the numbers one through nine describe a basic cycle of human experiences, as well as number attributes that describe human characteristics and abilities. When we divide the major arcana into rows of nine, ten starts a second row and a second cycle of nine, which includes the numbers ten through eighteen. Card nineteen, the Sun, represents a transition to a new cycle of nine. Once the transition of the Sun (card nineteen) is completed, the cycle continues with double-digit numbers that start with the digit two.

### Nineteen – Transition from an End to a Beginning

Nineteen is a number of transition. It is the transition from double-digit numbers that start with one to double-digit numbers that start with two. Nineteen is the first number that cannot be derived from the addition of two single-digit numbers, which distinguishes it from all previous numbers. In the tarot, nineteen is the last number before the final resolution (Judgement, twenty) and integration (the World, twenty-one) in the major arcana.

In numerology, the number nineteen is a karmic number that warns of unbalanced ego. Karmic numbers, in general, warn of an ego not harmonized with an individual's spiritual nature. Analyzing the digits of nineteen, the first digit, one, keeps the focus on self. The negative attribute of one is expressed as unbalanced ego that has a tendency to overvalue or undervalue self and abilities. The second digit, nine, expresses an innate desire to give selflessly to a group; however, over-giving can result in resentment, another unbalanced expression of ego. Ironically, the root number of "ego" is nine (Chart Sixty-four, page 88), a number that draws attention to the opposite of the individual ego, the group. This fact emphasizes that any consideration of ego must also consider its implied opposite, the group. Nine shows ego has the ability to give to others, but its prime concern is with self. As ego expresses in a more balanced way, the separateness of self becomes less important.

The ego is necessary to help us survive in a body, but how we survive does not have to be dictated by ego. A key word for the number nine is "ending," suggesting that ego's sense of separateness can end, freeing us to be complete within the totality.

The ultimate freedom is freedom from the negative aspects of ego, which promote separateness. A blending and balancing of the attributes of one and nine where both the individual and the group benefit is possible when ego blends with spirit, seeing others as a part of self. The termination of separateness allows unification of self and spirit—the ultimate expression of balance.

The interactive and reflective nature of the duality matrix promotes the changes made by spirit that restore balance. As we imagine what we want in life, the nature of the duality matrix under the right circumstances manifests these things as a part of our personal reality. We witness the response of the matrix, seeing the projections of our energy, and can thus evaluate ourselves in what we have created. The reflective nature of the duality matrix continually mirrors and promotes in many ways the inclusive nature of the divine.

The natural propensity of ego to focus on self makes it difficult for ego to embrace its place as a part of a much larger whole. As spirit and ego blend, spirit expresses its true nature. Spirit sees others as part of a whole. Nineteen, as a transition, brings balance so ego and spirit can progress toward unity, allowing a blending of what once appeared dualistic in nature.

### Chart One Hundred Forty-nine
### Nineteen

| 14 | 9 | 14 | 5 | 20 | 5 | 5 | 14 = 86/14/5 |
|----|---|----|---|----|---|---|--------------|
| N  | I | N  | E | T  | E | E | N            |
| 5  | 9 | 5  | 5 | 2  | 5 | 5 | 5 = 41/5     |

\* Translation of full numbers 8, 6, 1, 4, 5:
The Power (8) of ego needs to Harmonize (6) with an Individual's (1) spiritual nature to create and express a stable Foundation (4) of Freedom (5).

\* Translation of root numbers 4, 1, 5:
The Process (4) of blending the individual Self (1) with the spiritual self promotes Freedom (5).

A balanced ego blended with spirit promotes personal freedom, allowing for a more complete expression of our potential and true nature. In the light of divine love, imbalance cannot remain.

Let's look at "divine love" and unconditional love next.

### Chart One Hundred Fifty
### Divine Love

```
              63                              54
 4    9   22   9   14   5      12   15   22   5  = 117/9
 D    I   V    I   N    E       L    O    V   E
 4    9   22   9    5   5       3    6   22   5  = 18/9
           9 (54)                     9 (36)
```

\* Translation of full numbers 1, 1, 7, 9:
The Individual (1) and the Divine (1) are united within the Spiritual (7) embrace of unconditional Love (9).

\* Translation of root numbers 1, 8, 9:
The Individual (1) expresses the Power (8) of spirit by the grace of divine Love (9).

### Chart One Hundred Fifty-one
### Unconditional Love

```
                151                                  54
21 14  3  15 14  4   9 20   9 15 14   1  12 12  15 22   5 = 205/7
 U  N  C   O  N  D   I  T   I  O  N   A   L   L   O  V   E
 3  5  3   6  5  4   9  2   9  6  5   1   3   3   6 22   5 = 16/7
                  7 (61)                          9 (36)
```

\* Translation of full numbers 2, 0, 5, 7:
The Duality, (2) in the Reflection (0) of Change (5), sees the truth of its Spiritual (7) loving and divine nature.

\* Translation of root numbers 1, 6, 7:
By unconditional love, the Individual (1) expresses the true Beauty (6) of his Spiritual (7) origins.

The one of nineteen represents the self, so let's look at numerology of "self" next.

## Chart One Hundred Fifty-two
## Self

| 19 | 5 | 12 | 6 = 42/6 |
|----|---|----|----------|
| S  | E | L  | F        |
| 1  | 5 | 3  | 6 = 15/6 |

* Translation of full numbers 4, 2, 6:
A Foundation (4) of Balance (2) begins with the Self (6).

* Translation of root numbers 1, 5, 6:
An Individual's (1) personal Choices (5) need to be handled responsibly with the guidance of our Vision (6).

One of six's key words is responsibility. The root number of "self" (6) shows that the self is responsible (6). It is up to us to take responsibility for who we are and the way we conduct ourselves. Let's take a look at the phrase "self image" next.

## Chart One Hundred Fifty-three
## Self Image

|   | 42 |    |   |   | 35 |   |   |             |
|---|----|----|---|---|----|---|---|-------------|
|19 | 5  | 12 | 6 | 9 | 13 | 1 | 7 | 5 = 77/14/5 |
| S | E  | L  | F | I | M  | A | G | E           |
| 1 | 5  | 3  | 6 | 9 | 4  | 1 | 7 | 5 = 14/5    |
|   | 6 (15) |   |   |   | 8 (26) |   |   |         |

* Translation of full numbers 77, 1, 4, 5:
Spiritual Intelligence (77), along with a sense of Self (1), guides us, providing the Foundation (4) for how we use our personal Freedom (5).

* Translation of root numbers 1, 4, 5:
If we use Ego (1) to Build (4) a false self-image, personal Freedoms (5) are taken away.

On the esoteric level of "self image", we see the number for Christ consciousness (77). Christ consciousness is our name for the divine pattern that Jesus embodied, one of many possible divine spiritual patterns self can identify with.

The karmic number fourteen of "self image" warns us there is a danger of misusing spiritual intelligence and freedom. The word "power" (Chart One Hundred Forty, page 178) is another word with a 14/5 karmic warning. "Power" has the root number five showing its basic energy is expressed through change. Our ability to accept and make positive changes increases our personal power.

"Image" has a root number of eight, whose key word is power. An image that reflects the true nature of the self is very powerful.

### Sun – Ultimate Trust in our Divine Nature

The Sun (19/10/1) is the second card of transition. The Wheel of Fortune, 10/1, is the first (Chapter Thirteen). Sun's numbers, which reduce to one, are a transition to the next level—a new beginning. As card nineteen, the Sun is the divine (1) bringing an end (9) to the ego's dualistic point of view. The Sun archetype is also a transition to the next spiritual level, representing the final transformation of egocentric identity. An ultimate trust in our divine nature is what allows for the last transition. This last transition is from egocentric duality to the unity of our true nature in preparation for ascension to the next dimension of divine expression.

The Wheel of Fortune, the tenth card and the first card of transition, brings balance to spirit by divine direction and the dynamics of karma. The Sun, the second card of transition, brings balance by acceptance of our full nature, thereby revealing the unity of all that is.

The sun is the strongest source of light in our solar system. The numbers of "light" (Chart Ninety, page 120) showed us that the divine emanation of unconditional love is seen as light within the Duality. The strongest form of unconditional divine love within the Duality is sunlight. Sunlight is necessary for all life on earth by the process of photosynthesis. Light from the sun is absorbed into the body and transformed into vitamin D, a necessary component for good health. These are a few of the many ways divine love supports life.

We know that without the sun's light and heat, we could not survive on this planet. Let's look at the numerology of "Sun".

Chart One Hundred Fifty-four
Sun

| 19 | 21 | 14 = 54/9 |
|----|----|-----------|
| S  | U  | N         |
| 1  | 3  | 5 = 9     |

\* Translation of full numbers 5, 4, 9:

Man's (5) Process (4) of creating within the Duality would End (9) without the sun.

The root number nine of "Sun" is also the root number of "me", "I", and "ego". Within divine unity, we have the choice to be separate. The Sun archetype burns away all the ways we identify ourselves as separate. Ego self, after it has traveled through the preceding archetypes, returns to a place that exists within a unified perspective where ego blends with spirit. For us to have ultimate trust in the divine implies that we recognize, understand, and believe in unity as the true nature of all that is. The numerology of "separate" follows.

Chart One Hundred Fifty-five
Separate

```
19   5   16   1   9   1   20   5 = 76/13/4
S    E   P    A   R   A   T    E
1    5   7    1   9   1   2    5 = 31/4
```

\* Translation of full numbers 7, 6, 1, 3, 4:
The Spiritual (7) Vision (6) of the Divine (1) Creates (3) within a Foundation (4) of unconditional love.

\* Translation of root numbers 3, 1, 4:
Within divine vision is the impulse of Creative (3) consciousness to create the Individual Ego (1) that Structures (4) self-identity.

"Who am I?" is a question we commonly attempt to answer. Self identity makes a distinction between us and others. Ultimately, the me and I of self identity fade as ego blends more fully with spirit. Let's look at the word "identity" next.

Chart One Hundred Fifty-six
Identity

```
9   4   5   14   20   9   20   25 = 106/7
I   D   E   N    T    I   T    Y
9   4   5   5    2    9   2    7 = 43/7
```

\* Translation of full numbers 1, 0, 6, 7:
The Divine (1) Reflects (0) the Truth (6) of Identity (7) throughout the Duality.

\* Additional translation of full numbers 1, 0, 6, 7:
The Divine (1) Reflects (0) itself also by the Truth (6) of Spirit (7).

\* Translation of root numbers 4, 3, 7:
Identity is a Construct (4) of Creative (3) Intelligence (7) activated when spirit enters the Duality.

Divine vision includes the impulse to create the ego, which structures identity and sense of self when spirit incarnates into a body. Whose identity is being structured and why? Divine identity is being structured so that it can know itself. By knowing our true nature, we know the divine. The divine knows itself by our true nature being reflected throughout the Duality. Another way divinity knows itself is by the insight of spiritual awareness the Duality reflects back to it.

Without the heat and light from our sun, life could not survive on this planet. The archetype of the Sun (19/10/1) is an aspect of the Magician (1), the archetype of the divine. The sun, our star, is the physical manifestation of divine love. It is said that looking directly at the divine will blind physical eyes, which is also true of the sun. The sun, as a metaphor for divine love, "burns" off the last vestiges of ego. In a blaze of divine light, our ego loses hold over us. As the child on the Sun card, we are free again to be beings of light.

The Sun expresses as divine emanation. Divine emanation promotes integration: the integration of ego and spirit, of physical and spiritual, and of re-integration of duality to singularity. The archetypes progress from divine intention, to divine engagement, to divine emanation.

In a spread when two or more cards in the first triad of progression appear (in any order), it signals that divine energy is active. For example, when card 1, the Magician, and 19, the Sun, appear in a spread, the reader should consider the presence of divine intention and divine emanation. Divine intention, the Magician, is actively facilitating creativity. Divine emanation, the Sun, is actively facilitating the integration of ego with spirit, physical with spiritual, duality with singularity.

**Translation Review**

The Power of the ego needs to Harmonize with an Individual's spiritual nature to create and express a stable Foundation of Freedom. The Process of blending the individual Self with the spiritual self promotes Freedom. The Individual and the Divine are united within the Spiritual embrace of unconditional Love. The Individual expresses the Power of spirit by the grace of divine Love. The Duality, in the Reflection of Change, sees the truth of its Spiritual loving and divine nature. By unconditional love, the

Individual expresses the true Beauty of his Spiritual origins.

A Foundation of Balance begins with the Self. An Individual's personal Choices need to be handled responsibly with the guidance of our Vision. Spiritual Intelligence, along with a sense of Self, guides us, providing the Foundation for how we use our personal Freedom. If we use Ego to Build a false self-image, personal Freedoms are taken away.

Man's Process of creating within the Duality would End without the sun. The Spiritual Vision of the Divine Creates within a Foundation of unconditional love. Within divine vision is the impulse of Creative consciousness to create the individual Ego that Structures self-identity.

The Divine Reflects the Truth of Identity throughout the Duality. The Divine Reflects itself also by the Truth of Spirit. Identity is a Construct of Creative Intelligence activated when spirit enters the Duality.

**Applying the Revealed Information**

**Acquired Meanings – New Meanings Revealed by Numerology**

The beginning and the end, ultimate trust in our divine nature, the final release of egocentric identity, the assimilation of our personal journey through life into a cohesive whole, the relationship between creative consciousness, the ego and self-identity, the beauty of spirit within physical form, our true light of being.

**Relevant Questions**

How does the dynamic between what is beginning and what is ending affect me? What area of my life do I need to bring into the light? What is the best way for me to work on balancing my ego? What is the relationship between my creative consciousness, my ego, and my self-identity? What are they focused on right now? How do I currently express my true light of being? What is my divine path centered around at this time?

**Practical Application**
Reading: the Five of Wands, the Sun, the Two of Wands.

Interestingly, I pulled two cards in the suit of wands with the Sun card. Wands represent the element of fire. If the querent's life is in turmoil, the way the querent perceives his or her life is affected. No matter what the querent's life experiences are, they are the best for his or her personal spiritual growth. One of five's key words is change. Out of the confusion, what choice can be made to bring about changes that will bring positive personal experiences?

The man in the Two of Wands faces to the left toward the Sun card. Perhaps he is asking, "What light can you shed on my world?" Light, as in knowledge, can help resolve the question of what action should be taken. Reviewing options and making changes that allow for a fuller expression of self will help the querent make the best choice. The querent can then move more fully into the light of his or her true being.

**Just a Thought**
The ego promotes the belief that we are separate from everything, including the divine and each other. There are, however, many spiritual practices that believe all separateness is an illusion. "Me", "I", and "ego", three words we use to identify self, also have a root number of nine, as does the word "Sun". In the view of the unbalanced ego, it sees itself as "the be all and end all."

**Sun Dynamics:**
Illuminating
Embracing
Assimilating

# Chapter Twenty-Three

## Commentary: The Number Triads and the First Triad of Progression

In consideration of the Sun as card nineteen, we have now examined the third component of the first triad. In the major arcana, there are three number triads. The three number triads are: one, ten, nineteen (1/10/19); two, eleven, twenty (2/11/20); and three, twelve, twenty-one (3/12/21). These triads show not only a numerical progression, but also a progression of meaning. The progression of meaning is derived from the numbers themselves, as well as from the major arcana cards assigned to these numbers.

Two or more cards of a triad within a reading (they don't have to be in any particular order) indicate an important process. In a case where two out of three cards in the same triad are drawn, the third card may be implied.

The first triad of numbers is 1, 10, 19. Ten and nineteen reduce to the single-digit one by addition; 19 is reduced as $1 + 9 = 10$, ten is reduced as $1 + 0 = 1$. The corresponding triad of cards is: the Magician (1), the Wheel of Fortune (10), and the Sun (19).

The second triad of numbers is 2, 11, 20. Eleven and twenty reduce to the single-digit two by addition; 11 is reduced as $1 + 1 = 2$, 20 is reduced as $2 + 0 = 2$. The corresponding triad of cards is: the High Priestess (2), Justice (11), and Judgement (20).

The third triad of numbers is 3, 12, 21. Twelve and twenty-one reduce to the single-digit three by addition; 12 is reduced as $1 + 2 = 3$, 21 is reduced as $2 + 1 = 3$. The corresponding triad of cards is: the Empress (3), the Hanged Man (12), and the World (21).

We will examine the triads in the order of the cards and their chapters starting with the Sun.

# First Triad of Progression (1, 10, 19): Presence of Divine Energy

The "Magician" (one), "Wheel of Fortune" (ten), and the "Sun" (nineteen) have the same root number of one. These three cards show a progression of the number one as it moves toward integration: one, the divine; ten, one paired with zero (0), divine potential; nineteen, one, the beginning of a cycle, and nine, the ending of a cycle. In nineteen, the divine creates endings while re-integrating all that it has created to bring about a new beginning and new potential (1, new beginning, 9, endings, 1 + 9 = 10, new beginnings, 1, and new potential, 0).

These three cards show three types of divine expression or divine interaction with the Duality. Each archetype in this group expresses different aspects of divine energy. The three aspects of divine energy are intention, engagement, and emanation. Together, the three archetypes progress toward divine emanation, which is the specific expression of the archetype, the Sun. Similarly, the Magician is divine intention; the Wheel of Fortune is divine engagement.

The Magician in the context of this triad is divine intention. Divine intention expresses as creation: the creation of divine reflection or the Duality. In the Duality, we see the creation of the four elements, fire, water, air, earth, and other groups of four that are foundations within the Duality, such as directionality (north, south, east, west) and basic components of life (carbon, oxygen, hydrogen, nitrogen) (Chapter Three, page 34).

The Wheel of Fortune expresses as divine engagement. Karma, the interaction of the divine with the Duality, reflects back to us the result of our actions. The mechanisms of karma create the opportunity to change how we act. Divine engagement expresses as karma, the catalyst of change, bringing about spiritual growth and the expression of potential.

The Sun expresses divine emanation in the form of light. Light carries within it the vibration of unconditional love. Life thrives in light. The Sun archetype reflects a sense and feeling of well being as we accept our unity with the divine.

# Chapter Twenty-Four

## Twenty and Judgement

*The dynamics of a dimensional matrix provide an abundant energy source for the individual within the Duality for co-creation.*

### Twenty – The Reflection and Potential

Twenty contains the seeds of divine unity and the reflected dimensions of duality. The number two suggests separateness, something other than the number one. Two can be other, as in another person, another object, or another dimension. The Duality is our dimension, but it is ultimately a construct of the divine. Spirit expresses within the broad spectrum of the Duality, but is not limited to physical form and ego. As the divine expresses within dimensions, spirit expresses within the dimensions of duality. But ultimately, any dimension is contained within the divine and the unity of the one.

The number 20 brings the focus to the dynamic of the number two. The addition of a zero to make twenty expands the concepts of two into a spiritual level. Two represents a basic dichotomy. It has tension or conflict. It has the potential for resolution. It implies a resolution by containing the possibility to return to one and becoming a unity. The drive toward unity is why the inevitability in any duality is to return to the unity of one. Having dealt with the digit 2, we continue with the question of the meaning of the digit 0 in 20.

Zero, if you recall, raises the expression of the digit on the left to a higher level. The two of twenty represents differentiation, or the separateness of the other. The zero, as infinite potential (Chapter Two), adds the possibility for rediscovering unity.

How can we be two in the midst of divine unity? Are we spirit beings, physical beings, or both? In the number twenty, this last question is resolved within the continuum represented by our symbol for the glyph 0: two things, represented by two points, one at the top and one at the bottom of the 0, joined together as part of a continuum to form a complete whole.

The rediscovery of unity is an expression of divine potential represented by zero. Individual components, as part of a larger whole, are why the sum of two parts joined together can be so much more than the individual parts. An interpretation of 20 is: Twenty is the Duality (2) reflected within divine Potential (0). Divine potential is how zero brings the meaning of two back to the unity of the divine.

## Chart One Hundred Fifty-seven
## Twenty

| 20 | 23 | 5 | 14 | 20 | 25 = 107/8 |
|----|----|---|----|----|------------|
| T  | W  | E | N  | T  | Y          |
| 2  | 5  | 5 | 5  | 2  | 7 = 26/8   |

* Translation of full numbers 1, 0, 7, 8:
The Divine (1) Reflected (0) within manifested Spirit (7) contains Powerful (8) dimensional dynamics.

* Translation of root numbers 2, 6, 8:
The Duality (2) contains the Beauty (6) within Powerful (8) dimensional dynamics.

Divine energy present within the Duality grows into a dynamic that is not only powerful, but also endless, circular, and cyclical in nature. The number eight shows an energy pattern that is not only complete within itself, but also contains all the dimensional aspects of creation. The way the upper line flows down to become the lower half, then flows upward again reveals the dimensional aspects of the glyph eight. The dimensional aspects are part of the natural dynamic of divine energy being reflected as the Duality.

The word "dimension" has a root number of three. Three, as a result of one plus two, shows dimensions are rooted within what is created by the interaction of one and two. The Empress, three and the creative matrix, has an aspect of dimensionality where the spiritual becomes physical, where imagination becomes real, idea becomes invention, and concept becomes manifestation. A concept or idea that is brought from the imagination into manifestation uses the dimensional creative aspects of the Empress. Following is the numerology of the word "dimension".

## Chart One Hundred Fifty-eight
## Dimension

| 4 | 9 | 13 | 5 | 14 | 19 | 9 | 15 | 14 = 102/3 |
|---|---|----|---|----|----|---|----|------------|
| D | I | M  | E | N  | S  | I | O  | N          |
| 4 | 9 | 4  | 5 | 5  | 1  | 9 | 6  | 5 = 48/12/3 |

* Translation of the full numbers 1, 0, 2, 3:
The dimensional aspect of the Divine (1), its Reflection (0) as the Duality (2), is rooted in the Creative Matrix (3).

\* Translation of the root numbers 4, 8, 1, 2, 3:
The dynamics of a dimensional Matrix (4) provide an Abundant (8) energy source for the Individual (1) within the Duality (2) for co-Creation (3).

The word dimension implies two or more spaces of indeterminate measure and potential: the divine dimension of unity and the reflected dimension of the Duality. Divine potential expresses within dimensions. As two returns to the unity of one, consider dimensionality in this light. If dimensions can return to unity, then dimension is an illusion. The number eight is a circle twisted over itself in the center. The dimensions of the spiritual and the physical are illustrated by the glyph 8. The top circle is the spiritual dimension, and the bottom circle is the physical dimension. The glyph for eight also represents the reflection of the divine and pure potential. The Duality appears to those in it to be an independent dimension, represented by the lower half of the glyph eight, but it is still ultimately the one. Untwisting the figure eight returns the reflection to unity. Everything as unity of the whole is represented in duality by a circle. Everything is the one; there are no exceptions.

### Judgement – The Many of the One, Resolution, and Divine Grace

The many forms of duality appear real from the perspective of the corporeal. Duality is not the ultimate truth, but is the context within which spirit functions when in physical form. Duality forms the basis that allows spirit to see itself in many different manifestations.

In Justice, non-judgment allows ego to get closer to unity with spirit. It does this within the context of a physical body. The process of unification continues within the dynamics of Judgement when spirit returns to the state of resolution after leaving the physical. Judgement is the archetype in which divine grace and recognition of truth dissolve guilt and regret. Regret is a result of the ego's expectations. The last vestiges of regret dissolve within divine grace and truth. Divine grace and truth also bring resolution of any remaining conflict.

The angel on this card holds a trumpet with a banner. The banner has a red, equal-armed cross in a field of white. The equal-armed cross is a symbol of earth and all things physical. White is the color of purity. The archetype of Judgement brings resolution of earthly existence into the field of pure spirit.

Judgement also shows the angel sounding the trumpet and people of different ages and gender appearing to hear the sound, rising from coffins. If these people are no longer living, what can they "hear" that is causing them to "rise?" Hearing is a function of spirit, a response to vibration, as well as a function of physical ears. Let's take a look at the numerology of the word "hearing".

### Chart One Hundred Fifty-nine
### Hearing

| 8 | 5 | 1 | 18 | 9 | 14 | 7 = 62/8 |
|---|---|---|----|---|----|----------|
| H | E | A | R  | I | N  | G        |
| 8 | 5 | 1 | 9  | 9 | 5  | 7 = 44/8 |

\* Translation of full numbers 6, 2, 8:
The ability to respond to vibration is a function of the Body (6), as well as Spirit, and what We (2) use to recognize the call of the Creator (8). (Creator has a root number of 8).

\* Translation of root numbers 4, 4, 8:
Spirit made Manifest (4) in Form (4) cannot ignore the call of the Creator (8).

In the numerology of "hearing", the number six represents the body because of the six points of reference from a body's point of view: top, bottom, left, right, front, and back.

The divine sends out a signal that we respond to. This signal is a vibration rather than an actual sound. In order for the boundaries of form to be removed and resolution take place, spirit manifesting in the physical must emerge by raising its rate of vibration. The slower the rate of vibration within the Duality, the denser objects are. Spirit slows its vibration within the Duality so it can take solid form.

Spirit responds to the vibrational "call" of divinity, no matter what form spirit takes. Let's take a look at the numbers of the word "call".

### Chart One Hundred Sixty
### Call

| 3 | 1 | 12 | 12 = 28/10 |
|---|---|----|------------|
| C | A | L  | L          |
| 3 | 1 | 3  | 3 = 10/1   |

\* Translation of full numbers 2, 8, 10:
Spirit Cooperates (2) with the Power (8) of the divine Call (10).

"Call" is a word that represents the vibration of divinity as shown by its root number ten. This is the ultimate calling. Regardless of what form our spirit takes, we hear, recognize, and respond. If spirit is done with this incarnation, it responds to the call by rising, leaving the physical body.

Chart One Hundred Sixty-one
Rise

| 18 | 9 | 19 | 5 = 51/6 |
|----|---|----|----------|
| R  | I | S  | E        |
| 9  | 9 | 1  | 5 = 24/6 |

\* Translation of full numbers 5, 1, 6:
As Man (5) hears the call of Divinity (1) at the moment of death, the Beauty (6) of that vibration makes spirit rise, leaving the physical form.

\* Translation of root numbers 2, 4, 6:
Our (2) Foundation (4) in Vision (6) causes this innate response.

People sometimes "pray" (another 24/6 word) that those who have passed on will hear the call and rise to heaven. Our (2) Foundation (4) in spiritual vision encourages people to Pray (6). Let's look at "Judgement" next.

Chart One Hundred Sixty-two
Judgement

| 10 | 21 | 4 | 7 | 5 | 13 | 5 | 14 | 20 = 99/18/9 |
|----|----|---|---|---|----|---|----|--------------|
| J  | U  | D | G | E | M  | E | N  | T            |
| 1  | 3  | 4 | 7 | 5 | 4  | 5 | 5  | 2 = 36/9     |

\* Translation of 9, 9, 1, 8, 9:
Unconditional Love (9) sends an Initiate's (9) Individual (1) Power (8) into the World (9).

\* Translation of root numbers 3, 6, 9:
Listening to the Communications (3) of our inner Vision (6) promotes the embracing of Unconditional Love (9).

Unconditional love is the vehicle that carries divine energy through the Duality supporting us and all that is. Unconditional love is the vehicle of resolution.

"Judgement" has a root number of nine, the number of ending. To end something is to have resolution. "Resolution" has a root number of five. Five is the number of change. It takes change to bring about resolution. Judgement is the final resolution, a last gift before wholeness.

**Translation Review**

The Divine Reflected within manifested Spirit contains Powerful dimensional dynamics. The Duality contains the Beauty within Powerful dimensional dynamics.

The dimensional aspect of the Divine, its Reflection as the Duality, is rooted in the Creative Matrix. The dynamics of a dimensional Matrix provide an Abundant energy source for the Individual within the Duality for co-Creation. The ability to respond to vibration is a function of the Body, as well as spirit, and what We use to recognize the call of the Creator.

Spirit made Manifest in Form cannot ignore the call of the Creator. Spirit Cooperates with the Power of the divine Call. As Man hears the call of Divinity at the moment of death, the Beauty of that vibration makes spirit rise, leaving the physical form. Our Foundation in Vision causes this innate response. Unconditional Love sends an Initiate's Individual Power into the World. Listening to the Communications of our inner Vision promotes the embracing of Unconditional Love.

**Applying the Revealed Information**

**Acquired Meanings – New Meanings Revealed by Numerology**

The final resolution, the circular dimensional dynamics of energy, responding, rising to the call, rising up, the vision within unconditional love, divine grace, embracing unconditional love.

**Relevant Questions**

What is the basic conflict within me? What cycle is promoted by this conflict? What is calling me at this time? How should I respond? How can I bring forgiveness into my life? What are the foundation principles of unconditional love? How are they influencing me at this time? How will accepting divine grace change my life?

**Practical Application**
Reading: the Empress, Judgement, the Five of Cups.

In the Five of Cups, all is laid bare when the emotion of regret responds to the call of Judgement. No matter what choices were made or what the previous personal hardships entailed, divine grace lifts the querent in the final call. Divine forgiveness and personal growth happen when we rise to the challenge of delving deeply into unresolved issues with love, understanding, and compassion. By divine grace (Judgement) we are newly created (the Empress).

**Just a Thought**
Our personal interactions call on us to grow on all levels, but perhaps especially on an emotional one. The emotional responses and reactions to life are one of the driving dynamics within personal reality. As humans, we express many patterns of emotion, some of which keep us stuck. Repeating patterns of negative emotions keep us from understanding and truth. The illusions of duality evaporate as we respond to the call of unconditional love and divine grace.

## Divine Grace
The meaning of Judgement, after taking into consideration the numerical implications and its position as the twentieth card, includes divine grace. The phrase divine grace holds such hope—especially the hope for absolution. We often find it hard to forgive ourselves or allow ourselves to be forgiven. The archetype of Judgement is the act of divine grace absolving and forgiving all our actual or perceived transgressions. By this absolution, we embrace oneness with divine spirit once again.

**Judgement Dynamics:**
Responding
Rising
Resolving

# Chapter Twenty-Five

## Commentary:
## Second Triad of Progression (2, 11, 20): Resolution

The "High Priestess" (two), "Justice" (eleven), and "Judgement" (twenty) have the same root number of two. These three cards show a progression of the number two as two expands toward resolution: two, the reflection of the divine and duality; eleven, the higher spiritual aspect of two; twenty, divine potential expanding toward resolution and ultimate unity. Two has innate conflict, but in eleven—the higher spiritual vibration of two—two has expanded toward an expression in which there is no conflict. In twenty, two paired with zero uses divine potential to expand beyond two's limitations toward resolution of conflict and ultimate unity.

Each archetype expresses different facets of resolution. The three archetypes progress toward resolution of regret, which is the particular expression of the archetype Judgement. Similarly, the High Priestess is resolution of the illusory nature of appearance; Justice is resolution of conflict.

The High Priestess expresses as duality (Chapter Four). In this archetype, the illusion of the appearance of duality is resolved. Continuity brings apparent opposites together, resulting in the resolution of the difference between appearance and truth.

Justice expresses as non-judgment (Chapter Fourteen). This archetype, as non-judgment, brings resolution of conflict. Conflict is often brought about by judgment. Non-judgment, within a spiritual context, is indicated by the double-digit number of Justice, card eleven.

Judgement expresses as divine grace and resolution. Judgement as expectation not met is often expressed as regret (Chapter Twenty-Four). In this archetype, divine grace brings dissolution of regret and the recognition of truth resulting in resolution. The archetypes of the second triad express different facets of resolution moving toward unity: the resolution between appearance and reality; the resolution of judgment; the resolution between expectation and truth.

In a spread when two or more cards of the second triad of progression appear in any order, it evokes the divine process of recognition of truth and the resolution of regret. For example, when card 2, the High Priestess, and card 20, Judgement, appear in a spread, the reader should consider the processes of resolution. The High Priestess brings to mind processes of the resolution between appearance and reality. Judgement evokes processes involved in the resolution of any remaining conflict and regret.

## Chapter Twenty-Six

### Twenty-One and the World

*The divine manifesting in physical form embraces uniqueness as innately beautiful.*

**Twenty-One – The Unifying Dynamics of Divine Energy**

The number twenty-one brings focus to the dynamic interaction between divine reflection (2) and the divine (1). This interaction has a never-ending process of evolution. Evolution is defined by Google's web dictionary as "the gradual development of something, especially from a simple to a more complex form." The creative matrix (3)—the result of the interaction between one and two—allows for the development of these more complex forms. The creative matrix brings forth ever more complex forms within the Duality. As energies blend or combine, the resulting synergy creates a whole that is greater than the sum of its parts. An example of this is water, a liquid which is a combination of hydrogen and oxygen, two gasses. The result is a fluid that gives life to this planet. The dynamic co-operative interaction of two components combining into a different whole has examples everywhere in the Duality; we see countless illustrations of two re-creating the unity of one.

Chart One Hundred Sixty-three
Twenty-One

|    |    |   | 107 |    |    |    | 34 |   |         |
|----|----|---|-----|----|----|----|----|---|---------|
| 20 | 23 | 5 | 14  | 20 | 25 | 15 | 14 | 5 | = 141/6 |
| T  | W  | E | N   | T  | Y  | O  | N  | E |         |
| 2  | 5  | 5 | 5   | 2  | 7  | 6  | 5  | 5 | = 42/6  |
|    |    |   | 26  |    |    |    | 16 |   |         |

\* Translation of full numbers 1, 4, 1, 6:
The Divine (1) manifesting in physical Form (4) embraces Uniqueness (1) as innately Beautiful (6).

\* Translation of root numbers 4, 2, 6:
The divine Serves (4) the Duality (2) through the spiritual Vision (6) of the individual.

Four, two, six is an important number trinity in numerology, though commonly expressed in its numerical order 2, 4, 6, where the expanding energy of two occurs explicitly. The components needed to convert raw energy into a functioning physical form are in this trinity. Six is the numerical expression of form taking on a more complex function. The translation of the conventional order 2, 4, 6, would be: The Duality (2) matrix materializing in physical Form (4) supports the Function (6) of energy within our reality.

In number trinities, we see examples of the expansion and unification of divine energy. In the numerical trinity 2, 4, 6 we observe the energy of 2 expanding and unifying into the number 6; in the trinity 3, 6, 9 we observe the energy of 3 expanding and unifying into the number 9. In the equations 2 + 2 = 4 + 2 = 6, two expands its energy to ultimately express within six. Six is the result of two's expanded energy. It also expresses the ability of separate parts to unify into a form that functions on a whole new level. We see examples of expansion and unification within these number trinities when the interaction between divine and divine reflection is expressed. The numerical trinities also demonstrate how creative dynamics express in many ways and in many forms.

Divine energy appears in the Duality as solid when energy converts into matter, maintains a fixed volume and shape, and reflects light. The unifying dynamics of divine energy encourage creation within the Duality. In this particular case, the unifying dynamic brings energy into physical form. It becomes a solid. The word "solid" has a root number of five (change), showing energy within solid matter has the innate ability to change. For example, ice, a solid, can change to water, a liquid, then to water vapor, a gas. Spirit uses this same dynamic, by its divine attributes, to manipulate energy into a solid that functions in a particular form.

### Chart One Hundred Sixty-four
### Solid

| 19 | 15 | 12 | 9 | 4 = 59/14/5 |
|----|----|----|---|-------------|
| S  | O  | L  | I | D           |
| 1  | 6  | 3  | 9 | 4 = 23/5    |

\* Translation of full numbers 5, 9, 1, 4, 5:
Change (5) Initiates (9) the Individual (1) into the Foundation (4) of Freedom (5) of choice.

\* Translation of root numbers 2, 3, 5:
The Duality's (2) Creative (3) matrix, as a part of this foundation, promotes Change (5).

The initial change is the divine reflecting itself. Change must exist so there can be choice. The ability to make a choice implies personal freedom. Therefore, change gives the individual the freedom to choose. The creative matrix, by its nature of being the resulting combination of the divine and the divine's reflection (1 + 2 = 3), serves as the facilitator of change and choice. The combination of the divine and its reflection resulting in something else begins the never-ending dynamic of expansion.

Solid implies form. The word "form" has a root number of seven, which implies form is spiritual in nature. Spirit and divine energy unified to become form in the Duality. There is no form that does not contain spirit and divine energy. The divine is the unifying energy within all form and spirit that has the ability to manifest as an individual. The divine integrates all. Let's look at the numerology of "integration" next.

Chart One Hundred Sixty-five
Integration

| 9 | 14 | 20 | 5 | 7 | 18 | 1 | 20 | 9 | 15 | 5 = 132/6 |
|---|----|----|---|---|----|---|----|---|----|-----------|
| I | N | T | E | G | R | A | T | I | O | N |
| 9 | 5 | 2 | 5 | 7 | 9 | 1 | 2 | 9 | 6 | 5 = 60/6 |

* Translation of full numbers 1, 3, 2, 6:
The Individual (1) Creates (3) within the Duality (2) by means of the mechanics of Integration (6) and imagination.

* Translation of root numbers 6, 0, 6:
The mechanics of the Integration (6) of divine Potential (0) within the Duality Matrix allow imagination to manifest Form (6).

* Alternate translation of root numbers 6, 0, 6:
Imagination (6) Reflects (0) Vision (6).

Imagination, as a part of the "spirit mind," is the part of us that is centered in spirit. It is intrinsically connected to our vision, as in our ability to discern the spiritual. Imagination reflects what we are able to discern on a spiritual level.

We imagine what we want. The integration of energy combines with divine potential by our imagination to manifest a form with a function. The mechanics of energy integration with divine potential within the duality matrix allow imagination to manifest form as the result of a conceived function. The unifying dynamics of divine energy integrate freedom of choice, change, and imagination into unique physical forms, which have innate beauty.

## World – Total Integration and Unity

On the World card, the circle represented by the green wreath is a symbol of growth, harmony, and unity. Red lemniscates appear at the top and bottom of the wreath. Red is the color of energy, power, and love. The lemiscate is a symbol of the divine, the divine reflection, and their ultimate unity. The divine and the divine reflection are united in the totality of the wreath. The expression of this unity reaches the next level of creativity in the dynamics of the World.

The dynamics of the World are illustrated in the number twenty-one. The number 21 invokes the interaction of divine reflection and the divine; the numbers proceed in order from left to right: two re-joins the one, becoming all inclusive and returning to the original unity. In 12, one, suggesting unity, comes first, followed by two, suggesting division. Similarly, in the numbers for the World archetype, a division suggested by 2 leads to unity suggested by 1. The intuitive meaning of the numbers recapitulates the process of unification.

The archetype of the World expresses creativity on a spiritual plane. The World, the twenty-first card, $2 + 1 = 3$, is related to the archetype of the Hanged Man, the twelfth card, $1 + 2 = 3$. The basic attributes of the number three (creative expression) expand within the Hanged Man and the World. The Hanged Man (Chapter Fifteen, page 130) and the World illustrate ways in which the numbers one and two create on the one hand paradoxes and on the other hand unity as the expanded expression of the number three. The expression of three, associated with the Empress card, has evolved into the paradoxes of the Hanged Man, card twelve. In card twenty-one, the expression of the number three has evolved into the integrating and unifying energy of the World, resolving these paradoxes. Numerology reinforces the meanings of the archetypes of the Tarot.

The word "Empress" with the root number of five (change) (Chart Thirty-eight, page 51) brings changes to the World archetype through her ever-expanding creation. The new dimensions within the World archetype give the Empress more "space" to express in new ways. The Empress continues to express her potential within the new spiritual dimensions of the World. The World archetype, always in a state of expansion, embraces creativity and change as necessary for the evolution of all dimensions. Following is the numerology of "World".

### Chart One Hundred Sixty-six
### World

| 23 | 15 | 18 | 12 | 4 = 72/9 |
|----|----|----|----|----------|
| W  | O  | R  | L  | D        |
| 5  | 6  | 9  | 3  | 4 = 27/9 |

* Translation of full numbers 7, 2, 9:
When Spirituality (7) and ego are Balanced (2), Ascension (9) into unity is achieved.

* Translation of root numbers 2, 7, 9:
The illusion of Duality (2) (the dual nature of things) is expressed by divine Intelligence (7) and Love (9).

"World" has a root number of nine. Within the unity of the World, duality is ended (number nine's key word is Ending), and the next dimension of creativity is begun. Nine, made up of threes (3 + 3 + 3), symbolizes the creative expansion of three and the Empress. World, as an archetype, ends a cycle and leads to a new beginning.

In the archetype of the World, duality becomes unity once again. Let's look at "unity" next.

### Chart One Hundred Sixty-seven
### Unity

| 21 | 14 | 9 | 20 | 25 = 89/17/8 |
|----|----|---|----|--------------|
| U  | N  | I | T  | Y            |
| 3  | 5  | 9 | 2  | 7 = 26/8     |

* Translation of full numbers 8, 9, 1, 7, 8:
As the Powerful (8) vibration of Unconditional Love (9) emanates from the Divine (1), unconditional love becomes a part of everything, resulting in the Spiritual (7) Energy (8) that is an innate part of all that is.

The archetype of the World achieves true unity when ego and spirit blend. Duality resolves to become one. The archetypal energy of the World cannot be embraced successfully without true unity. "Unity" comes first with a root number of eight, then "World" with a root number of nine.

On the World card, a naked figure is dancing in the center of a circle created by the wreath. Following is the numerology of "naked".

## Chart One Hundred Sixty-eight
## Naked

| 14 | 1 | 11 | 5 | 4 = 35/8 |
|----|---|----|---|----------|
| N  | A | K  | E | D        |
| 5  | 1 | 11 | 5 | 4 = 26/8 |

\* Translation of full numbers 3, 5, 8:
The divine Created (3) Man (5) Naked (8).

\* Translation of root numbers 2, 6, 8:
The Duality (2) seeks to create Form (6) by using the interaction between spiritual energy and divine Power (8) flowing into the Duality, which eventually flows back again into divine unity.

We are spiritually and physically naked before the divine. Nothing is hidden. Of course, we are also literally naked when we are born. In the eyes of the divine, we also leave the material world naked, in the sense that our true self is revealed when we shed our physical body and ego persona. In our true "naked" form, we are most powerful.

The banner around the naked figure covers the lower half of the torso, preventing us from knowing if the figure is fully female or male. Therefore, the figure may be both. Interestingly, the word "androgynous" has a root number of nine, as does "World". The root number of "androgynous" suggests that after we have completed (9) our roles in gender, we return to the spiritual state of androgyny, signaling the end (9) of our existence within the Duality. The androgynous figure also alludes to the idea that we are a combination of male and female no matter what the gender of our physical bodies. Male and female attributes are balanced and fully expressed within the spiritual as well as the physical by the time we progress to expression in the World archetype.

## Chart One Hundred Sixty-nine
## Androgynous

| 1 | 14 | 4 | 18 | 15 | 7 | 25 | 14 | 15 | 21 | 19 = 153/9 |
|---|----|---|----|----|---|----|----|----|----|------------|
| A | N  | D | R  | O  | G | Y  | N  | O  | U  | S          |
| 1 | 5  | 4 | 9  | 6  | 7 | 7  | 5  | 6  | 3  | 1 = 54/9   |

\* Translation of full numbers 1, 5, 3, 9:
Divinity (1) within Man (5) Creates (3) the desire for Ascension (9).

\* Translation of root numbers 5, 4, 9:
Change (5) is a Foundation (4) of Ascension (9) within the Duality.

\* Alternate translation of root numbers 5, 4, 9:
Diversity (5) of Form (4) is the illusion of our World (9).

Once the cycle of incarnation has been completed and spirit returns to a state of indeterminate gender with the potential of either gender, ascension and realization of unity is next. If we see everything as divine, then ultimately we see that divine energy is all there is. If we see everything as divine, then ultimately we see the underlying unity: all is the same, all is one. Divine energy is the all and the everything.

**Translation Review**
The Divine manifesting in physical Form embraces Uniqueness as innately Beautiful. The divine Serves the Duality through the spiritual Vision of the individual. Change Initiates the Individual into the Foundation of Freedom of choice. The Duality's Creative matrix, as a part of this foundation, promotes Change. The Individual Creates within the Duality by means of the mechanics of Integration and imagination. The mechanics of the Integration of divine Potential within the Duality Matrix allow imagination to manifest Form. Imagination Reflects Vision.

When Spirituality and ego are Balanced, Ascension into unity is achieved. The illusion of Duality (the dual nature of things) is expressed by divine Intelligence and Love. As the Powerful vibration of Unconditional Love emanates from the Divine, unconditional love becomes a part of everything, resulting in the Spiritual Energy that is an innate part of all that is. The divine Created Man Naked. The Duality seeks to create Form by using the interaction between spiritual energy and divine Power flowing into the Duality, which eventually flows back again into divine unity. Divinity within Man Creates the desire for Ascension. Change is a Foundation of Ascension within the Duality. Diversity of Form is the illusion of our World.

**Applying the Revealed Information**

**Acquired Meanings – New Meanings Revealed by Numerology**
The dynamic interactions between energies, the expansion of energy for new creation, infinite possibilities, the unity of all things within the divine, the dissolving of paradox, the divine perfection of duality, inclusion, creative evolution.

**Relevant Questions**
Out of all the possibilities, what is most likely? If this (whatever "this" is) is an illusion, what is the reality? What is the dual nature of ...? In what way is my reality perfect for me? What needs to expand within me so that I can come closer to experiencing the unity of all that is?

**Practical Application**
Reading: the Seven of Pentacles, the World, the Three of Wands.

The querent takes stock of what has been created. Does the querent have enough to live in the manner he or she desires? Unconsciously, the interactions between imagination, intention, and manifestation are a part of creating the life he or she wants, but there are literally infinite possibilities as conscious and unconscious come together to create the querent's world.

Plans are made and actions taken, while ultimately all the components of creation unify to form a reality. The Three of Wands indicates the querent must wait for the results. Once the querent sees the results, then he or she can make changes.

**Just a Thought**
I thought it interesting that the number seven came up in the Seven of Pentacles because seven is the number of spirituality. The number seven reminds us of the spiritual nature underlying the physical world, represented by the suit of Pentacles. The Three of Wands, in this case, can represent creative energy represented by the number three, and how an individual spirit expresses creativity in the world.

**World Dynamics:**
Dissolving
Expanding
Unifying
Evolving

# Chapter Twenty-Seven

## Commentary:
## Third Triad of Progression (3, 12, 21): Unification

The tarot numbers of these three cards—the Empress (three), the Hanged Man (twelve), the World (twenty-one)—have the same root number of three. These three cards show a progression of the number three as it moves toward the integration and unity of what is created: three, the creative principle; twelve, paradox; twenty-one, unification. The cycle completes with the return to unity of all the divine created.

Different aspects of creativity are expressed in each archetype. The different aspects of creativity are fertility, paradox, and unity. The three archetypes progress toward unity, which is the particular expression of the archetype the World. Similarly, the Empress personifies creativity as fertility; The Hanged Man personifies creativity as paradox.

The Empress, creativity (Chapter Five), expresses as diversity. Because the Empress as 1 + 2 = 3 is the created result of the divine combined with divine reflection, this archetype represents divine energy added to something to create a similar, yet unique thing, which engenders diversity.

The Hanged Man, creativity of the expanded perspective, expresses as paradox (Chapter Fifteen). The resolution of antithetical ideas within a paradox leads to a new understanding of the Duality by creative thinking. The result is the expansion of the mind.

The World, unity (Chapter Twenty-Six), expresses as the integration and unification of divine creation. In the World, the illusion of diversity is dissolved, revealing the true state of unity.

In a spread when two or more cards of the third triad of progression appear in any order, it evokes the divine processes of creativity and unification. For example, if card 3, the Empress, and card 12, the Hanged Man, appear in a spread, the reader should consider how creative energy is expressed. The Empress is creativity expressed as diversity. The Hanged Man is creativity of the expanded mind as it searches for the resolution of paradox.

The Empress (3), the Hanged Man (12), and the World (21) form the last triad of progression. The archetypes illustrate how the cards express divine creativity. This forms the triad of: Empress, creativity; Hanged Man, paradox; and World, unity.

The Empress, creativity, expresses diversity. The Hanged Man, paradox, expresses what is created within a new context. The World, unity, expresses the integration and unification of what is created. These three archetypes progress from diversity, to paradox, to unity.

# Chapter Twenty-Eight

## Commentary:
## The Three Archetypes of Paradox

The Three Archetypes of Paradox: The Fool, The High Priestess, The Hanged Man.

We have considered the major arcana as archetypes. As archetypes, we should also look at them as representations of experiences that promote spiritual growth, as well as representations of our reality. Physicists say the universe is always in a state of becoming. The archetypes also reflect a similar dynamic state, as cultural and personal influences expand our interpretations and understandings.

The Fool, the High Priestess, and the Hanged Man promote spiritual growth by posing a particular kind of puzzle that we call a paradox. Paradox has an interesting dynamic within the Duality. The dynamic of paradox is made possible by the Duality being the reflection of the divine. Being a part of the reflection gives a unique perspective, as does looking in a mirror. Our perspective is reversed when we look in a mirror, but this perspective is only temporary. The dichotomy of perspective in the following analogy illustrates the limitation of any one perspective. Picture a coin that has a different carving on the front and back. If you show someone the two different sides on different occasions, and he doesn't know better, he would probably say there are two different coins. But we know he sees two sides of the same coin. How can the coin be simultaneously different and yet the same? We know how this is possible because we understand the coin has a different image on the front and back. The metal of the center of the coin is the same. It is not differentiated. In this analogy, we also understand the coin is the same coin (as opposed to two different coins) because it is made from one piece of metal. We can follow this same analogy using energy in place of the coin. Energy is all the same. It can express one way on the original side, the side of the divine, but express differently on the other side, the side of the Duality. However, it is connected and originally undifferentiated, just like the metal in the center of the coin. It is all the same energy.

When we discover a paradox, the divine is asking us to see a connection or sameness. The divine differentiates itself when it creates its reflected energy, but it is still the same energy. The divine does not separate the original energy from the reflected energy. The energy can be expressed differently, but it is not separate. Differentiation is a natural result of reflection. It is natural to differentiate based on perspective.

As spirit inhabiting a body, we differentiate ourselves from other bodies or things because we are part of the reflection. Reflection creates differentiation.

Spirit inhabiting a body includes having an ego. Ego leads beyond differentiation to separation. The ego's perspective of separateness makes it difficult to dissolve the illusion of separation, which we experience within the Duality. It is not natural for spirit to see itself as separate. Only our ego identity sees itself as separate from everything else.

By understanding a paradox, therefore resolving the dichotomy of differentiation and separation, we expand the mind and discover oneness. The recovery of connection and oneness brings us closer to the divine. We get closer to the divine because we see we are ultimately one with all of creation.

The three cards of paradox are the Fool, the High Priestess, and the Hanged Man. The Fool is a paradox because it represents the all and the nothing simultaneously. The High Priestess is a paradox because she represents the two of the one, or the divine reflection. The Hanged Man is paradox because he sees through the illusion of reflection and differentiation from an inverted or reversed position.

### The Fool

The archetype of the Fool is where the major arcana begin. As a representation of our reality, it is "the beginning" of all that exists. The Fool is the original paradox because it symbolizes the void or emptiness and also includes infinite potential. As infinite potential, the Fool is full. As zero, the number most commonly associated with the Fool, it is empty. The Fool represents both a state of nothingness and a state fullness. The Fool encompasses all potential and all possibility, therefore it is the potential of what is possible. Paradoxes also reflect possibilities that come with understanding. In and of itself, a paradox is nothing but a contradictory statement or idea. In this way, it is empty. A paradox, however, holds potential. Potential becomes possibility when the paradox is understood. As we understand the paradox of the Fool, the Fool becomes full in the context of the potential spiritual understanding that it brings us.

## The High Priestess

The High Priestess is a paradox because she is both two and one. She initiates differentiation; she is where the differentiation of divine energy starts. She is the focal point at the intersection of the lines of the lemniscate, the point of transition from the unity of the Magician to the duality of the High Priestess. As the point of origin of differentiated energy (energy that is different but not separate), she becomes both two and one.

Two things happen when divine energy reflects itself. The mirroring, or reflecting, causes reversal and differentiation. Everything that is the divine is mirrored or reflected in the High Priestess. Because reflecting causes reversal, reflection implies a dual nature: the original and the reversed form. Differentiation occurs simultaneously with reflection because the unity of the divine has manifested in the reflected form. Furthermore, differentiation is an illusion created by perspective. Reflecting results in energy having a dual nature and differentiation.

The lemniscate is a symbol describing a cosmology. On the left side of the lemniscate, divine energy is undifferentiated, all the same. As energy passes through the "X," it becomes differentiated because of the reversed flow as it returns to the divine. Everything in the reflection is in the original, as it is in a mirror image. Also, everything in the mirror image is reversed. This means that everything in the mirrored image has all the characteristics of the original, plus reversal.

The original divine elements interacting with their reversed counterparts results in the creation of two dimensions on the right side of the lemniscate. This interaction of one dimension (left side of the lemniscate) and two dimensions (right side of the lemniscate) can be expressed as the equation $1 + 2 = 3$. The creative principle as the equation $1 + 2 = 3$ is the expression for the potential of multi-dimensionality. The interaction of the original divine energy and the differentiated energy create the potential for many dimensions.

The High Priestess, as the "X" in the center of the lemniscate, translates divine energy into two dimensions, as well as differentiating it. On the reflected side, the expression of the continuum as gradations of polarity, gradations of light, and gradations of magnetism adds a dimension to the originally undifferentiated energy. Differentiated energy within the reflection creates dimension. Physicists know that our universe is multidimensional. The adding of dimension within the Duality in this case opens the door for the possibility of infinite dimensions.

Usually when we come across a paradox of the High Priestess, it presents one thing as two that from all appearances are different. The idea is to find the one thing, or commonality, that make the two one again.

### The Hanged Man

The Hanged Man represents a paradox because he sees truth in reversal: up is down; left is right. He sees through the illusion of reflection from his inverted and reversed position. The Hanged Man begs the question, what perspective leads to the truth?

The illustration of the Hanged Man shows a person suspended by one leg with a yellow halo around his head. The halo around the Hanged Man's head represents his insightful understanding. Another interpretation is that the halo symbolizes that he has become enlightened. Either way, at face value, it becomes difficult to imagine how hanging upside-down leads to clear thought, never mind enlightenment.

From our perspective, the Hanged Man sees everything reversed. The effect of mirroring includes left becoming right and up becoming down. But these effects are the result of our point of view, as a part of the reflected Duality. To us, mirroring includes distortions, just as hanging upside-down includes distortions.

The Hanged Man is a symbol of enlightenment: the idea that when you are on the divine side, you are not compensating for mirroring or distortion because you are one with the source. If we consider that the Duality is a reflection, then the Hanged Man's revelation of truth makes more sense. To perceive a truth, we need to appreciate different points of view. The resolution of mirroring, accomplished by changing one's perspective, reveals the true nature of the Duality.

The Hanged Man can be applied to various scenarios. One scenario is a person changing his perspective in terms of how he thinks about something. The other scenario is seeing things from a divine perspective. The two scenarios represent two ends of a spectrum. Our exposure to the paradoxes of the Hanged Man always brings us closer to resolving duality. As we get closer to resolving duality, we get closer to our divine nature and the divine.

The human eye acts as our own personal Hanged Man. The image of what we see is turned upside-down and backwards as it is projected onto the retina. Our brain then orients the image back to an upright position. Before the brain reorients the image, we see as the Hanged Man sees, which is without the distortion of reflection. We know and recognize the image as a representation of greater truth because it is without the reflection distortion, even though it is only fleeting. The function of our brain to reorient the image of the retina makes holding the true image impossible.

Both the High Priestess and the Hanged Man give us the opportunity to gain insight into the true nature of duality by getting us to look for the sameness or oneness of differentiated energy.

### The Expression of the Fool in the Archetypes of Paradox

All of the major arcana represent different potentials that are aspects of the Fool, but one of the most fascinating and enigmatic potentials lies in paradox. Paradoxes promote the dissolution of duality by their resolution. The High Priestess and the Hanged Man both express different aspects of paradox and its potential to bring about profound realizations. The High Priestess takes oneness, then creates differentiation and duality. The Hanged Man takes reality and turns it upside-down. The basic paradox represented in the High Priestess is that apparent differences are actually undifferentiated. The basic paradox represented in the Hanged Man is that apparent reality is not real. If all differentiation is the result of a change and reality is not real, then what is the underlying truth?

The Hanged Man suggests that the way to resolve both paradoxes and discover the underlying truth is to come to multiple realizations that culminate in a different understanding of reality. There is a logic from our perspective which reinforces our idea of what is real. If all that is, which includes us, is made up of that which is all the same, then everything we call reality would seem real because it is literally a part of us, and we are a part of it. However, the form we see ourselves in and the form we see reality take may not be the ultimate form. We always see things from our own limited perspective. Because we see ourselves and reality from a particular perspective, we are seeing the illusion. Our reality is what we make it. Therefore, the reality we see is not ultimately real. By the resolution of the paradoxes of the High Priestess and the Hanged Man, illusions of differentiation and apparent reality dissolve into the truth of unity and the truth of the ultimate form of reality.

### The Illusion of Paradox

A paradox is a statement that expresses a dual nature that appears contradictory within the original statement. In the absence of unity, non-unity is implied. As suggested in this book, the only appearance of non-unity is in the Duality. Duality makes paradox possible. Because unity is the ultimate reality, the dual nature of the Duality is an illusion. If duality is an illusion, then all paradoxes must also be illusory because they are at their core a statement of dualism. If the truth is that only unity exists, then everything else is an illusion.

# Chapter Twenty-Nine

## Discoveries

I have studied metaphysics and other related subjects for many years. The experience has given me a unique perspective into tarot and other related subjects. In multiple spiritual practices, there are core perceptions of reflection: what goes around comes around, as above so below, as within so without, etc. The archetypes of the tarot embody some of these perceptions. New discoveries about how the archetypes embody different spiritual awareness were numerous, but a few stand out.

## The Duality Matrix

Throughout this book, I have referred to our reality as the Duality. I give our reality this name because our reality is a reflection of the divine, making it a dual image of divine energy. The Duality is made up of an interactive grid. This grid is called the duality matrix. The duality matrix can be thought of as the grid of energy that gives rise to our reality in three dimensions. I came across the idea of a grid as a matrix for creation in one of Jane Robert's "Seth" books.

The term duality matrix came to me as I was writing Chapter Five: Three and the Empress. To review, the Empress as the third card is associated with the number three. Three is the first result of an interaction between two numbers, in this case one and two. The numerical equation for this is $1 + 2 = 3$. $1 + 2 = 3$ expresses the basic creative formula. I have repeatedly observed this equation as a foundational idea of the duality matrix.

The number three in numerology represents the geometric form of the two-dimensional triangle. The constant repeating of the triangular form results in a grid of triangles. This pattern creates the basic foundation of creation in two dimensions. But in the Duality, objects are also created in three dimensions. How do you create three-dimensional objects from a two-dimensional grid? You add a fourth point in space above or below the grid.

The addition of a fourth point allows for the creation of three-dimensional objects using the three points of the triangle as the base. If the triangles that make up the grid are right-angle triangles, it is possible to make a square out of pairs of triangles. The square adds more possibilities for creation in three dimensions; for example, by becoming a cube.

The duality matrix is responsive and interactive. Some of the ways that it responds are described by the effects of gravity in space, or the theory of general relativity. The duality matrix responds to gravity produced by the mass of a planet and other celestial bodies. Time is also affected by the duality matrix's response to gravity.

The duality matrix is also interactive on a more personal level. When a person's imagination, intent, and focus come together in a specific way to create an object, the duality matrix responds on a microcosmic level. This response allows the object the person wants to create to come into his or her personal reality and three-dimensional space. By conducting experiments, we see other ways in which the duality matrix is interactive and responsive. The duality matrix responds to our mental activity, whether apparent or not.

## The Lemniscate and the Magician

The figure eight laid on its side, or lemniscate, is a symbol used in three of the major arcana cards: the Magician, Strength, and the World. As I worked my way through the analysis of the archetypes, the mysteries of the lemniscate slowly revealed themselves. One of the mysteries revealed involves the movement of divine energy. I associate the lemniscate with energy because the symbol invokes the idea of flow: something flowing away and returning, and flowing away again and returning, ad infinitum, reminding us that the lemniscate is a symbol of infinity. Recognizing the Magician as the archetype of the divine, we can explore how the lemniscate is a symbol of divine energy dynamics.

The lemniscate describes much more than the idea of infinity. Its shape describes the pattern and dynamics of energy and what it creates. It is often said that everything at some point returns to its source. The lemniscate illustrates this pattern. If one follows the line of the lemniscate, there is a moving away and a return to the beginning. The symbol describes a repeating movement away from and back to a source. Another symbol of outgoing and returning energy is the circle. But the lemniscate is not imaged as a circle. There is something more being described by this symbol.

Another mystery revealed is the change in direction that the energy flow takes, and what the change in direction implies. The lemniscate is made up of one continuous line. By following the line as it is drawn, the direction of flow changes, so the outgoing energy changes direction in order to return to the source. The energy of a circle also returns to the source. But unlike a circle, a lemniscate contains a crossover point. What does the crossover mean?

The High Priestess and the attributes of her number—two, differentiation and distinction—provided the answer. The water element on the High Priestess card continues the idea of flow and something, in this case energy, moving from one area to another. As energy flows like water through the "X" at the center of the lemniscate into the Duality, it becomes differentiated (Chapter Four). The energy remains divine energy, but as the lemniscate envisions, changes appear as it flows through the "X" into the Duality.

The configuration of the lemniscate results in a left side and a right side. The right side is the Duality. In the Duality, we observe differentiation and make distinctions. If the energy on the left and right sides is the same, then the difference we see is an illusion. Flow led to the idea of a continuum: minute changes that we can't distinguish until they contrast enough for the differences to become apparent. The perceived contrast misleads us to conclude that the differences are real. The concept of the continuum explains how, despite appearances, there is no actual difference. The divine's undifferentiated energy is unified, regardless of the perception of our senses.

## Two and the Nature of Reflection

The unity of the divine differentiates when the divine creates its reflection. Divine energy takes on a dual nature when the divine projects energy outward from itself. The reflection of the divine appears. Some spiritual philosophies posit that everything is made of divine energy. The energy underlying the perceived differentiated energy, as seen in the Duality, is unified, divine energy. But the appearance of a reflection implies a second existence: where there was one, there are now two. The appearance of the number two denotes a change of some kind. In this case, the change is the differentiation of divine energy.

The number two implies that there is an original, and that there is something that is different from the original. Divine energy repeating itself does not explain the differentiated energy that makes up the "something" that is different. However, divine energy being reflected, which gives energy the properties of reflection, does explain the difference between divine energy and reflected divine energy. Reflection is the key to the differentiated energy that makes up the Duality. The flow of energy depicted by the lemniscate led me to discover the nature of reflection and how it impacts once unified energy.

The explanation of how reflection impacts energy is contained in the expression $1 + 2$. Starting with $1 + 2$, we can deduce the basic mechanics of reflection as they apply to the creation of the Duality. The sum $1 + 2$ creates a paradigm of the origin of divine reflection. The number one represents the divine. The number two represents its reflection: reflected energy and also divine energy.

To summarize, number 2 includes a 1. The number 2 in the expression $1 + 2$ must represent the original divine energy and the reflected divine energy. 1 + 2 can also be expressed as the divine energy (1) plus the quantity of divine energy and reflected divine energy (2).

The lemniscate as a diagram shows that the flow of energy changes direction. The change of direction is a direct result of reflection. When something is reflected, as in a mirror image, left becomes right; a clockwise motion becomes counterclockwise. In other words, direction is reversed. The reflected energy retains the original properties and characteristics of the divine, but also displays additional properties and characteristics such as reversals. While the Duality is made up of differentiated energy, it is also made up of the original divine energy.

The original divine energy, on the left side of the lemniscate, flows outward. As the energy moves away from the point of origin, it reverses its flow, creating the right side. The reversal of flow, shown in the lines of the lemniscate, creates the dual nature of the reflected energy. Hence, the name for the reflection is the Duality. The "X" in the middle of the lemniscate is where the dynamics of reflection and reversal begin.

The reflected energy is the same energy, but has additional characteristics. A reflection, as in a mirror image, is a reproduction of the original and only contains elements that are contained in the original. When it comes to energy being reflected, however, something interesting happens. Reversal, as a result of reflection, adds some interesting attributes to the energy that is reflected. The act of reflection adds polarity, positive and negative in the case of an electric charge, magnetism, active and passive characteristics to the energy, and the possibility of paradox.

(I use the artificial orientation of left and right because we read from left to right and because the lemniscate is drawn horizontally. In this case, we associate left with the starting point.)

## Strength, the Lemniscate, and Number 8

The second card with the lemniscate is Strength, card number eight. On Strength, the lemniscate is shown above the woman's head. Appearance of a lemniscate on card number eight and the similarities of the two symbols call for the interpretation of the relationship between the lemniscate and the glyph 8. The discovery of the relationship between the number eight and the leminscate is explored in this section.

By focusing on the glyph 8 and the lemniscate, we see how they visualize the flow of energy. The similarities begin with the configuration of the two glyphs, one in a horizontal position and the other in a vertical position.

We reference divine energy as coming from above. The cosmology of ancient times embraced the idea of heaven and earth, above and below. The orientation of the figure 8 reinforces this idea that energy comes from "above" and is manifested "below." The Magician card illustrates this idea further. The Magician represents mankind's ability to draw undifferentiated energy from the divine (the "above") and manifest it in the Duality (the "below") as differentiated energy. The glyph 8 diagrams the flow of this energy.

Energy movement described by the glyph for eight is ultimately a description of divine energy movement. Divine energy coming from above is mankind's explanation for where we conceptualize divine location to be. The idea of up and down is only given as a point of reference to the human body. The appearance of the lemniscate on the Magician card, in fact, suggests the paradigm should be conceived of as horizontal. In the creative act, divine energy moves horizontally, as in the lemniscate. The lemniscate shows us that divine energy is projected outward and moves away from the source. Because the Duality is a reflection of the divine, our personal energy also moves horizontally away from us as the source.

The paradigm of the lemniscate is re-enacted in the Duality. While we describe energy as coming from "above" to express "below," ultimately our creative energy moves horizontally, just as divine energy moves. This means that while the glyph for eight illustrates energy coming from "above" and manifesting "below," that energy ultimately projects outward as a personal expression of creative energy and is envisioned as a lemniscate.

As mentioned before, the reflective dynamic applies to the duality matrix, which the lemniscate and glyph for eight illustrate. The reflection occurs when we create an object in physical form. We see the created object because the duality matrix reflects that energy back to us, showing us our creation. In the Duality, we project energy outward when we create, as does the divine.

The quote, "As above, so below, as within, so without, as the universe, so the soul," by Hermes Trismegistus can apply to the reflective energy dynamic. Conventional understanding of "as within, so without" is that one creates his external reality as a mirror image of his internal reality. Reflection implies that all elements that are part of the original (as within) are present in the reflection (so without). But in the context of this discussion, it can also mean that our self-expression derives from divine energy because we are part of the divine.

### The Lemniscate on the World

The third card with the lemniscate is the World. The World card shows a green circular wreath with red lemniscates entwined at the top and bottom. The green of the wreath, the color of growth, suggests the circle is expanding. In any circle form, a circular motion of energy whirls around without end, but no change occurs that we would identify with growth. Growth as a form of expansion can occur in several ways: circle to a larger circle; circle to a column; circle to a sphere. This section explores the discovery of how the lemniscate invokes the idea of expansion and growth.

The lemniscate draws our attention because it is red. Red is the color of energy. The colors on the World, green and red, imply growth (green) within a closed circle (the wreath) of energy (red). The lemniscate, in contrast to the circle, invokes the idea of multi-dimensions. The reflection of divine energy—the right side of the lemniscate—is the creation of a new dimension. The wreath, drawn as a circle on a piece of paper, is two-dimensional and doesn't evidence another dimension. A circle that does have another dimension, as in three dimensions, is a sphere. But a circle as a symbol can imply four or more possible dimensions. A four-dimensional circle is a hypersphere. We know energy can express multi-dimensionally, as it does within the Duality and all creation. By adding dimensions to a circle, the circle expands and achieves growth. The red lemniscate on the green wreath suggests that growth occurs within the existence of a multi-dimensional circle.

The lemniscate is a circle with a twist, both figuratively and literally. As an icon, its meanings include infinity, hence divinity. Its graphics, made with one continuous line, reiterate the meaning of infinity; the line doesn't end. In geometry, it can be described as a sine wave with a circle's arc, which doubles back on itself. This configuration implies the infinite flow of energy, as well as a self-replicating chain. The presence of the lemniscate on the green wreath associates replication with the circle. A circle that self-replicates as one continuous line makes an unending chain of circles.

The different descriptions of the lemniscate—in the previous paragraph, the sine wave in particular—suggest an interesting idea. The sine wave with three or more repeated, rounded arcs doubled back on itself creates a strand of DNA. The lemniscate that makes an unending chain, imagined in three dimensions with arcs and twists, results in strands that appear to cross over each other in the same way as strands of DNA.

The lemniscate on the World card reminds us that there are many dimensions. As physical beings, we have access to only a few. As spirit beings, many more dimensions become accessible. The dancing figure in the center of the wreath is partially encircled by a piece of material. If the two ends of the material are re-attached, it forms a lemniscate. The image of the figure stepping over the end of the broken lemniscate evokes the idea of breaking free. The figure transcends duality and is stepping beyond it into another dimension of creativity. Creativity ultimately has no bounds or limitations. In the archetype of the World, not only is duality resolved when spirit and ego blend, but the next level of creative possibility is revealed. New dimensions beyond our three-dimensional space become available when duality resolves to become one again with the divine. Beyond the physical world, we are multi-dimensional spirits creating in a multi-dimensional universe.

**THE END**

# Glossary

**All That Is** – Everything that has been and is being created; our world, our universe.
**Arcana** – One or the other of a group of tarot cards.
**Archetype** – The original model after which all similar things are patterned.
**Ascension** – The act of rising to a higher level.
**Beauty** – The innate natural state of being of all that is.
**Biopolymers** – Nucleic acids in all living things.
**Consciousness** – The collective power of the subconscious and conscious.
**Construct** – An ideal object where the existence of the thing may be said to depend on the subject's mind.
**Continuum** – A coherent whole characterized as a progression of values or elements varying by minute degrees.
**Core Vibration** – The single-digit number that shows the basic characteristics of a word or phrase.
**Divine or Divinity** – Refers to God, Goddess, All That Is, a higher power.
**Duality** – Our world; duality with a lowercase "d" refers to the dual nature of some thing.
**Esoteric** – Something known by a restricted number of people.
**Expression** – Words that describe the characteristics or attributes of the final digits in a numerological analysis.
**Four Directions** – North, South, East, West.
**Four Elements** – Fire, Water, Air, Earth.
**Full Numbers** – Full numbers for the English alphabet are one through twenty-six.
**Gematria** – Obtaining hidden meanings from the geometric shapes of letters and from the numerical values of both words and phrases.
**Hexagram** – A six-pointed star.
**Innate** – Inborn; natural.
**Key Word** – A word or words that describe the essence of a number.
**Lemniscate** – The symbol of eternity or infinity.
**Manifestation** – A perceptible, outward, or visible expression.
**Master Numbers** – Any repeating double-digit number.
**Metaphysics** – A traditional branch of philosophy concerned with explaining the fundamental nature of being and the world that encompasses it.
**Matrix** – An environment or material in which something develops.
**Mundane** – Of the earthly world instead of the spiritual or heavenly world.

**Notariqon** – The hidden meanings obtained from abbreviations and first letters of words provided by their corresponding numbers.

**One** – An individual; the divine, God, Goddess, All That Is; the number.

**Paradox** – A self-contradictory statement that upon examination proves to be true.

**Polarity** – The direction of a magnetic or electric field.

**Querent** – The person who the reading is for.

**Root Number** – The reduction of the double-digit numbers ten through twenty-six to a single-digit through addition. Also a word's root number is the final digit arrived at after the reduction of the sum of the numbers of the word's individual letters.

**Tarot Suits** – Wands, Cups, Swords, Pentacles.

**Temperance** – Moderation or self-restraint.

**Temurah** – Finding words within words and from anagrams.

**Tetractys** – A mathematical idea and a metaphysical symbol.

**Vision** – Conceiving of and/or the discernment of spiritual awareness and insight.

# The Foundation Principles

Throughout this book, certain concepts called foundation principles become apparent. These concepts are the basic tenets, within the context of this book, of creation, the Duality, spirituality, and existence.

*Foundation Principle of Divine Potential:*
All That Is is contained within divine potential.

Chapter Two: Zero and the Fool states, "The infinite potential within zero is expressed by the one, the divine." Without a change from the state of the un-manifested, there would be no expression of potentiality. The translation of the full numbers of the word "zero" translate as, "The Beautiful Foundation of Divine Potential is the first and original." The divine, as the result of this change, creates a vehicle for the expression of infinite potential. Potential is reflected as possibility within divinity and the Duality. All creation and all creativity exist as a result of the expression of infinite potential.

*Foundation Principle of Change:*
Everything changes except the origin and the divine.

In Chapter Two, the Duality exists because change exists. Change exists because the divine made a reflection of itself which added some unique attributes to the reflected energy. The nature of origin never changes. The nature of the divine never changes.

*Foundation Principle of Unconditional Love:*
Unconditional love permeates all of existence as potential.

In Chapter Three: One and the Magician, the full numbers of the phrase "free will" translate as, "Divine energy Initiates the creation of its Reflection with the emanation of Unconditional Love." Unconditional love is the first key. All potential is unlocked by the expression of unconditional love.

*Foundation Principle of Free Will:*
Free will is a part of spirit's initiation into the Duality.

In Chapter Three, the translation of the numbers of "free will" indicates that free will is necessary for the full expression of potential. The nature of the Duality allows for individual self-expression. Free will and unconditional love unlock spirit's expression of potential. Free will is the second key.

*Foundation Principle of Reflection:*
Reflection exists as an outward projection of divine energy creating the Duality, polarity, reversals (mirroring), and paradox.

Also in Chapter Three, reflection is synonymous with the Duality. All that encompasses the divine is also present in divine reflection as well as differentiated energy that has unique qualities.

*Foundation Principle of Paradox:*
Certain expressions of energy are true and not true simultaneously.

In Chapter Four: Two and the High Priestess, paradox is only possible as a condition of the Duality. This is due to the reflection principle expressed within the archetype of the High Priestess, the holder of secret mysteries.

*Foundation Principle of Creation:*
The Creative Trinity—the numbers 1, 2, 3—is the result of the divine (1) plus the divine reflection (2) creating something unique (3).

In Chapter Five: Three and the Empress, three represents divine energy's impetus toward creativity, expression, and diversity.

## List of Key Words

Following is a list of key words for the numbers 1-9, 11, and 22.

One – active, unity, initiating, original.

Two – duality, choice, reflection, differentiation.

Three – creative trinity, expression, support matrix.

Four – manifestation, foundation, physical, work.

Five – re-generation, change, expansiveness, freedom, man.

Six – vision, harmony, beauty.

Seven – spirit, spirituality, trust, intelligence.

Eight – power, dynamic, continual, reflective.

Nine – unconditional love, ending, altruistic, faithful, generous.

Eleven – spiritual understanding, illumination, mystical visionary.

Twenty-two – master architect, material, matter, practical visionary.

## List of Analyzed Words by Chapter

Chapter One    1
   Tarot, archetype, free will.

Chapter Two    15
   Zero, potential, circle, hold, pause, Fool, good, choice.

Chapter Three    26
   One, will, EAFW, wand, magic, free will, Magician, intention, carbon.

Chapter Four    38
   Two, reflection, duality, mirror image, dead end, High Priestess, free will, Magician.

Chapter Five    49
   Three, create, time, Empress, exist, support matrix.

Chapter Six    57
   Four, tetractys, Emperor, initiation, physical manifestation, compassion.

Chapter Eight    69
   Five, devotion, pentagram, Hierophant, key, mentor.

Chapter Nine    78
   Six, male, female, conception, heart, love, lover, Lovers.

Chapter Ten    87
   Seven, divine will, ego, personal will, Chariot.

Chapter Eleven    94
   Eight, model, energy, Strength, lion.

Chapter Twelve    101
   Nine, balance, Hermit, hexagram, harmony, staff, inner nature, cycle.

Chapter Thirteen    109
   Ten, transition, higher, begin, Wheel of Fortune, change, karma, movement.

Chapter Fourteen     119
    Eleven, mature, light, Justice, recompense, scales, balance, right, wrong, sword.

Chapter Fifteen     129
    Twelve, creative, beauty, Hanged Man, paradox, perspective.

Chapter Sixteen     140
    Thirteen, fulfillment, process, transformation, rose, Death, beyond, ascension.

Chapter Seventeen     148
    Fourteen, limitation, nature, Temperance, universal law.

Chapter Eighteen     156
    Fifteen, life, matter, diversity, Devil, spirit manifestation, temptation, flexibility.

Chapter Nineteen     165
    Sixteen, consequence, dynamic, Tower, rigid, control, divine nature, curiosity, fall, lightning.

Chapter Twenty     175
    Seventeen, growth, Star, blueprints, power.

Chapter Twenty-One     182
    Eighteen, structure, construct, Moon, symbol, dreams, subconscious, context.

Chapter Twenty-Two     190
    Nineteen, divine love, unconditional love, self, self image, Sun, separate, identity.

Chapter Twenty-Four     202
    Twenty, dimension, hearing, call, rise, Judgement.

Chapter Twenty-Six     212
    Twenty-one, solid, integration, World, unity, naked, androgynous.

## Alphabetized List of Analyzed Words

```
1   14   5   18   15   7   25   14   15   21   19 = 153/9
A    N   D    R    O   G    Y    N    O    U    S
1    5   4    9    6   7    7    5    6    3    1 = 54/9


1   18   3    8    5   20   25   16   5 = 101/2
A    R   C    H    E   T    Y    P    E
1    9   3    8    5   2    7    7    5 = 47/11 (2)


1   19   3    5   14   19   9   15   14 = 99/18/9
A    S   C    E   N    S    I   O    N
1    1   3    5   5    1    9   6    5 = 36/9


2    1   12   1   14   3    5 = 38/11
B    A   L    A   N    C    E
2    1   3    1   5    3    5 = 20/2


2    5   1   21   20   25 = 74/11
B    E   A   U    T    Y
2    5   1    3   2    7 = 20/2


2    5   7    9   14 = 37/10
B    E   G    I   N
2    5   7    9   5 = 28/10/1


2    5   25  15   14   4 = 65/11
B    E   Y    O   N    D
2    5   7    6   5    4 = 29/11


2   12   21   5   16   18   9   14   20   19 =136/10/1
B    L   U    E   P    R    I   N    T    S
2    3   3    5   7    9    9   5    2    1 = 46/10/1


3    1   12  12 = 28/10
C    A   L   L
3    1   3   3 = 10


3    1   18   2   15   14 = 53/8
C    A   R    B   O    N
3    1   9    2   6    5 = 26/8
```

```
3   8   1   14  7   5 = 38/11
C   H   A   N   G   E
3   8   1   5   7   5 = 29/11

3   8   1   18  9   15  20 = 74/11
C   H   A   R   I   O   T
3   8   1   9   9   6   2 = 38/11

C   H   O   I   C   E
3   8   6   9   3   5 = 34/7

3   9   18  3   12  5 = 50/5
C   I   R   C   L   E
3   9   9   3   3   5 = 32/5

3   15  13  16  1   19  19  9   15  14 = 124/7
C   O   M   P   A   S   S   I   O   N
3   6   4   7   1   1   1   9   6   5 = 43/7

3   15  14  3   5   16  20  9   15  14 = 114/6
C   O   N   C   E   P   T   I   O   N
3   6   5   3   5   7   2   9   6   5 = 51/6

3   15  14  19  5   17  21  5   14  3   5 = 121/4
C   O   N   S   E   Q   U   E   N   C   E
3   6   5   1   5   8   3   5   5   3   5 = 49/13/4

3   15  14  19  20  18  21  3   20 = 133/7
C   O   N   S   T   R   U   C   T
3   6   5   1   2   9   3   3   2 = 34/7

3   15  14  20  5   24  20 = 101/2
C   O   N   T   E   X   T
3   6   5   2   5   6   2 = 29/11

3   15  14  20  18  15  12 = 97/16/7
C   O   N   T   R   O   L
3   6   5   2   9   6   3 = 34/7

3   18  5   1   20  5 = 52/7
C   R   E   A   T   E
3   9   5   1   2   5 = 25/7
```

```
3  18  5   1   20  9   22  5 = 83/11
C  R   E   A   T   I   V   E
3  9   5   1   2   9   22  5 = 56/11


3  21  18  9   15  19  9   20  25 = 140/5
C  U   R   I   O   S   I   T   Y
3  3   9   9   6   1   9   2   7 = 49/5


3  25  3   12  5 = 48/12/3
C  Y   C   L   E
3  7   3   3   5 = 21/3


D  E   A   D       E   N   D
4  5   1   4       5   5   4 = 10/1
   5 (14)              5 (14)


4  5   1   20  8 = 38/11
D  E   A   T   H
4  5   1   2   8 = 20/2


4  5   22  9   12 = 52/7
D  E   V   I   L
4  5   2   9   3 = 43/7


4  5   22  15  20  9   15  14 = 104/5
D  E   V   O   T   I   O   N
4  5   4   6   2   9   6   5 = 41/5


4  9   13  5   14  19  9   15  14 = 102/3
D  I   M   E   N   S   I   O   N
4  9   4   5   5   1   9   6   5 = 48/12/3


4  9   22  5   18  19  9   20  25 = 131/5
D  I   V   E   R   S   I   T   Y
4  9   22  5   9   1   9   2   7 = 68/14/5


             63                    54
4  9   22  9   14  5     12  15  22  5 = 117/9
D  I   V   I   N   E     L   O   V   E
4  9   22  9   5   5     3   6   22  5 = 18/9
       9 (54)                9 (36)
```

```
          63                    79
4   9  22   9  14   5    14   1  20  21  18   5 = 142/7
D   I   V   I   N   E    N    A   T   U   R   E
4   9  22   9   5   5     5   1   2   3   9   5 = 16/7
        9 (54)                      7 (25)


          63                    56
4   9  22   9  14   5    23   9  12  12 = 119/11
D   I   V   I   N   E    W    I   L   L
4   9  22   9   5   5     5   9   3   3 = 56/11
        9 (36)                      2 (20)


4  18   5   1  13   19 = 60/6
D   R   E   A   M   S
4   9   5   1   4    1 = 24/6


D   U   A   L   I   T   Y
4   3   1   3   9   2   7 = 29/11


4  25  14   1  13   9   3 = 69/15/6
D   Y   N   A   M   I   C
4   7   5   1   4   9   3 = 33/6


E   A   F   W
5   1   6   5 = 17/8


5   7  15 = 27/9
E   G   O
5   7   6 = 18/9


5   9   7   8  20 = 49/13/4
E   I   G   H   T
5   9   7   8   2 = 31/4


5   9   7   8  20   5   5  14 = 73/10/1
E   I   G   H   T   E   E   N
5   9   7   8   2   5   5   5 = 46/10/1


5  12   5  22   5  14 = 63/9
E   L   E   V   E   N
5   3   5  22   5   5 = 45/9
```

| | | | | | | |
|---|---|---|---|---|---|---|
| 5 | 13 | 16 | 5 | 18 | 15 | 18 = 90/9 |
| **E** | **M** | **P** | **E** | **R** | **O** | **R** |
| 5 | 4 | 7 | 5 | 9 | 6 | 9 = 45/9 |

| | | | | | | |
|---|---|---|---|---|---|---|
| 5 | 13 | 16 | 18 | 5 | 19 | 19 = 95/14/5 |
| **E** | **M** | **P** | **R** | **E** | **S** | **S** |
| 5 | 4 | 7 | 9 | 5 | 1 | 1 = 32/5 |

| | | | | | |
|---|---|---|---|---|---|
| 5 | 14 | 5 | 18 | 7 | 25 = 74/11 |
| **E** | **N** | **E** | **R** | **G** | **Y** |
| 5 | 5 | 5 | 9 | 7 | 7 = 38/11 |

| | | | | |
|---|---|---|---|---|
| 5 | 24 | 9 | 19 | 20 = 77 |
| **E** | **X** | **I** | **S** | **T** |
| 5 | 6 | 9 | 1 | 2 = 23/5 |

| | | | |
|---|---|---|---|
| 6 | 1 | 12 | 12 = 31/4 |
| **F** | **A** | **L** | **L** |
| 6 | 1 | 3 | 3 = 13/4 |

| | | | | | |
|---|---|---|---|---|---|
| 6 | 5 | 13 | 1 | 12 | 5 = 42/6 |
| **F** | **E** | **M** | **A** | **L** | **E** |
| 6 | 5 | 4 | 1 | 3 | 5 = 42/6 |

| | | | | | | |
|---|---|---|---|---|---|---|
| 6 | 9 | 6 | 20 | 5 | 5 | 14 = 65/11 |
| **F** | **I** | **F** | **T** | **E** | **E** | **N** |
| 6 | 9 | 6 | 2 | 5 | 5 | 5 = 38/11 |

| | | | |
|---|---|---|---|
| 6 | 9 | 22 | 5 = 42/6 |
| **F** | **I** | **V** | **E** |
| 6 | 9 | 4 | 5 = 24/6 |

| | | | | | | | | | |
|---|---|---|---|---|---|---|---|---|---|
| 6 | 12 | 5 | 24 | 9 | 2 | 9 | 12 | 9 | 20 | 25 = 133/7 |
| **F** | **L** | **E** | **X** | **I** | **B** | **I** | **L** | **I** | **T** | **Y** |
| 6 | 3 | 5 | 6 | 9 | 2 | 9 | 3 | 9 | 2 | 7 = 61/7 |

| | | | |
|---|---|---|---|
| 6 | 15 | 15 | 12 = 48/12/3 |
| **F** | **O** | **O** | **L** |
| 6 | 6 | 6 | 3 = 21/3 |

```
6   15   21   18 = 60/6
F   O    U    R
6   6    3    9 = 24/6

6   15   21   18   20   5    5    14 = 104/5
F   O    U    R    T    E    E    N
6   6    3    9    2    5    5    5 = 41/5

         34             56
6   18   5    5    23   9    12   12 = 90/9
F   R    E    E    W    I    L    L
6   9    5    5    5    9    3    3 = 45/9
    7 (25)             2 (20)

6   21   12   6    9    12   12   13   5    14   20 = 130/4
F   U    L    F    I    L    L    M    E    N    T
6   3    3    6    9    3    3    4    5    5    2 = 49/13/4

7   15   15   4 = 41/5
G   O    O    D
7   6    6    4 = 23/5

7   18   15   23   20   8 = 91/10/1
G   R    O    W    T    H
7   9    6    5    2    8 = 37/10/1

              39                  28
8   1    14   7    5    4    13   1    14 = 67/13/4
H   A    N    G    E    D    M    A    N
8   1    5    7    5    4    4    1    5 = 40/4
              30                  10

8   1    18   13   15   14   25 = 94/13/4
H   A    R    M    O    N    Y
8   1    9    4    6    5    7 = 40/4

8   5    1    18   9    14   7 = 62/8
H   E    A    R    I    N    G
8   5    1    9    9    5    7 = 44/8
```

```
8   5   1   18  20 = 52/7
H   E   A   R   T
8   5   1   9   2 = 25/7

8   5   18  13  9   20 = 73/10/1
H   E   R   M   I   T
8   5   9   4   9   2 = 37/10/1

8   5   24  1   7   18  1   13 = 77/14/5
H   E   X   A   G   R   A   M
8   5   6   1   7   9   1   4 = 41/5

8   9   5   18  15  16  8   1   14  20 = 114/6
H   I   E   R   O   P   H   A   N   T
8   9   5   9   6   7   8   1   5   2 = 60/6

8   9   7   8   5   18 = 55/10
H   I   G   H   E   R
8   9   7   8   5   9 = 46/10/1

         32                      130
8   9   7   8   16  18  9   5   19  20  5   19  19 = 162/9
H   I   G   H   P   R   I   E   S   T   E   S   S
8   9   7   8   7   9   9   5   1   2   5   1   1 = 72/9
      5 (32)                    4 (40)

8   15  12  4 = 39/12/3
H   O   L   D
8   6   3   4 = 21/3

9   4   5   14  20  9   20  25 = 106/7
I   D   E   N   T   I   T   Y
9   4   5   5   2   9   2   7 = 43/7

9   14  9   20  9   1   20  9   15  14 = 120/3
I   N   I   T   I   A   T   I   O   N
9   5   9   2   9   1   2   9   6   5 = 57/12/3
```

```
              60                    70
     9   14  14   5  18   14   1  20  21  18   5 = 139/13/4
     I   N   N   E   R    N    A   T   U   R   E
     9   5   5   5   9    5    1   2   3   9   5 = 13/4
           6 (33)                7 (25)

     9   14  20   5   7   18   1  20   9  15   5 = 132/6
     I   N   T   E   G    R    A   T   I   O   N
     9   5   2   5   7    9    1   2   9   6   5 = 60/6


     9   14  20   5  14   20   9  15  14 = 120/3
     I   N   T   E   N    T    I   O   N
     9   5   2   5   5    2    9   6   5 = 48/12/3


    10   21   4   7   5   13   5  14  20 = 99/18/9
     J   U   D   G   E    M    E   N   T
     1   3   4   7   5    4    5   5   2 = 36/9


    10   21  19  20   9    3   5 = 87/15/6
     J   U   S   T   I    C    E
     1   3   1   2   9    3    5 = 24/6


    11   1   18  13   1 = 44/8
     K   A   R   M   A
    11   1   9   4   1 = 26/8


    11   5   25 = 41/5
     K   E   Y
    11   5   7 = 23/5


    12   9   6   5 = 32/5
     L   I   F   E
     3   9   6   5 = 23/5


    12   9   7   8   20 = 56/11
     L   I   G   H   T
     3   9   7   8    2 = 29/11


    12   9   7   8  20   14   9  14   7 = 100/1
     L   I   G   H   T    N    I   N   G
     3   9   7   8   2    5    9   5   7 = 55/10/1
```

251

```
12   9   13   9   20   1   20   9   15   14 = 122/5
L    I   M    I   T    A   T    I   O    N
3    9   4    9   2    1   2    9   6    5 = 50/5


12   9   15   14 = 50/5
L    I   O    N
3    9   6    5 = 23/5


12   15   22   5 = 54/9
L    O    V    E
3    6    4    5 = 18/9


12   15   22   5   18 = 72/9
L    O    V    E   R
3    6    4    5   9 = 27/9


12   15   22   5   18   19 = 91/10/1
L    O    V    E   R    S
3    6    4    5   9    1 = 28/10/1


13   1   7   9   3 = 33/6
M    A   G   I   C
4    1   7   9   3 = 24/6


13   1   7   9   3   9   1   14 = 57/12/3
M    A   G   I   C   I   A   N
4    1   7   9   3   9   1   5 = 39/12/3


13   1   12   5 = 31/4
M    A   L    E
4    1   3    5 = 13/4


13   1   20   20   5   18 = 77/14/5
M    A   T    T    E   R
4    1   2    2    5   9 = 23/5


13   1   20   21   18   5 = 78/15/6
M    A   T    U    R    E
4    1   2    3    9    5 = 24/6
```

```
13   5   14   20   15   18 = 85/13/4
M    E   N    T    O    R
4    5   5    2    6    9 = 31/4

M    I    R    R    O    R    I    M    A    G    E
4    9    9    9    6    9    9    4    1    7    5 = 72/9
     1 (46)                             8 (26)

13   15   4    5    12 = 49/13/4
M    O    D    E    L
4    6    4    5    3 = 22/4

13   15   15   14 = 57/12/3
M    O    O    N
4    6    6    5 = 21/3

13   15   22   5    13   5    14   20 = 107/8
M    O    V    E    M    E    N    T
4    6    4    5    4    5    5    2 = 53/8

14   1    11   5    4 = 35/8
N    A    K    E    D
5    1    11   5    4 = 26/8

14   1    20   21   18   5 = 79/16/7
N    A    T    U    R    E
5    1    2    3    9    5 = 25/7

14   9    14   5 = 42/6
N    I    N    E
5    9    5    5 = 24/6

14   9    14   5    20   5    5    14 = 86/14/5
N    I    N    E    T    E    E    N
5    9    5    5    2    5    5    5 = 14/5

15   14   5 = 34/7
O    N    E
6    5    5 = 16/7
```

```
16   1   18   1   4   15   24 = 79/16/7
P    A   R    A   D   O    X
7    1   9    1   4   6    6 = 34/7

16   1   21   19   5 = 62/8
P    A   U    S    E
7    1   3    1    5 = 17/8

16   5   14   20   1   7   18   1   13 = 95/14/5
P    E   N    T    A   G   R    A   M
7    5   5    2    1   7   9    1   4 = 41/5
```

```
                100                          56
16   5   18   19   15   14   1   12   23   9   12   12 = 156/12/3
P    E   R    S    O    N    A   L    W    I   L    L
7    5   9    1    6    5    1   3    5    9   3    3 = 57/12/3
              1 (37)                        2 (20)

16   5   18   19   16   5   3   20   9   22   5 = 138/12/3
P    E   R    S    P    E   C   T    I   V    E
7    5   9    1    7    5   3   2    9   22   5 = 75/12/3
```

```
             93
16   8   25   19   9   3   1   12
P    H   Y    S    I   C   A   L
7    8   7    1    9   3   1   3
             39
                                       146
         13   1   14   9   6   5   19   20   1   20   9   15   14 = 237/12/3
         M    A   N    I   F   E   S    T    A   T    I   O    N
         4    1   5    9   6   5   1    2    1   1    9   4    5 = 93/12/3
                                        56

16   15   20   5   14   20   9   1   12 = 112/4
P    O    T    E   N    T    I   A   L
7    6    2    5   5    2    9   1   3 = 40/4

16   15   23   5   18 = 77 (14/7)
P    O    W    E   R
7    6    5    5   9 = 32/5
```

```
16   18   15    3    5   19    19 = 95/14/5
P    R    O    C    E    S    S
7    9    6    3    5    1    1 = 32/5

18    5    3   15   13   16    5   14   19    5 = 113/5
R     E    C    O    M    P    E    N    S    E
9     5    3    6    4    7    5    5    1    5 = 50/5

18    5    6   12    5    3   20    9   15   14 = 107/8
R     E    F    L    E    C    T    I    O    N
9     5    6    3    5    3    2    9    6    5 = 53/8

18    9    7    9    4 = 47/11
R     I    G    I    D
9     9    7    9    4 = 38/11

18    9    7    8   20 = 62/8
R     I    G    H    T
9     9    7    8    2 = 35/8

18    9   19    5 = 51/6
R     I    S    E
9     9    1    5 = 24/6

18   15   19    5 = 57/12/3
R     O    S    E
9     6    1    5 = 21/3

19    3    1   12    5   19 = 59/14/5
S     C    A    L    E    S
1     3    1    3    5    1 = 14/5

19    5   12    6 = 42/6
S     E    L    F
1     5    3    6 = 15/6

           42                   35
19    5   12    6    9   13    1    7    5 = 77/14/5
S     E    L    F    I    M    A    G    E
1     5    3    6    9    4    1    7    5 = 14/5
        6 (15)            8 (26)
```

```
19   5   16   1   9   1   20   5 = 76/13/4
S    E   P    A   R   A   T    E
1    5   7    1   9   1   2    5 = 31/5


19   5   22   5   14 = 65/11
S    E   V    E   N
1    5   4    5   5 = 20/2


19   5   22   5   14   20   5   5   14 = 109/10/1
S    E   V    E   N    T    E   E   N
1    5   22   5   5    2    5   5   5 = 55/10/1


19   9   24 = 52/7
S    I   X
1    9   6 = 1


9    9   24   20   5   5   14 = 96/15/6
S    I   X    T    E   E   N
1    9   6    2    5   5   5 = 33/6


19   15  12   9   4 = 59/14/5
S    O   L    I   D
1    6   3    9   4 = 23/5


               91
19   16  9    18  9   20
S    P   I    R   I   T
1    7   9    9   9   2
               37
                              146
         13   1   14   9   6   5   19   20   1   20   9   15   14 = 237/12/3
         M    A   N    I   F   E   S    T    A   T    I   O    N
         4    1   5    9   6   5   1    2    1   2    9   6    5 = 93/12/3
                              56


19   20  1    6   6 = 52/7
S    T   A    F   F
1    2   1    6   6 = 16/7


19   20  1    18 = 58/13/4
S    T   A    R
1    2   1    9 = 13/4
```

```
19  20  18   5  14   7  20   8 = 111/3
 S   T   R   E   N   G   T   H
 1   2   9   5   5   7   2   8 = 39/12/3

19  20  18  21   3  20  21  18   5 = 145
 S   T   R   U   C   T   U   R   E
 1   2   9   3   3   2   3   9   5 = 37/10/1

19  23  15  18   4 = 79/16/7
 S   W   O   R   D
 1   5   6   9   4 = 25/7

19  21   2   3  15  14  19   3   9  15  21  19 = 160/7
 S   U   B   C   O   N   S   C   I   O   U   S
 1   3   2   3   6   5   1   3   9   6   3   1 = 43/7

19  21  14 = 54/9
 S   U   N
 1   3   5 = 9

                125                          85
19  21  16  16  15  18  20    13   1  20   8   9  24 = 210/3
 S   U   P   P   O   R   T     M   A   T   R   I   X
 1   3   7   7   6   9   2     4   1   2   9   9   6 = 12/3
             8 (35)                         4 (31)

19  25  13   2  15  12 = 86/14/5
 S   Y   M   B   O   L
 1   7   4   2   6   3 = 23/5

20   1  18  15  20 = 74/11
 T   A   R   O   T
 2   1   9   6   2 = 20/2

20   5  13  16   5  18   1  14   3   5 = 100/1
 T   E   M   P   E   R   A   N   C   E
 2   5   4   7   5   9   1   5   3   5 = 46/10/1

20   5  13  16  20   1  20   9  15  14 = 133/7
 T   E   M   P   T   A   T   I   O   N
 2   5   4   7   2   1   2   9   6   5 = 43/7
```

```
20   5   14 = 39/12/3
T    E   N
2    5   5 = 12/3

20   5   20   18   1   3   20   25   19 = 131/5
T    E   T    R    A   C   T    Y    S
2    5   2    9    1   3   2    7    1 = 32/5

20   8   9    18   20   5   5    14 = 99
T    H   I    R    T    E   E    N
2    8   9    9    2    5   5    5 = 45/9

20   8   18   5    5 = 56/11
T    H   R    E    E
2    8   9    5    5 = 29/11

20   9   13   5 = 47/11
T    I   M    E
2    9   4    5 = 20/2

20   15   23   5    18 = 81/9
T    O    W    E    R
2    6    5    5    9 = 27/9

20   18   1   14   19   6   15   18   13   1   20   9   15   14 = 183/12/3
T    R    A   N    S    F   O    R    M    A   T    I   O    N
2    9    1   5    1    6   6    9    4    1   2    9   6    5 = 66/12/3

20   18   1   14   19   9   20   9   15   14 = 139/13/4
T    R    A   N    S    I   T    I   O    N
2    9    1   5    1    9   2    9   6    5 = 49/13/4

20   23   5   12   22   5 = 87/15/6
T    W    E   L    V    E
2    5    5   3    22   5 = 42/6

20   23   5   14   20   25 = 107/8
T    W    E   N    T    Y
2    5    5   5    2    7 = 26/8
```

```
              107                    34
20   23   5   14   20   25   15   14   5 = 141/6
T    W    E   N    T    Y    O    N    E
2    5    5   5    2    7    6    5    5 = 42/6
              8 (26)                 7 (16)


20   23   15 = 58/13/4
T    W    O
2    5    6 = 13/4


                         151
21   14   3   15   14   4   9   20   9   15   14   1   12
U    N    C   O    N    D   I   T    I   O    N    A   L
3    5    3   6    5    4   9   2    9   6    5    1   3
                         7 (52)


              54
     12   15   22   5 = 205/7
     L    O    V    E
     3    6    22   5 = 16/7
              9 (36)


21   14   9   20   25 = 89/17/8
U    N    I   T    Y
3    5    9   2    7 = 26/8


                    121                         36
21   14   9   22   5   18   19   1   12   12   1   23 = 157/13/4
U    N    I   V    E   R    S    A   L    L    A   W
3    5    9   22   5   9    1    1   3    3    1   5 = 67/13/4
                    58                          9


23   1    14   4 = 42/6
W    A    N    D
5    1    5    4 = 15/6


              53              21              99
23   8   5   5   12   15   6   6   15   18   20   21   14   5 = 173/11
W    H   E   E   L    O    F   F   O    R    T    U    N    E
5    8   5   5   3    6    6   6   6    9    2    3    5    5 = 20/2
              8 (26)          3 (12)          9 (36)
```

| 23 | 9 | 12 | 12 | = 56/11 |
|---|---|---|---|---|
| **W** | **I** | **L** | **L** | |
| 5 | 9 | 3 | 3 | = 20/2 |

| 23 | 18 | 15 | 14 | 7 | = 77/14/5 |
|---|---|---|---|---|---|
| **W** | **R** | **O** | **N** | **G** | |
| 5 | 9 | 6 | 5 | 7 | = 32/5 |

| 23 | 15 | 18 | 12 | 4 | = 72/9 |
|---|---|---|---|---|---|
| **W** | **O** | **R** | **L** | **D** | |
| 5 | 6 | 9 | 3 | 4 | = 27/9 |

| 26 | 5 | 18 | 15 | = 64/10/1 |
|---|---|---|---|---|
| **Z** | **E** | **R** | **O** | |
| 8 | 5 | 9 | 6 | = 28/10/1 |

# Bibliography

French, Karen, L., *The Hidden Geometry of Life: The Science and Spirituality of Nature,* Watkins Publishing, London.

Goodwin, Matthew Oliver, *Numerology the Complete Guide, Volume One: The Personality Reading,* New Castle Publishing Company, Inc., North Hollywood, California, 1981.

Goodwin, Matthew Oliver, *Numerology the Complete Guide, Volume Two: Advanced Personality Analysis and Reading the Past, Present, and Future,* New Castle Publishing Company, Inc., North Hollywood, California, 1981.

Lawrence, Shirley Blackwell, Msc.D., *The Secret Science of Numerology: The Hidden Meanings of Numbers and Letters,* The Career Press, Inc., Pompton Plains, New Jersey, 2001.

*Merriam Webster's Collegiate Dictionary, Tenth Edition,* Merriam Webster, Inc., Springfield, Massachusetts, 1993.

Millman, Dan, *The Life You Were Born to Live: A Guide to Finding Your Life Purpose,* H.J. Kramer Publishing, Inc., Tiburon, California, 1993.

Pollack, Rachel, *Seventy-Eight Degrees of Wisdom: A Book of Tarot,* Thorsons Publishing Group, 1980, 1983, revised 1997.

Pollack, Rachel, *Tarot Wisdom: Spiritual Teachings and Deeper Meanings,* Llewellyn Publications, Woodbury, Minnesota, 2008.

Websites:
http://lubomir.name – website of Australian Astrologer Lubomir Dimitrov.

## About the Author

Carey Croft is a professional numerologist and tarot reader. Continuing her study of several metaphysical subjects, she became interested in tarot and eventually took classes with internationally known tarot master and author Rachel Pollack. In 2010, after several years of study with Pollack, Croft earned her Professional Tarot Reader Certificate. She continues to study tarot with Pollack and other tarot professionals. Croft currently conducts a bi-monthly tarot forum with co-founder Annie Wellington at her home in upstate New York.

www.ingramcontent.com/pod-product-compliance
Lightning Source LLC
Chambersburg PA
CBHW070638160426
43194CB00009B/1495